CONTEMPORARY ARAB FICTION

This book introduces Western readers to some of the most significant novels written in Arabic since 1979. Despite their contribution to the development of contemporary Arabic fiction, the authors discussed remain relatively unknown to the English-speaking reader.

Fabio Caiani examines the work of the Moroccan Muḥammad Barrāda, the Egyptian Idwār al-Kharrāṭ, the Lebanese Ilyās Khūrī and the Iraqi Fuʾād al-Takarlī. Their most significant novels were published between 1979 and 2002, a period during which their work reached literary maturity. They all represent pioneering literary trends compared to the novelistic form canonized in the influential early works of Naguib Mahfouz. Until now, some of their most innovative works have not been analysed in detail – this book fills that gap.

Relying on literary theory and referring to comparative examples from other literatures, this study places its findings within a wider framework – defining what is meant by innovation in the Arabic novel and the particular socio-political context in which it appears.

This book will enrich significantly the existing critical literature in English on the contemporary Arabic novel.

Fabio Caiani teaches Arabic in the Department of Middle Eastern Studies at the University of St. Andrews.

ROUTLEDGE STUDIES IN MIDDLE EASTERN LITERATURES

Routledge Studies in Middle Eastern Literatures is a monograph series devoted to aspects of the literatures of the Near and Middle East and North Africa, both modern and pre-modern. It is hoped that the provision of such a forum will lead to a greater emphasis on the comparative study of the literatures of this area, although studies devoted to one literary or linguistic region are warmly encouraged. It is the editors' objective to foster the comparative and multi-disciplinary investigation of the written and oral literary products of this area.

1. SHEHERAZADE THROUGH THE LOOKING GLASS
Eva Sallis

2. THE PALESTINIAN NOVEL
Ibrahim Taha

3. OF DISHES AND DISCOURSE
Geert Jan van Gelder

4. MEDIEVAL ARABIC PRAISE POETRY
Beatrice Gruendler

5. MAKING THE GREAT BOOK OF SONGS
Hilary Kilpatrick

6. THE NOVEL AND THE RURAL IMAGINARY IN EGYPT, 1880–1985
Samah Selim

7. IBN ABI TAHIR TAYFUR AND ARABIC WRITERLY CULTURE
A ninth-century bookman in Baghdad
Shawkat M. Toorawa

8. RELIGIOUS PERSPECTIVES IN MODERN MUSLIM AND JEWISH LITERATURES
Edited by Glenda Abramson and Hilary Kilpatrick

9. ARABIC POETRY
Trajectories of modernity and tradition
Muhsin J. al-Musawi

10. MEDIEVAL ANDALUSIAN COURTLY CULTURE IN THE MEDITERRANEAN
Three ladies and a lover
Cynthia Robinson

11. WRITING AND REPRESENTATION IN MEDIEVAL ISLAM
Muslim horizons
Julia Bray

12. NATIONALISM, ISLAM AND WORLD LITERATURE
Sites of confluence in the writings of Mahmūd al-Masadī
Mohamed-Salah Omri

13. THE ORAL AND THE WRITTEN IN EARLY ISLAM
Gregor Schoeler
Translated by Uwe Vagelpohl
Edited by James Montgomery

14. LITERATURE, JOURNALISM AND THE AVANT-GARDE
Intersection in Egypt
Elisabeth Kendall

15. THE THOUSAND AND ONE NIGHTS
Space, travel and transformation
Richard van Leeuwen

16. ARAB CULTURE AND THE NOVEL
Genre, identity and agency in Egyptian fiction
Muhammad Siddiq

17. LITERARY MODERNITY BETWEEN MIDDLE EAST AND EUROPE
Textual transactions in 19th Century Arabic, English and Persian literatures
Kamran Rastegar

18. POPULAR CULTURE AND NATIONALISM IN LEBANON
The Fairouz and Rahbani nation
Christopher Stone

19. CONTEMPORARY ARAB FICTION
Innovation from Rama to Yalu
Fabio Caiani

CONTEMPORARY ARAB FICTION

Innovation from Rama to Yalu

Fabio Caiani

LONDON AND NEW YORK

First published 2007
by Routledge
2 Park Square, Milton Park, Abingdon, Oxon, OX14 4RN

Simultaneously published in the USA and Canada
by Routledge
605 Third Avenue, New York, NY 10017

Routledge is an imprint of the Taylor & Francis Group, an informa business

Typeset in Times New Roman by
Newgen Imaging Systems (P) Ltd, Chennai, India

British Library Cataloguing in Publication Data
A catalogue record for this book is available from the British Library

Library of Congress Cataloging in Publication Data
A catalog record for this book has been requested

ISBN13: 978–0–415–41456–2 (hbk)

TO CATHERINE

CONTENTS

PREFACE

This study aims at introducing Western readers to some of the most significant novels written in Arabic since 1979, by Muḥammad Barrāda, Idwār al-Kharrāṭ, Ilyās Khūrī and Fuʾād al-Takarlī. Despite their contribution to the development of contemporary Arabic fiction, these writers remain relatively unknown to non-Arab readers. Some of their most innovative works have not been analysed in detail, so that even Western students of Arabic fiction are often oblivious of these writers' literary value. They all represent literary tendencies which are innovative as compared to the novelistic form canonized in the influential early works of Naguib Mahfouz. Mahfouz's death (30 August 2006) should serve as an inspiration for literary critics to investigate the new trends in operation within the Arabic novel, the literary form which Mahfouz, more than anybody else, demonstrated to be the most apt at engaging with the problems of the contemporary world. Although this study does not ignore the socio-political content and context of the literature, it aims principally at a close textual analysis.

The transliteration of Arabic most commonly used in academic publications in the Anglo-Saxon world is adopted here. Titles of Arabic books and names of Arab authors have therefore been transliterated according to the table found following this preface, with the notable exception of Najīb Maḥfūẓ, whose name, transliterated Naguib Mahfouz, is relatively well known even in the West.

TRANSLITERATION OF ARABIC LETTERS

Letter	Name	Transliteration
ا	*alif*	*ā*
ب	*bāʾ*	*b*
ت	*tāʾ*	*t*
ث	*thāʾ*	*th*
ج	*jīm*	*j*
ح	*ḥāʾ*	*ḥ*
خ	*khāʾ*	*kh*
د	*dāl*	*d*
ذ	*dhāl*	*dh*
ر	*rāʾ*	*r*
ز	*zāʾ/zāy*	*z*
س	*sīn*	*s*
ش	*shīn*	*sh*
ص	*ṣād*	*ṣ*
ض	*ḍād*	*ḍ*
ط	*ṭāʾ*	*ṭ*
ظ	*ẓāʾ*	*ẓ*
ع	*ʿayn*	*ʿ*
غ	*ghayn*	*gh*
ف	*fāʾ*	*f*
ق	*qāf*	*q*
ك	*kāf*	*k*
ل	*lām*	*l*
م	*mīm*	*m*
ن	*nūn*	*n*
ه	*hāʾ*	*h*
و	*wāw*	*w / ū*
ي	*yāʾ*	*y / ī*
ء	*hamza*	*ʾ*

ACKNOWLEDGEMENTS

This book is an edited and revised version of a PhD thesis submitted in 2005 at the University of St. Andrews (Scotland).

The research would not have been possible without the help received from different institutions which I wish to thank: the University of Ca' Foscari (Venice, Italy), the Honeyman Foundation, SAAS (Students Award Agency for Scotland) and BRISMES (British Society for Middle Eastern Studies).

I would like to thank the two external examiners of my thesis – Professor Roger Allen and Dr Robin Ostle – for their useful comments and advice, which helped me greatly in preparing the present monograph.

I am grateful to the publisher Brill for allowing me to integrate it in the present study material taken from my article 'Polyphony and Narrative Voice in Fuʾād al-Takarlī's *al-Rajʿal-baʿīd*', which was published in the *Journal of Arabic Literature* (Vol. XXXV, No. I, 2004: 45–70). Chapter V of this book, on metafiction, includes a discussion of Ilyās Khūrī's novel *Yālū*. Such discussion forms the basis for my article '"My Name is Yālū." The Development of Metafiction in Ilyās Khūrī's Work', which at the time of writing has not yet been published but will appear in the journal *Middle Eastern Literatures*. I wish to thank the publisher Taylor & Francis for allowing me to include this material in the present work.

I had the pleasure of meeting both Idwār al-Kharrāṭ and Fuʾād al-Takarlī to discuss their works: I am very grateful to them for their help, encouragement and remarkable kindness. I am also grateful to Muḥammad Barrāda for having kindly provided me with a copy of his novel *Luʿbat al-nisyān.*

Ai miei genitori e a mio fratello and to all my friends, my heartfelt thanks for their constant support.

It is thanks to Catherine Cobham of the University of St. Andrews that I began studying literature, and she has been a continuous source of inspiration ever since. I wish to thank her for having so capably supervised my thesis and helped me turn it into this book, the merits of which owe much to my collaboration with her.

1
INTRODUCTION
On literary innovation (part 1)

In 1997, the May/June issue of the prestigious Lebanese literary magazine *al-Ādāb* was dedicated to the topic of experimentation and innovation in the Arabic novel.[1] In his brief introduction, editor-in-chief Samāḥ Idrīs first explains that he wants this special issue to deal with the 'new' and the 'lively' in the Arabic novel through an analysis of specific examples, instead of relying on Western literary theories. He then adds that the impressive response of readers, writers and critics to such topics[2] shows a growing interest in new novelistic styles which, unlike old techniques, keeps abreast with a life which has become unpredictable, quickly changing (Idrīs 1997: 19).

Our approach to the same topic (innovation within the realm of contemporary Arabic fiction) has some features in common with Idrīs's: in particular, we will rely on a close textual analysis of certain novels which present significant innovative features. However, we will also refer to literary theories and draw parallels between the Arabic novels studied and non-Arabic fictional texts.

The focus of this study is a number of novels published in recent decades (the first in 1979, the last in 2002)[3] which were written by Arab authors of different nationalities who, according to most critics (Arab and Western scholars of modern Arabic fiction), have significantly contributed to innovation in the Arabic novel in the period under consideration. The Iraqi novelist Fuʾād al-Takarlī (b. 1927, Baghdad) has received less critical attention than others and the innovative elements in his work (wrongly but maybe inevitably, as will be shown in the following section) have often been overlooked. The other main writers whose work is analysed here are Idwār al-Kharrāṭ (b. 1926, Alexandria), Ilyās Khūrī (b. 1948, Beirut) and Muḥammad Barrāda (b. 1938, Rabat).[4]

This study aims at filling a gap in the field of criticism (in English) of the contemporary Arabic novel. The gap is both quantitative and qualitative. First of all, studies in English focusing on writers of the preceding generations, dominated by Naguib Mahfouz (1911–2006), outnumber those on the generation of writers under consideration here. More importantly, it is evident that Arabic fiction is today often read by Western academic and non-academic readers alike for extra-literary reasons. In other words, Arabic novels are usually read (often in translation) and analysed not as *works of art* in their own right but because they are seen as interesting documents from diverse points of view: anthropological, socio-political, feminist,[5] historical and so on. Of course, all of these approaches are legitimate and all can add something substantial to our understanding of Arab societies, as well as enriching their parent disciplines. Nonetheless, if the literary, artistic and technical elements in these novels are overlooked, then their most crucial aspect is not taken into account. These works all deal with social, political and historical phenomena but they do so quite differently to, say, history books, journalistic articles or academic essays.[6] The difference is the form the author has decided to give them and this form is that of a novel, a work of fiction which we should evaluate by considering how a specific *form* gives life to a specific *content*. In other words, we will consider the *aesthetics* of these works, relying on a close textual analysis of technical aspects such as narrative voice, structure, style, and mood. The present study is therefore divided into chapters dedicated explicitly to formal aspects of the novels read. According to our reading, the most significantly innovative aspects of these texts are

1 narrative fragmentation;
2 polyphony;
3 intertextuality and
4 metafiction.

To each of these literary aspects corresponds a more or less well formulated corpus of critical material (developed mainly in the West) – in some cases a theory of literature, in others only a critical method. We will refer to this material throughout this work. For example, once we acknowledge that a common feature of many texts analysed is the presence of more than one narrative voice, it is impossible for us to ignore what M. M. Bakhtin and other Western critics have written about this literary phenomenon. Nevertheless, our dependence on these works (and the general critical concepts they generate) means neither that we will rigidly apply the critical methods employed by Western scholars engaging with similar formal aspects, nor that we will necessarily reach the same conclusions.[7] We simply found these general and much debated concepts useful as starting points from which to carry out a rigorous formal analysis of the novels and a discussion of their contents. This analysis is obviously our main goal, but we also aim to define as clearly as possible what we mean by these critical concepts, which are often referred to in discussions of Arabic fiction without being properly defined.

Moreover, we have deliberately chosen the general term *content* as opposed to more specific words such as *message* or *meaning* because we believe that the obsessive search for a message in a novel (and more generally in a work of art) can be dangerously misleading: if in a novel the message is not clearly spelled out (and it rarely is), readers can easily find what they wish to find; once this message is found (or once the more sophisticated reader's theory or ideology is confirmed), it is easy to dismiss the other features of the work as insubstantial ornaments – mere embellishments. We believe that a literary approach, more than any other perhaps, helps the reader of fiction to avoid such mistakes and simplifications. To resist the tyranny of the message does not mean to disregard the content of a novel: none of the novels here considered is an exercise in pure form, devoid of any connection with its non-fictional context. This content, or more accurately the *raison d'être* of a novel, could well be something very different from a straightforward message (and in the best fiction it usually is). We are thinking here of those authors who deform their fictional texts in order to make political statements. This is not to say that all authors who deal with political issues in their fiction or even explicitly articulate political discourses are doomed to failure. The problem arises when the political element emerges as an alien feature which has been artificially introduced and does not have much to do with the surrounding fictional text.[8] We will discuss this later, giving examples of successful and unsuccessful political arguments made through fictional texts and, in the final chapter of this study, we will draw our conclusions on the argument. Here it will suffice to refer to the ideas of two novelists about literature and art in general. Al-Kharrāṭ writes in an article about commitment in art (referring to his own experience as an Arab writer of fiction) that a truly artistic experience is 'a striving towards knowledge'. According to him, literature should be there to ask questions (as we strive towards knowledge), rather than to provide answers. He then says that literary works should fulfil this questioning task in an artistic fashion: they should not conform to a political cause (Kharrāṭ 2001). The Czech novelist Milan Kundera writes: 'I have always, deeply, violently, detested those who look for a position (political, philosophical, religious, whatever) in a work of art rather than searching it for an *effort to know*, to understand, to grasp this or that aspect of reality' (Kundera 1993: 91).

'Aspect of reality' is a crucial phrase for our study. As seen earlier, Ṣ. Idrīs too refers to novels which strive to deal with real life: for all their innovative and, at times, radical features, these novels primarily engage with their wider socio-political context (the notable exception is, as we will see, a novel which promotes an inward, self-referential discourse). Again, we read in Kundera that 'apprehending the real world is part of the definition of the novel' (Kundera 1993: 53), but we could have cited many other critics and writers to confirm that the novel, despite its self-referential elements, is mainly concerned with the world in which we live (according to Bakhtin the concern with the present is one of the features which separates the novel from the epic: cf. the essay 'Epic and Novel' in Bakhtin 1975: 3–40). This is certainly the case with the novels we have studied: the metaphor of art as a mirror held up to the world is generally still valid (although it is often questioned), even if at times the mirror which the innovative Arabic novel holds up has two glasses – one reflecting the world and the other itself and its own history, with references to the non-Arabic novel and the Arab literary heritage. The nature of such texts seems to be further enriched (and complicated) by a necessity born out of certain socio-political circumstances typical of the Arab world.

We will see how literary innovations and representations of reality are at times paired with a preoccupation with historiography. In her book on the connection between history and fiction in the works of the Egyptian novelists Mahfouz, Jamāl al-Ghīṭānī and Ṣun^{c}allāh Ibrāhīm, the Egyptian scholar Samia Mehrez writes about the power the state in developing countries exercises over the narratives (both historiographical and literary) of society and reality, and she reflects on the role of the writer of fiction as follows:

> the Arab contemporary writer comes to occupy a larger and more crucial space, despite (or perhaps because of) all the restrictions, limitations, and censorship he or she may encounter. [. . .] The position of the writer as 'underground historian' is indeed what characterizes much of the literary output in the contemporary Arab world.
>
> (Mehrez 1994: 7–8)

This tendency towards some sort of alternative historiography is evident in some of the novels we analyse here (especially the works by Khūrī and Barrāda). Even when in other texts (by al-Takarlī and al-Kharrāṭ for example) this urge to repair the omissions of the official historiography is generally resisted by the author, it is necessary for us to keep it in mind as it is a feature clearly much more relevant in the Arab world than in the West.[9]

The particular socio-political situation of the Arab world has another effect on the writing of fiction, pushing certain authors towards politically aware, if not directly militant, positions. As early as 1975, the Syrian sociologist and novelist Ḥalīm Barakāt articulates this militant attitude clearly when he addresses 'the gap between [. . .] Arab society as it exists in reality, and as it ought to be in order to confront trying challenges':

> A writer could not be part of Arab society and yet not concern himself with change. [. . .] the theory of influence which sees writers as agents of social change, applies more accurately to contemporary Arab novelists than the theory of reflection, which sees writers as objective and detached observers holding a mirror to reality.
>
> (Barakāt 1975: 126–7)

He then concludes his argument, foreseeing the birth of what he defines the Arabic 'novel of revolutionary change', as follows:

> Novels of revolutionary change invalidate the hypothesis that literature reflects reality [. . .] Such novels invalidate also the hypothesis that there is a conflict between art and political commitment. Literature can subordinate politics to creative and reflective thinking, and undertake the task of promoting a new consciousness.
>
> (Barakāt 1975: 137)

Similarly today, a writer like Khūrī, for instance, does not content himself with creating a narrative which reflects on its own nature and at the same time engages with politics and history. He, like others, harbours the ambition that such a narrative will have an impact on the use of language and will contribute to promoting cultural changes:

> Writing in times of transition takes the form of a journey towards what we do not know and towards the shock of writing what we know, which will lead us to discover how writing changes things and does not only reflect them.
>
> (Khūrī 1990: 8)

While this attitude of full commitment might be understood, if not appreciated (considering the situation of general crisis in which the Arab world finds itself today), it is also true that some critics have stigmatized it as paternalistic. For instance, according to Stefan Meyer, Pierre Cachia states that 'most Arab writers look upon themselves as nothing less than cultural and social guides for their contemporaries' (Meyer 2001: 5).[10] Meyer suggests that what Cachia allegedly says about the Arab modernists of the beginning of the last century is relevant today too. This is questionable, despite the fact that the passages quoted from Barakāt may seem to confirm it.[11] An increasing number of Arab writers today (including the novelists discussed in this study) are alienated not only from the centres of political power, but also from their societies (as Meyer rightly points out – Meyer 2001: 6). For this reason and given a series of obvious practical problems (e.g. illiteracy) which contribute to limiting the readership of fiction, these writers are well aware that the impact of their fiction on the general public, to which it is primarily addressed, is not as strong as they might wish.[12] In fact, a cynical commentator could speculate that Arabic novels have a wider readership in the West than in the Arab world. While it is impossible today to establish precise statistics for the readership of contemporary Arabic fiction,[13] there are indications that this fiction has a considerable impact beyond the bounds of its readership: novels are adapted for television, cinema and theatre;[14] writers enjoy a relatively high public profile in the press, media, literary cafes, and so on; both official censors and Islamist protestors have shown great enthusiasm in banning and burning novels, as well as attacking novelists (consider for example, the 1994 stabbing of Mahfouz, the cultural 'war' surrounding the 2000 Egyptian reprint of Ḥaydar Ḥaydar's novel *Walīma li-aᶜshāb al-baḥr* 'Banquet for Seaweed' (1983) and the 2001 action by the Egyptian Ministry of Culture in taking off the market three novels considered obscene).[15]

As far as the connection between political power and writers is concerned, however, the case of Egypt will help us to illustrate our point further. Under Nasser, the political elite controlled and at times cracked down on writers and intellectuals but also gave them a certain autonomy and power (basically, employing them) in exchange for their support in articulating the regime's policies

(Jacquemond 2003: 31–7). During the later years of Nasser's rule, writers became increasingly disillusioned with the leadership's strategies. Under Sadat, they were progressively excluded from the centres of power (Jacquemond 2003: 39–42). If we now consider the situation under Mubarak, we can see that (after a first decade which roughly reproduced the conditions existing under Sadat) his leadership has recently shifted to a more inclusive approach but this does not resolve the two major problems (which were already prominent under Nasser): if the patronage offered by those in power defends intellectuals from the attacks of the radical Islamic movement on the ascendancy, it obviously limits their independence and freedom to criticize the government;[16] more importantly perhaps, as Richard Jacquemond points out, the promoters of this policy (promotion of the values of the *nahḍa* – such as patriotism, tolerance, rationalism, freedom, political reform – from above, as it were) do not seem to realize how ineffective it is in reaching its targets (Jacquemond 2003: 45). As a result of this situation, writers like the novelists studied here, who promote secular ideas, social equality, democracy, political and religious tolerance, now find themselves in the middle of a double process of alienation: on the one hand, they have been ostracized by the political authorities, which still exert pressure on them in various ways;[17] on the other hand, they are increasingly alienated from some sections of the general public who, having become disillusioned with secular ideas, seem to embrace a more radical religious discourse. As a result of all these changes, the attitude of the novelists, who are fully aware of their position in society, is much less paternalistic than Meyer seems to imply. The general attitude of Arab writers has changed: rather than envisaging guiding their fellow citizens from above, they are more receptive towards their concerns, while still producing discourses critical of what they feel are dangerous trends (like radical Islamic thought). A writer like Khūrī would embrace as his own what the late Italian novelist Italo Calvino says about politics and literature:

> Literature is necessary to politics above all when it gives a voice to whatever is without a voice, when it gives a name to what as yet has no name, especially to what the language of politics excludes or attempts to exclude.
>
> (Calvino quoted in Mehrez 1994: 80)

Such writers are part of that 'small group of Arab secular intellectuals who', along with some religious reformers, according to Waïl Hassan, 'challenge canonical interpretations [of religious texts] embraced unquestioningly by traditional clerics and by fundamentalists [and] advocate reforms in the areas of women's rights, social organization and political institutions. And those progressive intellectuals', Hassan adds, 'also see themselves as actively committed to resisting neo-colonialism as well as political despotism at home' (Hassan 2002: 56). By acting in this way, let us note very clearly (albeit in passing), these authors not only assume a sort of intellectual responsibility in writing about politically dangerous topics but are also ready to pay personally for their commitment. The imprisonment of Arab writers is well documented and the late ᶜAbd al-Raḥmān Munīf once publicly stated that he felt almost ashamed of having spent only a few months in prison, whereas most of his colleagues had paid a much heavier price.[18] The task of literature as expressed earlier by Calvino can hardly involve a paternalistic attitude, and it also leads us, incidentally, to another main concern for Arab writers: the literary language.[19] This concern can range from Khūrī's plan to make the literary language closer to the colloquial and therefore available to a wider public, to al-Kharrāṭ's sophisticated wordplay and interplay between numerous linguistic varieties. There is no doubt that the authors studied here pay much attention to the formal aspect of their work, engaging with questions of literary technique much more than earlier generations. This trend probably has to do with the fact that engaging with form and technique is inherent in any sophisticated literary discourse, even when it deals directly or indirectly with politics.[20] We will return to the connection between political engagement and fiction later in this introduction when we talk about the concept of modernism.

To affirm that these novels are a sort of representation of reality does not mean that they can be ascribed to literary realism – that they try to produce 'the illusion of reality' in the same way as the European nineteenth-century mainstream novel. This effect relies on a kind of writing which represents verisimilar situations and plausible characters. Within modern Arabic literature we can generally relate such an effect to Mahfouz's early novels. Of course, such *realistic* writing is not limited to actual facts but often deals with metaphysical reality: it is not incidental that Henry James, a novelist so concerned with the workings of the mind, was the one to highlight this quality of fiction – the illusion of reality.[21] The Egyptian critic Sabry Hafez has underlined how at the beginning of the twentieth century the Arabic novelistic tradition, which was clearly heavily influenced by, if not entirely imported from the West,

> perceived itself as an equivalent of reality or as its reproduction in verbal form. Its starting point was a belief in the infallibility of mimesis, which was seen as a trustworthy representation of life with its verisimilitude as the ultimate proof of its plausibility and relevance to the reader's experience. The quest for literary excellence involved the exact reproduction of the condition of reality in a manner that convinced the reader that what he was reading had actually happened.
>
> (Hafez 1994: 102)

In the texts under scrutiny here, this traditional representation of reality is subverted, questioned, its limitations exposed. This questioning is sometimes paired with a questioning of the workings of fiction itself, but the reference to the non-fictional, wider context is never completely banished: the mode of representation is different, new, but it is still related to that context.[22] We will see in the next chapter how al-Kharrāṭ and Khūrī, whose writing can hardly be considered *realistic* (in the manner of the early Mahfouzian or the nineteenth century European novel), implicitly claim that their way of writing is more truly *realistic* (i.e. capable of representing a reality efficiently) than that of their predecessors. Their first response to their sense that the *realistic* mode is no longer adequate to represent their reality is their use of narrative fragmentation, which upsets the main ingredients of traditional Mahfouzian writing: *linear* development, *clear* exposition, *solid* temporal and spatial settings. Further aesthetic choices will be shown to subvert other cardinal elements of the Mahfouzian model: *verisimilar* scenarios and plots, *credible* characters, *reliable* narrative voice (usually only one), and so on.

We have already alluded to the kind of literary innovation these novels display, but it is now necessary to address the issue more directly. In the period we have chosen to survey, a significant number of novelists have experimented with new ways of narrating. These writers, we argue, can be defined as innovative. The comparison is obviously made with the writers of preceding generations, and especially with those who have contributed most to establishing the features of the mainstream Arabic novel, to canonizing it and to shaping its forms. Roger Allen writes in his monograph on the Arabic novel (first published in 1982) about 'transformations in fictional perspectives' which developed after 1967 as follows:

> Such is the quality and quantity of experimentation in the realm of the Arabic novel in recent decades that it is clearly impossible to include here discussion of the multifarious ways in which novelists are making use of contradictions, fractured or cancelled time, and textual pastiche and subversion, to express in fiction a vision of contemporary society and their sense of alienation towards it. [. . .] it is quite clear that the fictional works of contemporary novelists [. . .] turn the act of reading into a process of discovery that is often complex.
>
> (Allen 1995: 123–4)

The major aim of the present work is to give an analysis of the most significant examples of this experimental and innovative way of writing fiction. The key feature of our selection of writers is neither the amount of critical recognition they have received, nor their influential legacy, nor their regional provenance, but rather the fact that they represent different ways of departing from the *realistic* writing imposed by the success of Mahfouz's early fiction.[23] Before we move on, let us make it clear that Mahfouz himself had moved away from a *realistic* narration and experimented with new techniques and forms much earlier than 1979. At the risk of oversimplifying, we can outline four main trends originating in Mahfouz's novels which have influenced the Arabic novel in general[24]: his first novels are historical and deal with the history of ancient Egypt; with the so-called Cairo Trilogy (1956–1957), Mahfouz successfully imposes a realistic style which is further explored in his novels of the 1960s (such as *al-Liṣṣ wa-'l-kilāb* [1962; *The Thief and the Dogs*, 1984] and *Mīrāmār* [1967; *Miramar*, 1978]), where the stress is more on the psychological portrayal of the characters. In the later novels, realism is also often transcended by symbolism and formal experimentation. The last significant trend was inaugurated with novels like *Layālī Alf layla* (1982; *Arabian Nights and Days*, 1995) and its overt intertextual use of the Arabic popular heritage, already evident in the title.[25]

We can see 1967, the year of the *naksa*, as a turning point in literary orientation throughout the Arab world, when the prevalent mode of realistic writing starts to seem inadequate to portray a rapidly changing reality and a general identity crisis. Like all such generalizations, this one must be taken as no more than a convention to simplify presentation of a complex historical reality. It is obvious, as we will see in the following paragraphs, that some kind of change in literary sensibility was already in the air well before 1967.[26] There is little doubt, nevertheless, that the *naksa* accelerated those changes. Other historical events also played an important role in destabilizing the writers' worldview and self-perception: it is impossible to ignore the impact (especially on Lebanese authors) of the long Lebanese Civil War (1975–1990) and the gradual destruction of Beirut, once a vibrant cultural centre for the whole Arab world, and of the many Gulf wars which destabilized Iraq.

To go back to the literary turning point of the 1960s, our analysis will not include a discussion of works published in the 1960s and 1970s, despite their undoubted importance. The so-called 1960s generation, including writers such as Jamāl al-Ghīṭānī (b. 1945), Ṣunᶜallāh Ibrāhīm (b. 1937), ᶜAbd al-Ḥakīm Qāsim (1935–1990) and Bahā᾽ Ṭāhir (b. 1935) played and continue to play an important innovative role in Egyptian fiction. There are various reasons for our omission of these writers: the first is that an increasing number of studies (even in English) have appeared treating works of these writers.[27] At the same time, only a small number of studies deal adequately with the early novels of al-Kharrāṭ (himself one of the members of the '1960s generation'), whose importance as innovative texts can hardly be overestimated. For instance, some critics mention his first novel, *Rāma wa-'l-tinnīn*, almost in passing as a very innovative work without substantiating these claims through critical argument: in short, the novel is a true turning point which has not attracted the critical attention it deserves.[28] Even more serious is the underestimation of all the works of al-Takarlī. Our analysis is intended as a contribution to the growing number of studies on the post-Mahfouz generation. Another reason for our focusing on Barrāda, al-Kharrāṭ, Khūrī and al-Takarlī, and exclusively on those works which appeared after 1979, is that we witness in them a maturation of the innovative writing which they had initiated earlier.[29] In other words, in the novels we have chosen to discuss, technical innovations are consistent and radical: early innovations are developed to the limit and new ones are introduced. For example, the early novelistic works by al-Kharrāṭ already display a new trend common to the works of many contemporary Arab authors (with the Egyptian al-Ghīṭānī as possibly the most eminent amongst them): the use of the Arab literary heritage as a source of inspiration. A large number of Arab novelists engage in a dialogue not only with the classical Arabic *turāth*, but also with the folk traditions. Even the most innovative of these writers display an awareness of belonging to a certain cultural heritage. It is curious how a novelist like al-Kharrāṭ can in the same interview easily dismiss the *realistic* novel in the style of early Mahfouz and at the same time state that he hopes he has contributed to the revival of the *Arabian Nights* type of narration (see later). The contribution of the *turāth* to contemporary fiction is one of the most significant features of the Arabic novel as it moves away from the realistic form of the period of its maturity. The reasons behind this trend are many and parallels can be made with the modern South American, African or Indian novel.[30] Whatever role politics have played in promoting it, this trend remains a cultural phenomenon of significance which should not surprise us at all: once Arab writers had adopted the literary genre of the novel (from the West), and brought its realistic form to maturity, they used this most plastic and healthily ill-defined of all literary genres (so fluid that it tends to subsume all other literary genres), as the ideal medium to explore their own literary heritage.[31] This development is suggested by Khūrī himself, who underlines how the first, marginal fictional experiments at the beginning of the *nahḍa* were given a form by Mahfouz employing a European model. After Mahfouz, novelists were more inclined to subvert the Mahfouzian form and relied on a sort of formless fiction which Khūrī relates to classical Arabic literature (Khūrī 1990: 4–5). While the connection between classical and modern Arabic literatures is not always evident and deserves to be studied more extensively, it is nonetheless of some significance that an author who, like Khūrī, is at times defined as postmodernist (and, according to Meyer, places 'no value on the attempt to forge an indigenous Arab literature', Meyer 2001: 117) makes such a statement.

Even when discussing the tendency of Arab writers to refer increasingly to their own cultural traditions, it is difficult to stay away from comparisons between the Arabic and the Western novel (one can think about the Western modernist motto 'make it new!', referring to the Western literary past). As we explained at the beginning of this introductory chapter, this study will occasionally include references and comparisons to the non-Arabic novel, with particular attention to the development of the Western novel. This is because Western literature exercised much influence on Arab writers throughout the twentieth century. Therefore, scholars who have dealt with the Arabic novel of the last few decades have obviously considered the possibility and the usefulness of drawing parallels between the changes in Arabic novelistic writing, and the evolution from social realism to modernism (and postmodernism) in the Western novel. Hassan has described such a comparative exercise as flawed because it does not adequately take into account the colonial context. Referring to Terri DeYoung's work on the Iraqi poet Badr Shākir al-Sayyāb, he writes:

> In the absence of any consideration of the colonial context, critics have tended hastily and unquestioningly to use Western periodization to describe the development of modern Arabic literature, thus reducing it, in DeYoung's words, to 'an inexorable sequencing not of its own making', as if those phases of modern Arabic literature (romanticism, realism, modernism)

> 'were simply repetitions of their Western counterparts ... that had to be "gotten through" so that one could arrive at the teleologically determined endpoint of modernism'
>
> (Hassan 2002: 58–9)

Similarly, Meyer, in his monograph on the experimental Arabic novel in the Levant, reiterates Hassan's doubts, debating at length whether it is useful to apply Western critical terms such as modernism and postmodernism to the Arabic novel, and concluding that

> while the investment of postmodernism in postcolonial theory produces a binary vision of the world and a unitary vision of both modernism and postmodernism, [our] examination of the experimental Arabic novel suggests that a more appropriate response would be to move to a unitary vision of the world and a multiple view of modernism
>
> (Meyer 2001: 277)

Here, we will refer to Meyer's most significant observations, which will serve us to contextualize further the texts analysed in this work without indulging in theoretical discussion about modernism and postmodernism and whether these terms can be applied to the Arabic novel. This debate is certainly important and Meyer does it justice with his thorough investigation, but we hope that we can achieve what he advocates[32] through our close textual analysis. Regarding the historical (colonial) context which Hassan wants us to consider, it has to be said that it obviously played and still plays an important role. As we have seen briefly earlier, Hassan discusses how the academic disciplines of postcolonial studies and Arabic literary studies can both improve through a tighter collaboration: the former can add to the latter 'interdisciplinary inquiry, theoretical sophistication and historical contextualization' (Hassan 2002: 59). Such contextualization does not, however, have to imply that Arab writers only did and do react to the Western discourse with their 'activity of resistance' (DeYoung quoted in Hassan 2002: 59). They have also reacted with enthusiasm to Western literature (see for example the influence of Russian authors on the pioneers of Egyptian and Iraqi fiction). If it is simplistic to ascribe uncritically the canonical development of Western fiction (from the historical novel to the postmodernist pastiche) to Arabic fiction, it is also simplistic to underestimate the role played by Western literature in the shaping of modern Arabic literature – to ignore how many influential Arab writers have sought inspiration in their reading of Western literature. Moreover, it is difficult to ignore the critical tools which Western literary criticism can provide, even when we are dealing with non-Western literatures (as we have underlined earlier). For example, while subscribing to DeYoung's critique on the uncritical application of Western periodization to Arabic literature, Hassan cannot avoid describing Arab poets as 'neo-classicists', 'romantics' and 'modernists', when he briefly refers to how the anti-colonial element is present in the development of modern

Arabic poetry. The contradiction between political rejection of, and cultural fascination with, the West is often only apparent to critics and theorists and not to Arab writers themselves, who usually acknowledge it quite freely.[33] This is all the more evident in authors who adopt the language of the colonial power in order to formulate a discourse which can often be critical of colonialism (the Egyptian Ahdaf Soueif, who writes her novels in English, is a case in point; the Algerian writer Kateb Yacine famously regarded the French language in which he wrote as his *butin de guerre*).

Apart from all this, Hassan draws our attention to the fact that one of the limits of postcolonial studies is that it is not always possible to refer to the 'activity of resistance' to Western discourse:

> the vast majority of Asian and African literary texts produced since the onset of modern European colonialism simply do not fall into any homogenous category. Even if we limit ourselves to the twentieth century, we realize that the number of works that fit within the paradigms of resistance privileged in postcolonial theory is scant.
>
> (Hassan 2002: 60)

In other words, many literary texts produced in the Arab world deal, just like their Western counterparts, with a wide range of subjects, some of which have little to do with the East–West, colonizer–colonized dichotomies (al-Takarlī's novels are a case in point).

In considering Western influence on the Arabic texts discussed here, the best insight is provided by an analysis of the concept of modernism. As we have said earlier, the writers discussed in this study can be regarded as modernists, in as much as it is possible to apply the concept of modernism as formulated by Western literary criticism to the Arabic novel's switch from realism to a more complex writing mode. Obviously, there are significant differences between Arab and Western writers, not least those concerning the status of writers within the two societies and the impact of their works on the general public. These differences play a role in shaping the novel in different ways. Meyer has stressed the prominence of the political and the *engagé* in modern Arabic literature as one of the major differences between Arabic and Western modernism: 'while textual ambiguity in Western modernism is rarely overtly political, in the Arab world, it is nearly always political in its intent and effect' (Meyer 2001: 46).

The importance of political commitment for Arab writers cannot be overestimated in the light of the observations we have made earlier about the historiographical elements in contemporary Arabic fiction. Obviously, this attitude can be regarded as either noble and indeed necessary (see earlier), or an impediment to literary creativity. In other words, novels with an overbearing political message become didactic and superficial (cf. Meyer 2001: 46). Some Palestinian novels, for example, suffer from this shortcoming because of their overtly political motivation, and some feminist writing becomes predictable because of its social concerns. While the *raison d'être* of these texts may be admirable from an ideological point of view (see Ḥ. Barakāt earlier), we are left to wonder whether an artistically rich and profoundly innovative novel written by writers who are skilled technicians in the art of fiction would have a bigger long term impact than a more simplistic and straightforward narrative. On the other hand, some critics, even when dealing with Western fiction,[34] welcome some form of political commitment and consider it a healthy element of fiction, especially today. For instance, the American critic John Brenkman, writing on literary innovation, compares two novelists who are often labelled 'postmodernist': Thomas Pynchon and Salman Rushdie. The former, whom Brenkman defines as the master of metafictional writing today, is guilty (still according to Brenkman) of indulging too much in metafictional practices *per se*. At the same time, Brenkman's critical reading exalts Rushdie's *Satanic Verses* (1988) as a novel in which we find metafictional references but also, crucially, a deep understanding of complex phenomena, continuous references to the real world and social criticism (in the best tradition of Menippean satire;[35] Brenkman 2006: 816–18). In the Arab context, the late Egyptian critic Magda al-Nowaihi seems to echo Brenkman's concerns that some so-called postmodernist texts risk being too solipsistic.[36] In her article about one of the novels we will analyse later, Barrāda's *Lu*ᶜ*bat al-nisyān* (1987; *The Game of Forgetting*, 1996), she welcomes the Moroccan author's efforts to create a novel which is experimental and metafictional whilst at the same time engaging with real, important issues:

> in distinction from western texts where postmodernity and commitment often seem to be mutually exclusive, we have here a narrative that is postmodern in sensibility and structure, but is also fiercely concerned with the here and now and committed to struggling for its improvement
>
> (Nowaihi 2000: 387–8)

Al-Nowaihi talks of an Arab writer who simultaneously accepts postmodernism but finds 'unacceptable some western postmodernist tendencies such as total relativism and the production of texts that are divorced from the surrounding reality' (Nowaihi 2000: 388).

The authors considered here try to find a successful solution to the dilemmas and contradictions highlighted earlier by giving birth to a work of fiction which: is very much concerned with 'the surrounding reality' but also reflects on its own form and history; deals with politics but also proposes innovative solutions to technical and formal literary problems; finds inspiration in Western or non-Arabic literatures, but also draws on its own cultural heritage.

At the beginning of this introduction we referred to a gap in the body of critical literature available in English on the Arabic novel. The present study aims at adding to the contribution towards filling that critical gap made in recent years by two major monographs:

1 *The Experimental Arabic Novel* by Stephan Meyer (2001);
2 *The Postcolonial Arabic Novel. Debating Ambivalence* by Muhsin Jassim al-Musawi (2003).

These two monographs are much broader in scope than the present study. They include analyses of a far higher number of texts and aim at a comprehensive general outline of the Arabic novel's development. This is especially true of Musawi's monograph, which does not focus exclusively on innovative and experimental fiction, but considers the post-Mahfouzian novel more generally. Meyer's volume on the other hand, whilst a true pioneering work in its field, focuses on the literature of 'the Levant' only. This study aims to carry out closer textual analysis and makes fewer overarching generalizations, and, as it focuses on novelistic innovation, Meyer's work will be more relevant to it. As we have mentioned earlier, more detailed textual analysis is what we feel is needed in our field today, where too often important concepts are left unarticulated and illustrative examples from texts are lacking. Our study's most important contribution is that it constitutes a detailed and thorough analysis of significant novels which are only partly considered by both Musawi and Meyer. For instance, an author as important as Khūrī is almost entirely ignored by Musawi, but not by Meyer. Meyer, on the other hand, does not write about al-Kharrāṭ, al-Takarlī and Barrāda (as they do not come from 'the Levant'). These two texts will provide useful reference points for this study, as our findings will fit in or contrast with the general conclusions they formulate. For example, Meyer's volume provides a solid framework in its introduction which clearly defines the main trends of innovation in the Arabic novel:

> They [experimental Arab writers] have reacted to the formal unity, ideological bias, omniscient viewpoint, and heroism of realist narratives and countered these with narratives that are fragmented, artistically determined, multiple-voiced, and that reflect a sense of cultural crisis, while still working from a standpoint that reflects the values and priorities of the *engagé*
>
> (Meyer 2001: 7)

On the other hand, it seems that the need to draw very general conclusions which might apply to the whole of Arabic literature makes the author formulate some questionable observations (e.g. regarding Arab writers' supposedly paternalistic and conservative attitudes). Meyer affirms that narrative fragmentation and abstraction do not necessarily point at a progressive way of thinking on the part of the author.[37] This is true, but surely the Arab authors who rely on fragmentation and abstraction do not do so because of the Islamic prohibition regarding the representation of the human form (Meyer 2001: 12–13). If one relies too much on these stereotypical concepts, one might well assume that Arabic classical literature, because predominantly Islamic, is characterized by over-abstraction, whereas everything in it is in fact tangible and concrete, and there is no abstraction even when the author is depicting the thought processes of a character/historical figure. Meyer claims that more complex novelistic forms are prevented from developing in the Arab world by virtue of the fact that 'the spirit of irony, paradox, criticism and particularly self-criticism within the society as a whole is still severely restricted.' He defines Arab culture (and that of the 'Third World' more generally) as 'a culture in which the privileges of ironic distance are not available' (Meyer 2001: 6). While we might agree that Arab society is, at this particular moment in its history, vulnerable to these shortcomings, it would be very difficult to ascribe to Arab culture as a whole a lack of 'ironic distance' (there is plenty of ironic distance from Abū Nuwās up to Nizār Qabbānī and beyond, to mention only two extremely popular poets).

We believe that a close textual analysis of innovative modern and contemporary Arabic novels will not only be valuable in itself, but will also help us to avoid drawing simplistic and over-generalized conclusions about Arab culture and society.

2

FRAGMENTATION

One of the main characteristics of most of the novels we have selected is that they are devoid of a traditionally ordered plot. A non-linear, non-chronological way of narrating is adopted and developed in a radical way, especially in the works of al-Kharrāṭ and Khūrī. This feature is so prominent that some critics have indicated the presence of an almost random or casual narrative. For instance, Roger Allen writes about Khūrī's novel *Riḥlat Ghāndī al-ṣaghīr* (1989; *The Journey of Little Gandhi*, 1994): 'There is little about this narrative that suggests an organizing principle based on chronology or any other criterion' (Allen 1995: 88). In this chapter we will try to show how and why these writers have chosen to depart from a traditional, more linear and logically ordered narration.

The lack of conventional order typical of most works by al-Kharrāṭ and Khūrī is well expressed by the term fragmentation. Western literary critics tend to agree that disruption of the linear flow of narrative (typical of the nineteenth century mainstream novel) is one of the formal features of literary modernism (cf., for example, Gerald Graff referred to in Barth 1980: 199). On the other hand, in his afterword to the English translation of Khūrī's *al-Jabal al-ṣaghīr* (1977; *Little Mountain*, 1989), Edward Said talks about the Lebanese writer as a typical postmodern author who writes formless works,[1] characterized by a 'combinatorial amalgam of different elements, principally autobiography, story, fable, pastiche, and self-parody' (Said 1989: 144). In the novels discussed here fragmentation is twofold. It influences: (1) Time. Literary fragmentation is perhaps most evident in the disruption of time. Most of the novels analysed here are not chronologically ordered; (2) Style and narrative technique. Fragmentation is also present in the continuous shifting from one literary style to another, and from one narrative mode to another. This last feature could be said to be present in virtually all novels (writers employ varying techniques in the course of their novels), but in our examples we will see that the sudden shifts from one technique to another, the juxtaposition of completely different literary styles and genres (see Said's comment earlier), is quite extraordinary. The merging of different styles and the imitation or importing of alien texts into the narrative will be discussed in more detail in Chapter 3, devoted to intertextuality.

Al-Kharrāṭ is usually regarded as being among the most innovative Arab writers of our time. One of the most prominent features of his prose is fragmentation, as defined earlier.[2] Our analysis of al-Kharrāṭ's works will focus mainly on what is sometimes referred to as the *Rāma* Trilogy (*Thulāthiyyat Rāma*). This includes al-Kharrāṭ's first two novels: *Rāma wa-'l-tinnīn* (first published in a limited edition in Cairo in 1979) and its sequel *al-Zaman al-ākhar* 'The Other Time' (1985). The Trilogy's last novel is *Yaqīn al-ᶜaṭash* 'Certainty of Thirst' (1996). Not only does our decision to study the Trilogy reflect the need to focus on al-Kharrāṭ's early novels (which, as we have seen in the introduction, have not been properly analysed in English), it also gives us the opportunity to study the development of the author's style by taking into consideration *Yaqīn*, a novel published in the 1990s (eleven years after *al-Zaman*) – the most prolific decade for al-Kharrāṭ as a novelist (*Yaqīn* is his thirteenth novel).

In these three novels, literary conventions such as spatial-temporal framing, chronological exposition of facts and plot do not occur or at least not in a traditional way. The systematic use of flash-backs and flash-forwards, the incessant shifting to and from undefined places and different periods of time, the juxtaposition of narrative techniques (speech, interior monologue, stream of consciousness, first and third person narratives), all combine to prevent the reader from immediately identifying the characters and their story. On the contrary, the novels are structured (or, better, deconstructed) in such a way that the reader becomes aware only gradually who the protagonists, namely Mīkhāᵓīl and Rāma, are. Al-Kharrāṭ does this deliberately, being more interested in the hero, Mīkhāᵓīl's, inner self and his subjective point of view.[3] Factual events are always seen, elaborated, interpreted, indeed experienced internally by Mīkhāᵓīl. This is part of the way these novels are narrated: nothing seems to be observed from an external, objective point of view. We could relate narrative fragmentation in al-Kharrāṭ's works to his strategy of mixing the two dimensions of human experience: the physical one (hard facts and tangible actions) and the metaphysical one (dreams, wishes, fears, thoughts). 'Accordingly', as we have underlined elsewhere,

> the Kharrāṭian hero coincides with Ernst Cassirer's definition of man as an ' "animal symbolicum" living in a "symbolic universe" ' who 'does not live in a world of hard facts ... He lives rather in the midst of imaginary emotions, in hopes and fears, in illusions and disillusions, in his fantasies and dreams' (Cassirer quoted in Gershoni and Jankowski 1986: 77). Hence, if on one level Mīkhāᵓīl experiences the sublime peaks and desperate lows of his ambivalent love story with Rāma, on another, parallel level, from the beginning of *Rāma* until the finale of [*Yaqīn*], he associates his beloved with mythological or religious figures. As a consequence of this, Rāma's character acquires a well-defined, multifaceted, mythological dimension. It is significant that the passages in which Rāma appears along with these images, or where these latter appear

clearly as symbols of Rāma, are at least as frequent as those passages conveying straight biographical information about the heroine.

(Caiani 2005: 37)

As we mentioned in the introduction, this representation of reality is to be found in Western modernist novelists (like James Joyce),[4] and in many ways al-Kharrāṭ can be defined as a modernist.

The author argues that there is no such a thing as 'objective reality' in his art. Hence, biographical information often appears in the *Rāma* Trilogy as something which the two main characters relate to each other incidentally. We shall, however, try to define briefly what the main story narrated in the novels is about. The main subject of the Trilogy is the love story between Mīkhāʾīl, a middle-aged Copt, and Rāma, a middle-aged Muslim, as remembered, reconsidered and relived by the former once their relationship has ended. The fact that this relationship belongs to the past of the characters is of major importance: we will see later how this affects the way al-Kharrāṭ tells the story. Another main consequence of this feature is that two of the Trilogy's main themes are those of loss and of the impossibility of perfect union (e.g. between two people, the individual and his society, man and God, man and himself, and so on). It is clear, from the beginning of *Rāma*, that the themes dealt with in the Trilogy can be interpreted allegorically and refer to philosophical, religious and socio-political themes which encompass and transcend the love story trope. For instance, the fact that Mīkhāʾīl is a Copt and Rāma a Muslim is not central to the story, but at the same time the confessional difference serves the author's discourse on Egyptian national identity which should, according to him, transcend religious beliefs. Apart from the symbolic value of the narration, Mīkhāʾīl's memories take us back to some key moments in his story with his beloved: the friendship stage of their relationship and their trip to Rome; their emblematic 'six days' spent in a hotel; their numerous farewells and re-encounters (e.g. while *Rāma* ends with what seems to be a definitive split of the couple, *al-Zaman* begins with the two meeting again by chance at a conference). These events are remembered randomly and interspersed with the protagonist's feelings and considerations, especially on his failures *vis-à-vis* Rāma.

As stated earlier, an unusual variety of literary techniques is employed in the narration and these are juxtaposed or even merge into one another. Not only does this juxtaposition facilitate the destruction of a clear spatial-temporal frame, it also makes it difficult to understand which part of the story has actually taken place and which is part of Mīkhāʾīl's thoughts, desires, illusions and dreams. Hence, we sometimes find the protagonist wondering:

> Did that [really] happen? Was he so happy? Had he experienced that joy? He did not know if he was recalling that image or if it was only the drama of a day-dream, an illusion that was more able to resist annihilation than the harshness of reality.
>
> (Kharrāṭ 1979: 254)[5]

From a technical point of view, this passage is narrated in indirect free style to convey Mīkhāᵓīl's thoughts,[6] but this is only one of the narrative techniques used by the author. The singular mixture of narrative techniques in al-Kharrāṭ's fiction is evident from the very beginning of *Rāma*. The novel starts conventionally when an omniscient narrator conveys Mīkhāᵓīl's actions and thoughts in the third person. Then extracts from a past conversation between Mīkhāᵓīl and Rāma follow and eventually the narration switches to the first person (Kharrāṭ 1979: 5–6). More remarkable than the variety of techniques used by the writer, however, is the suddenness with which he switches from one to the other. The next excerpt from *Rāma* is an example of the alternation of different techniques and styles which al-Kharrāṭ employs throughout the Trilogy:[7]

now Rāma is sleeping in his arms . . . sleeping.

You are sleeping in the arms of your lovers, Rāma, in your imprisoned dawn which comes with no flood of light, while your anxious awakening ebbs and flows over the mouth of your womb, incessantly.

She said to him: Why am I waking up? What's making me wake up?

Her eyes are shining with reproach, not expecting a reply. Is the bitterness in her eyes a residue of days and nights of frustration? Is it ambition which has folded its wings in a circle of rejection, an incomplete circle? Is it me she is rejecting, because I'm not doing anything, just lying on her long, narrow bed between the high rocks and the sand, while her arms are reaching forth to the luminous sea, but cannot reach it?

She said to him: Why are you looking at me?

He said: Let me look at you.

She said: Why? Why are you looking at me?

He said: I am making provision for the days of drought.

And of course I am still writhing with hunger, staring without quenching my thirst at the green and salty waters of the lake.

I am still calling you Rāma . . . *Anima* . . . *Mandala* . . . my woman . . . my harbour . . . my cave . . . *Kemi* . . . my dream, merciful Ment, Mut wife of Amun, Ma'at my mirror . . . my blessing . . . Mary full of grace . . . buried Demeter, her wet mouth raining blessing and mercy . . . her womb greedy for sperm, destined to the cycle of death and blazing pleasures . . . mother of the hawk . . . mother of patience . . . mother of the golden jasmine trembling on the waters . . . Rāma.

When she woke up, she looked in his eyes questioningly.

He said to her: You were with me.

She said to him: I too got used to taking you with me wherever I was.

He did not say to her: Liar!

But she knew, she accepted, silently.

He bent over her, kissing her full on the lips

(Kharrāṭ 1979: 104–5)

This lengthy passage shows the juxtaposition of third and first person narratives, interior monologue, stream of consciousness and dialogue (the passage also includes a sophisticated example of alliteration – inevitably lost in translation – which will be analysed in Chapter 4).[8]

The shift from one technique to another can sometimes point at a shift in content but not always: the passage we have just looked at is all focused on the protagonist's feelings towards his beloved. If we take the Trilogy as a whole, however, we can affirm that despite its technical structure remaining the same there is a clear development: in *al-Zaman* and *Yaqīn*, al-Kharrāṭ is increasingly inclined to engage with socio-political issues.[9] How does this change affect the fragmented stylistic nature of the texts? In *al-Zaman* the author follows two strategies to dramatize his socio-political concerns (extreme poverty, corruption, crisis of values, and so on): the first is to introduce abruptly into the narrative letters sent by readers to newspapers, or correspondence between members of Mīkhāʾīl's family. The other strategy is to formulate the political arguments by means of lively dialogues between Mīkhāʾīl and Rāma. In *Yaqīn*, al-Kharrāṭ abandons the insertion of letter texts and confines the political element mainly to Rāma's recounting to Mīkhāʾīl her trip to Upper Egypt, during which she investigated the aftermath of the sectarian violence suffered by Copts at the hands of Islamist radicals. Rāma's investigation gives shape to a substantial, linear subplot rather than the usual fragmented text. Here it will suffice to draw attention to the contrast between the sophisticatedly worded musings and direct free speech, which from *Rāma* to *Yaqīn* is made livelier by increasing use of the Egyptian vernacular. Such vivid and at times colloquial language is also used to depict domestic scenes, which, when they are juxtaposed with Mīkhāʾīl's lyrical flights, sometimes produce ironic effects.[10] However, even the passage quoted earlier, which is free of colloquialisms, shows a high level of heterogeneity on the linguistic and stylistic level.

Now that al-Kharrāṭ's fragmented narratives have been described in detail, their innovative value will be assessed. Novelists like the Egyptians Mahfouz and Idrīs and the Palestinian Ghassān Kanafānī (1936–1972), to mention only a couple of significant names, have all experimented with increasingly fragmented texts. For example, Kanfānī's novel *Mā tabaqqā la-kum* (1966; *All That's Left to You*, 1990) contains sudden shifting from one narrator to another, without clarifying markings. The Palestinian critic Fayṣal Darrāj attacks al-Kharrāṭ's critical works, in which the latter articulates the features of what he defines as the new literary sensitivity (*al-ḥasāsiyya al-jadīda*), features characteristic of al-Kharrāṭ's own fiction.[11] He talks about 'breaking the uninterrupted narrative sequence' and 'disrupting the linear temporal sequence' (Kharrāṭ 1993: 11–12). Darrāj's basic criticism of al-Kharrāṭ is that the latter's work both as a critic and a novelist is not as innovative as al-Kharrāṭ claims it to be. Darrāj suggests that the features which al-Kharrāṭ attributes to the 'new sensitivity' are already analysed in many critical studies predating al-Kharrāṭ's: Darrāj relates them to 'the stream of the subconscious, the psychological novel, spontaneous bursts of language [in the narrative]'.[12] More crucially, such features, argues Darrāj, are already present in many Arabic novels predating *Rāma*.[13] While it is certainly possible to say that some of the techniques al-Kharrāṭ employs were already being used by Arab authors before him, it is impossible to find a passage similar to the one quoted earlier in any of the novels referred to by Darrāj. Another obvious difference is the overall effect produced by the way all these techniques are merged together in al-Kharrāṭ's fiction. What Meyer writes about the fragmented narrative of al-Kharrāṭ's novel *Yā banāt Iskandariyya* (1990; *Girls of Alexandria*, 1993), is also relevant to his Trilogy:

> Fragmented and impressionistic as [it] may seem, the narrative as a whole conveys a feeling of unity and transcendence, its lyricism comparable to the work of Proust, Joyce and Virginia Woolf. The contrast with the carefully plotted, formalistic modernism of Mahfouz is considerable.
>
> (Meyer 2001: 213)[14]

To show how al-Kharrāṭ has taken some of these innovative features further than the novelists mentioned by Darrāj, we will compare al-Kharrāṭ's radical way of mixing different techniques with Fuʾād al-Takarlī's procedure of dividing his novel *al-Masarrāt wa-'l-awjāʿ* 'Joys and Pains' (1998) into different narrative blocks.[15] Al-Takarlī's ordered way of employing different narrative methods in this novel could be seen as an intermediate stage between the two forms of innovation: Mahfouz's pioneering attempts and al-Kharrāṭ's radical experimentation. In *al-Masarrāt*, a third person narrator and a first person narrator alternate in the four chapters ('blocks') of the work, each clearly confined to its particular section of the novel, making it easier to attribute a function to each of these narrating techniques. The first part (al-Takarlī 1998: 5–104) is a sort of chronicle (full of historical references and precise dates going from the beginning of the twentieth century to the first half of the 1970s) narrated by an omniscient third-person narrator. This opening section clearly functions as an historical introduction to the central story of the hero, Tawfīq, since it provides background information on the history of his family and on the time in which the action is set.[16] The second part (al-Takarlī 1998: 105–200), being Tawfīq's own diary, could hardly be more different from the first one. The second part focuses naturally more closely on Tawfīq's perspective and zooms in on a more limited period of time (1975–1978). The diary form also serves the author's discourse on the act of narrating, since Tawfīq from time to time asks himself why he thinks he is writing his diary. In the third part (al-Takarlī 1998: 201–317) we go back to a third person narration which, unlike the first chapter, focuses only on Tawfīq's life. Finally, the last section (al-Takarlī 1998: 319–464) is a first person narrative by Tawfīq himself and it is obviously limited to his point of view. While in *al-Masarrāt* the different techniques are limited to a well defined area and have precise functions, in al-Kharrāt's novels, all these techniques are mixed together.[17]

Moreover, *al-Masarrāt*'s various narratives, unlike *Rāma*'s, do not subvert the coherent, chronological exposition of the novel's action (which unfolds from the beginning of the twentieth century to the early 1980s, following a strict chronological order). In other words, the Egyptian writer experiments with an unconventional method of writing, more radical than the usual mixture of techniques a novelist is likely to use to provide his work with a sophisticated narrative structure. The reasons why he employs so many – and such rapidly alternating – techniques and styles are debatable. It is possible that al-Kharrāṭ is self-consciously indulging in displays of his technical mastery. However, other reasons are more likely. The first, which we have already explained earlier, is that al-Kharrāṭ intends to subvert a conventionally linear narrative in order to introduce more elements of human experience – in his words, 'to widen the concept of reality so that dream, myth and poetry are returned to it' (Kharrāṭ 1993: 12). After all, this has been the author's plan since his first collection of short stories *Ḥīṭān ᶜālya* ('High Walls') appeared. The collection, just like *Rāma* in 1979, was published at his own expense in 1959 and this testifies to the difficulties the writer had to face in getting his new fiction accepted.[18] With these short stories al-Kharrāṭ showed himself to be one of the most original voices on the Egyptian literary scene. As Sabry Hafez and Catherine Cobham have noted, 'the introspective and experimental style of the writing was out of keeping with the prevailing tradition which was still outward-looking, positive and based on national pride' (Hafez and Cobham 1988: 201–2). In the 1960s he was one of the editors of the independent literary magazine *Jālīrī 68* (Gallery 68), which was pivotal in promoting a literary new wave with which most of the writers of the '1960s generation' were associated. More recently, starting with the novel *Rāma*, he continues to fulfil his self-assigned role of avant-garde writer. Paradoxically perhaps, the author argues that his writing, which is generally defined as being opposed to the realistic style of preceding generations, is in fact much more faithful to reality – to what human experience really is. He writes in an article about his own work: ' "reality" in a literary work [is] more significant than fact; an inescapable interpolation of subjectivity is more fruitful here than a presumed but never attained objectivity' (al-Kharrāṭ 1998: 10).

To go back to al-Kharrāṭ's Trilogy, we can see that he further frustrates what might be the expectations of readers used to a more traditional type of fiction when the narration focuses at length on an episode which, as we are then telegraphically informed, has not happened at all. At a certain point in the first chapter of *Rāma*, Mīkhāᵓīl is recalling what is probably his first sexual encounter with Rāma. After he has painted a picture of two lovers submerged by extreme happiness and mutual fulfilment, he briefly states: 'None of that happened' (Kharrāṭ 1979: 26/*21*). This example leads us to consider another feature typical of al-Kharrāṭ's style. An episode is mentioned, sometimes only hinted at, and then after many pages the narration goes back to it and the reader learns some more about it. The episode we are referring to here is an excellent example, in that it is only alluded to briefly at the beginning of the novel, then after some two hundred pages

(Kharrāṭ 1979: 214/*198*) the narration goes back to it, and only at this point do we learn more details (this is indeed the couple's first sexual encounter and it has probably taken place in Rome). This way of narrating, which could be defined as cyclical since it is based on the gradual elaboration of recurrently narrated events, is taken further by al-Kharrāṭ when we find in both *al-Zaman* and *Yaqīn* references to episodes mentioned in *Rāma*. These references are often nothing but brief sentences which make the reader recall something he or she has already read. For instance, in this case the same sentence whispered by Rāma to Mīkhāᵓīl ('Put your hand on my breast', Kharrāṭ 1979: 214/*198*) indicates to us that we are reading about an episode which we have already come across (Kharrāṭ 1979: 25).[19] However, we would maintain that the point of this narrative technique is not to reveal key episodes in the life of the relationship between Rāma and Mīkhāᵓīl gradually but rather has more to do with al-Kharrāṭ's very particular concept of literary time.

Al-Kharrāṭ seems to push to the extreme a procedure also adopted by Khūrī, another novelist employing a fragmented style of writing. In Khūrī's novels, shifts connecting (and separating) the various episodes and stories which make up the narration are characterized by an often incomprehensible sentence (referring to facts previously unheard of) which is explained either shortly afterwards or pages later. This procedure is possibly intended to keep the reader's attention or increase his or her sense of expectation. For example, in *Mamlakat al-ghurabāᵓ* (1993; *The Kingdom of Strangers*, 1996), at the beginning of his encounter with the writer Salman Rushdie, the narrator says that he wanted to tell him the story of 'the village doctor' (Khūrī 1993: 96/*78*). After a couple of pages, he narrates the story.[20] The same technique is also to be found in other novels by Khūrī. Meyer quotes the Egyptian critic Ceza Draz analysing a similar procedure adopted by Ṣunᶜallāh Ibrāhīm in his novel *Najmat Aghusṭus* 'August Star' (1974): 'While the transitions from the surface level of narration appear to occur randomly, some conceptual association usually sparks them. This is often merely a single word, which acts like tripwire, causing the narrative shift' (Meyer 2001: 44).

Of course, this fragmented narrative, especially in al-Kharrāṭ's work, requires the reader to work much harder than he or she would normally do while reading a clearly plotted novel. He or she has to try to recollect the work's various components. The higher degree of commitment demanded from the reader is one of the main characteristics of these novels and is of course a widely acknowledged component of Western literary modernism.

One of the main differences between al-Kharrāṭ's novels and Khūrī's is that the latter expands his texts, embedding within them stories about different characters and situations, while the former writes what are basically variations on the same story. In fact, we could call the overall structure of the *Rāma* Trilogy variations on a theme, to borrow a musical term. In *Rāma*, for instance, each of the fourteen chapters could be considered as an independent, complete short story which at the same time is tied in with the others by the general theme (Rāma and Mīkhāᵓīl's relationship) and by recurrent episodes (the same applies to the other two novels of the Trilogy). More than that, the whole novel could be considered as the same short story rewritten in various ways. In fact, the first chapter of *Rāma, Mīkhāʾīl wa-'l-bajᶜa* (*Mīkhāʾīl and the Swan*), was first conceived as a short story (Hafez 1982: 241).[21] The author himself claims to have been inspired to adopt this sort of chain structure (where every link is formally perfect in itself and at the same time part of the whole) by both Arab art (the repetition of the same pattern on the walls of mosques, for instance) and by one of the classics of the Arabic popular literary heritage: *The Arabian Nights* (*Alf layla wa-layla*), in which one story evolves into another which evolves into another and so on.[22] Interviewed by the Egyptian critic Sabry Hafez, he talks about 'an inspiration and revival of this form that is embedded in our cultural heritage, and which I hope I have made contemporary and alive' (Hafez 1982: 242).[23]

Meyer has noted, in analysing the novels of Khūrī, that his 'preferred novelistic technique is to build the novel on the basis of a series of short stories that interweave and connect' (Meyer 2001: 130). It is clear that both Khūrī and al-Kharrāṭ use comparable techniques in order to 'undermine the classic structure of the novel' (Meyer 2001: 130).

The fact that the structure of al-Kharrāṭ's novels is based on the short story gives us the opportunity to address the problem of defining the literary genre of his writing. Labelling al-Kharrāṭ's narrative works can be problematic. It is not incidental, for instance, that the original subtitle of his novel *Turābu-hā zaᶜfarān* (1986; *City of Saffron*, 1989) is *Nuṣūṣ Iskandariyya* 'Alexandrian Texts'. The author warns us that we are dealing with *texts*, something which is not exactly a novel. *Amwāj al-layālī* 'The Waves of the Nights' (1991) looks like a collection of short stories, but named as *mutatāliya qiṣaṣiyya* 'a narrative sequence'.[24] In this case, the nine independent sections of the work seem to be linked by the same overall theme even if, unlike the Trilogy, they involve different characters. As many critics and writers have made clear, the genre of the novel is by definition very fluid and difficult to define.[25] It is evident that the Egyptian writer takes advantage of the ever-evolving nature of the novel, which represents an ideal literary space in which to experiment with his poetic fancy. In his critical work *al-Kitāba ᶜabra-'l-nawᶜiyya* 'Transgeneric Writing' (1994), al-Kharrāṭ studies the new literary form of the *qiṣṣa-qaṣīda* 'the poem story' (which he himself has contributed to creating). Indeed, he addresses the phenomenon of a literature which goes far beyond the conventional divisions of literary genres. As Boutros Hallaq has noted in his brief but incisive essay ('Transgénérique et modernité dans la littérature arabe'), transgeneric writing is by no means unique to al-Kharrāṭ and, moreover, can tell us a lot about his 'philosophical' attitude towards literature. Hallaq's analysis involves the balance between the political and the artistic in the contemporary Arabic novel which we have discussed in the introduction to the present work and will return to in its conclusion. It is significant to note that a sort of 'formless' (to borrow Said's and Khūrī's expression), genreless writing has started to emerge recently within Arabic literature. This style of writing, which cannot be easily defined, is not exclusive to al-Kharrāṭ and Khūrī, even if we can argue that they were amongst the first to adopt it consistently. The definition al-Kharrāṭ applies to some of his works ('texts') is also used to define a work like *Barārī al-ḥummā* (1985; *Praires of Fever*, 1993. Cf. Meyer 2001: 183) by the Palestinian poet Ibrāhīm Naṣrallāh (b. 1954). In talking about transgeneric writing, it is impossible not to refer to the strategy of European modernist writers who sought to encourage their readers to question culture, tradition and language itself. Their complex way of writing, characterized by a stratification of styles (cf. Ezra Pound's Canto I), was intended to fulfil this goal (cf. Rabaté 2001: 748–9; Litz and Rainey 2000: 90). Whether authors like al-Kharrāṭ and Khūrī have been influenced by this modernist technique is open to debate. Moreover, we should concede that, if their writing is possibly reminiscent of Joyce, Proust or Woolf's lyrical prose, it is also true that rhyming prose has occupied a very important position in the Arabic literary tradition (the *saj*ᶜ of the Koran and the *maqāmāt*). In Chapter 4, while dealing in more detail with al-Kharrāṭ's lyrical prose, we will expand on this topic.

We have noted earlier that the writing of Khūrī and that of al-Kharrāṭ have common features, while remaining quite distinct from one another. The main point that they have in common is narrative fragmentation, which produces the sense of ambiguity so typical of both writers. However, uncertainty and questioning have other implications in Khūrī's work. First of all, his novels differ significantly from al-Kharrāṭ's in that they focus much more on who is telling the story. *Mamlakat*, *Riḥlat* and his lengthy novel *Bāb al-shams*[26] (1998; *Gate of the Sun*, 2005) all begin with a character (in the first two, that of a writer) telling a story. Here, a first person narration is the privileged narrative technique, while in al-Kharrāṭ's work it is difficult to decide which narrative voice he favours. In Khūrī's work, therefore, a sense of disruption is not conveyed so much through the anarchic sequence of different techniques so typical of al-Kharrāṭ, but through a technique which is meant to reproduce that of oral story-tellers.[27] The Lebanese critic Samira Aghacy claims that the Lebanese writer is inspired by the *ḥakawātī* tradition of storytelling (Aghacy 1996: 164).[28] A consequence of this technique is that the narrator switches from one tale to another very often, sometimes suddenly. In Khūrī's narrative, the narrator is in the middle of telling one story when he or she associates a certain word or idea with another story, and this then becomes our focus of attention (sometimes these parenthetic stories are very brief). This characteristic reproduces a narration which is typically oral, at times deliberately casual and random. Khūrī embarks on this task in such a radical way that even his narrators admit to having gone astray with their narration, as is the case with the main narrator of *Bāb*, Khalīl, who is addressing his unconscious friend Yūnis:

> Why am I talking about Shams, when we're supposed to be talking about Mme Nada Fayyad? [. . .] I never meant to end up here. I wanted to tell you the story you don't know, and I don't know how the subject got changed, I must concentrate because one subject leads to another.
>
> (Khūrī 1998: 47/*40*)

This technique (successfully summarized by Khalīl with the Arabic sentence *al-kalām yajurr al-kalām* – 'one subject leads to another') is typical of most of Khurī's narrators, like the prostitute Alice in *Riḥlat*. The technique is poetically explained in this latter novel by the seemingly autobiographical unnamed narrator who comments on Alice's narration as follows: 'I'd listen to her and see her in front of me, but it was as though she weren't really there. She'd fade away into her words, as though her body vanished while the stories transformed into stories' (Khūrī 1989: 21/*17*). He thinks that Alice herself turns into a story and the same concept is underlined elsewhere in both *Riḥlat* and *Mamlakat* where narrators and authors are 'swallowed' into their own stories: in the eyes of the narrator of *Mamlakat*, Salman Rushdie has become a character in one of his own novels (Khūrī 1993: 102/*83*).[29]

Even if the overall effect of Khūrī's narrative is one of randomness (cf. Allen's comment quoted at the beginning of this chapter), he is by no means a casual writer: he takes great pains with his style and works on it meticulously. The result is a written fictional style containing many of the features of oral narrative, which, as we have just seen, allows him to introduce parenthetic stories, change suddenly from one tale to another and introduce other narrating voices. One of the reasons behind Khūrī's employment of this kind of fragmented narrative has to do with the inability of a well ordered, more traditional narration to reproduce the disrupted, shattered socio-political reality of his country after years of civil war. He applies the same technique even when dealing with the history of the Palestinian people, especially in *Bāb*. Critics have underlined how the highly fragmented society of the Arab countries has produced highly fragmented narratives.[30] For Khūrī too, the phenomenon of fragmentation is of paramount importance within modern Arabic literature and reflects a well defined socio-political crisis, as he explains: 'While watching everything crumbling and disintegrating in a fragmented society, dominated by all different forms of dictatorship, we [the Arabs] were in search of our language and our [familiar] features, but we didn't find anything but broken mirrors' (Khūrī 1999: 14). The poetical image of 'broken mirrors' finds an artistic counterpart in the writer's adoption of his characteristic oral-influenced style and multi-voiced, heterogeneous narration. Without forcing too many parallels between the colonial situation of Ireland and the Arab world's postcolonial one, it may be relevant to mention that Declan Kiberd, in his introduction to Joyce's *Ulysses*, refers to Leopold Bloom's Irish self as not a single, but a multiple self, because it is rendered by the cracked looking-glass (Oscar Wilde) left by the colonizer (Kiberd 1992: lxxviii–lxxix). If al-Kharrāṭ questions the concept of 'objective reality' through mixing up metaphysical and physical aspects of human experience, Khūrī openly questions 'reality', offering many versions of it and ultimately questioning the very stories his characters narrate. As with al-Kharrāṭ's Mīkhāʾīl, we are not sure whether to consider Khūrī's narrators reliable and believe them. The traditional image of an omniscient narrator who tells us the truth is explicitly negated here (cf. Ghandour 2000: 186–8 for the same observation referring to *Riḥlat*). The unnamed narrator of *Mamlakat* tells us: 'But I'm not writing a story [*qiṣṣa*]. I just let things come to me. I say that I'm telling the [tale] [*ḥikāya*] as it is, and I wanted to say also "nothing added, nothing removed," but I changed my mind' (Khūrī 1993: 21/*16*).

A fundamental element of Khūrī's novels is the fact that the reader is made continuously conscious that he or she is dealing with only a version, or several versions, of a story, which are not necessarily reliable. This feature is reinforced by the sense of ambiguity expressed by narrative fragmentation. In fact, such ambiguity echoes the Kharrāṭian 'Did that really happen?' so much that at a certain point in the last part of *Mamlakat*, the narrator, easily identifiable with the implied author, if not with Khūrī himself, states ironically: 'I won't say I don't know, for I have said that so many times in this novel' (Khūrī 1993: 102/*83*). Similarly, *Bāb*'s main narrator Khalīl is gradually forced to admit that he has lied about the reason why he is spending all his time in the Galilee Hospital: at the beginning of the novel he claims that through his stories he is going to give life back to his mentor Yūnis; then it becomes clear that he is also hiding from the family of his late lover Nahīla who want to kill him.[31] These lies and 'I don't know' and 'I'm not sure' are typical of Khūrī's story-tellers: in *Riḥlat*, the main autobiographical narrator (a writer who is gathering information about the story of a Beirut shoeshine nicknamed 'Little Ghāndī') finds himself lost in the middle of the various contradictory stories narrated to him by the prostitute Alice and other acquaintances of Ghāndī's. The novel begins and ends with the death of ᶜAbd al-Karīm, Little Ghāndī. He dies on 15 September 1982 and, as the author makes clear in the novel, this date was not chosen at random, since it was the day the Israeli army entered Beirut. Between the beginning and the end of the novel many stories are narrated, stories which are connected to Little Ghāndī's life to a greater or lesser degree. The novel is also the story of, among others, Alice herself and other 'little people' living their daily lives in the war. As the text says explicitly, *Riḥlat* is about 'those who couldn't escape' (Khūrī 1989: 25/*20*) from the war and the city – although most have originally come to it from outside. Little Ghāndī met Alice and told her his stories. The narrator hears them from Alice and others, and now – while narrating them to us – he tries to connect them together but keeps 'finding holes in the story', as he himself says (Khūrī 1989: 12/*7*). In a sense, the very act of narrating or writing itself is questioned here. The narrator himself alternately doubts and is convinced that his narrators are telling the truth (as a consequence, his own version of the story is fragmented).

As we mentioned at the beginning of this chapter, fragmentation in the texts studied here also results in the disruption of any chronological order. Having described in detail the general characteristics of the prose of Khūrī and al-Kharrāṭ, it is easy to understand how their texts can often be devoid of a rigid temporal framework. The lack of such a framework is much more dramatic than in other experimental, but still more traditional novels. Even if it is true that the metaphysical aspects of the characters' lives are presented, for example, through the use of interior monologue in a novel like Mahfouz's *al-Liṣṣ wa-'l-kilāb* (1962; *The Thief and the Dogs*, 1984), it remains impossible to compare it with the much more radical experimentation of *Rāma*.[32] Similarly, it is true that in some other works by Mahfouz the temporal frame is made less linear, through the use of flashbacks for instance (e.g. *Mīrāmār*, 1967; *Miramar*, 1978), but the subversion of time in Khūrī and al-Kharrāṭ is much more complete. It is as if the whirlpool of stories which forms Khūrī's fiction takes place in the absolute present time of narration, much as Mīkhā'īl's thoughts take place in an atemporal dimension, or in another absolute present time – that of remembering.[33] These texts only give an impression of presenting any linear narrative of events taking place one after the other, an illusion because if they do form a narrative, this is flattened, as it were, by the atemporality of remembrance.[34] In al-Kharrāṭ, this is the outcome of a conscious plan to give shape to a new fiction where temporal references are simply rejected. In one of his several works of literary criticism, al-Kharrāṭ explains that in his fiction he aims at capturing a moment, elusive and at the same time persistent, where the different temporal stages of a human being (childhood, boyhood, adulthood) converge (Kharrāṭ 1996b: 26–7).

To go back to the fragmented time, or atemporality, of the Kharrāṭian Trilogy, there is another fundamental aspect of this work which we have hinted at earlier: Mīkhā'īl's highs and lows with Rāma are remembered in the Trilogy, although the author would rather say that Mīkhā'īl's experiences are continuously lived anew[35] in a moment which is connected to the author's concept of literary time, as 'an ever renewing moment', or 'an absolute present' (*laḥẓa mutajaddada abadan*, Kharrāṭ 1996b: 26).[36] This looking back at the past is another aspect which the *Rāma* Trilogy and Khūrī's novels have in common. Here we will focus on al-Kharrāṭ, as Khūrī's ideas about the topic are more relevant to his metafictional method (see Chapter 5). We believe that what Walter Benjamin writes about Proust can, at least partially, be applied to al-Kharrāṭ as well:

> in his work Proust did not describe a life as it actually was, but a life as it was remembered by the one who had lived it. [. . .] the important thing for the remembering author is not what he experienced, but the weaving of his memory, the Penelope work of recollection.
>
> (Benjamin 1929: 204)

Writers like al-Kharrāṭ and Khūrī are interested in the mental processes of recollecting and remembering. But again, al-Kharrāṭ underlines how in remembering, and in his art, what is intangible, the dream, the thought, the memory are even more important than what can actually be touched. As Mīkhā'īl confesses in *al-Zaman*:

> When I talk about those matters now, they look luminous, their dimensions and limits clear. But there is nothing true in that, nor in the stream of days and nights with its confused waves, where there is hardly any light, and [only] fragments with uncertain sizes and broken shapes. Light comes only in dreams.
>
> (Kharrāṭ 1985: 44)

It is not incidental, therefore, that when al-Kharrāṭ writes about that absolute present where past, present and future merge to allow literary creation, he adds that he also aims at fusing 'the actual I' (*anā al-wāqiᶜī*) with the imaginary one (Kharrāṭ 1996b: 27). The connection between al-Kharrāṭ's conception of literary art *vis-à-vis* remembrance and the Proustian concept has not been lost on critics. At the same time, al-Kharrāṭ himself might be aware that, in trying to give the *dream* such a prominent position in his writing,[37] he invites the drawing of parallels between his work and surrealism (cf. Darrāj 1999: 64–7). André Breton writes in his *Manifesto of Surrealism*: 'I believe in the future resolution of these two states, dream and reality, which are seemingly so contradictory, into a kind of absolute reality, a *surreality*, if one may so speak' (Breton 1924: 14).[38] In his critical works, al-Kharrāṭ claims to create a style and images which are surrealist but also realist (Kharrāṭ 1996b: 28–9). In fact, we have seen earlier some examples where the physical and sensual elements are prominent in his ability to create images. As a consequence of this, Meyer is led to write that '[o]ne of the most striking aspects of [al-Kharrāṭ's] prose, despite its effusiveness and near overabundance, is the sense it conveys of being rooted in a strong realist tradition' (Meyer 2001: 211).

As noted earlier, even Barrāda's texts are fragmented but in a more conventional way, as chapters (and sections within chapters) are narrated by one narrative voice at a time. In other words, in novels like *Luᶜbat al-nisyān* and *al-Ḍawᵓ al-hārib*, we find many different narrative voices and styles, but these are well-confined into sections (as in al-Takarlī's *al-Masarrāt*). However, even if the structure of Barrāda's novels is more orderly than al-Kharrāṭ's,[39] the former's fiction is similar to the latter's for two main reasons (here we are not concerned with the similarities in style, which are not uncommon): first, shifts in time are systematic and so some concentration is required on the part of the reader to make sense of the chronology of events. This is especially true in *Luᶜbat*, albeit in a less impressionistic fashion than in al-Kharrāṭ's Trilogy. Second, the content of Barrāda's two novels explicitly focuses on recollection, memory and forgetfulness, and their connection with the creative act of writing (in *Luᶜbat*, the main characters explicitly play 'the game of forgetting/remembering' which is part of the self-referential structure of the novel). Al-Hādī and al-ᶜAyshūnī – the protagonists of *Luᶜbat* and *al-Ḍawᵓ* respectively – look back at their past because they want to make sense of their present, their life. This attempt is consciously carried out through creative, artistic activities with no sure successful outcome: the prevailing feelings are those of frustration and nostalgia for one's past, one's childhood (as we have seen earlier, al-Kharrāṭ guards us against seeing his evocative prose as the result of a nostalgic attitude, as he is more interested in depicting the process of memory, rather than the longing to regain the past). Al-Hādī, the leftist journalist clearly familiar with Proust and Freud, muses over the workings of involuntary memory, the feel of having lived already what is happening in the present, the power exercised by the unconscious and the need to write, even if he is suspicious of his ability to express feelings and experiences. Unlike the

Proustian hero, al-Hādī's feelings of frustration and nostalgia for his past are to be seen against the backdrop of disillusionment with the socio-political situation of post-Independence Morocco: the leftist activist al-Hādī has actively supported the nationalistic movement and is now contemplating the failure of his generation to change their society in a progressive way. Al-Hādī's is, however, not the only perspective through which the novel is narrated and part of the fragmentation of the Barrādian text has to do with the number of narrating characters, which is higher than in al-Kharrāṭ's Trilogy. As we will see in more detail in the next chapter, Barrāda tries to shape a sort of collective memory (the fictional depiction of which is intrinsically fragmented), whereas al-Kharrāṭ's text is fragmented because it depicts the thought process of an individual mind.

In conclusion, we would like to quote a passage from Barrāda's *al-Ḍawᵓ* which may encapsulate why authors such as himself, al-Kharrāṭ and Khūrī have felt the need to use a fragmented style to render their characters' past experiences faithfully (here, the narrator is an amateur writer, the painter al-ᶜAyshūnī):

> I tore up many pages because I found that they sounded certain, definitive, especially when I was dealing with my own experiences... whereas I can't help thinking that what I experienced, when it is not formulated in words, seems to me obscure, contradictory and lacking the logic which words impose on it. I said to myself: let's adapt to thoughts as they come, without wanting to order or link them. Let writing be [made up of] passages which blaze and fade in time to an internal rhythm. I would find myself dozing, I mean, I would write a page, or half a page, then I would resume writing only after a few months during which I would turn over what I had written in my mind: was it really conveying what I had experienced? Was its language close to mine or was it an echo of it? Would someone else understand these shattered fragments from a vast, multilayered space?
>
> (Barrāda 1993: 192–3)[40]

In this chapter we have mainly described the phenomenon of narrative fragmentation and tried to analyse the reasons behind it. In doing so, we have also touched upon some of the implications of such a style. For instance, in the works of Khūrī and Barrāda it might facilitate the introduction (and the questioning) of different narrators and numerous narrative voices. In al-Kharrāṭ's fiction, on the other hand, if the fragmented nature of the narrative is due to the focus on the subjective viewpoint of Mīkhāᵓīl, we might ask whether other perspectives emerge, and if they do, whether they are independent or dominated by Mīkhāᵓīl's. These problems are related to the concepts of narrative voice, multi-voicedness and polyphony, which we will explore in the following chapter.

3

POLYPHONY

According to Meyer, one of the innovative, modernist strategies introduced into the Arabic novel in the 1960s was a 'democratisation of narration, or polyphony' (Meyer 2001: 9).[1] He refers to Walid Hamarneh's observations on experimentation in the Arabic novel in the 1960s as follows: authors started to replace the common 'editorial omniscient third person narrator or the first person' (Hamarneh quoted in Meyer 2001: 9) with a multiple narration. He then offers an analysis of some novels by Kanafānī (*Rijāl fī-'l-shams*, 1963 [*Men in the Sun*, 1978]; *Mā tabaqqā la-kum*, 1966), Mahfouz (*Mīrāmār*, 1967) and Jabrā (*al-Safīna*, 1969 [*The Ship*, 1985]; *al-Baḥth ᶜan Walīd Masᶜūd*, 1978 [*In Search of Walid Masoud*, 2000]) as examples of such innovative experimentation. Meyer, like other critics before him (such as Sabry Hafez), mentions Jabrā's Arabic translation of William Faulkner's novel *The Sound and the Fury* (1929) as exercising a great influence on most, if not all, of these novelists.[2] What all these novels have in common with Faulkner's novel is a division of the narrative, whereby events are related by different voices or through the perspectives of more than one character.[3] The same technique is adopted in al-Takarlī's *al-Rajᶜ al-baᶜīd* (1980, *The Long Way Back*, 2001). This chapter will work towards an analysis of this novel, which can be considered as the finest example of narrative polyphony and multiple narration within contemporary Arabic fiction.

The technique of multiple narration can be applied in different ways, for different reasons and to produce different effects and results. One of the most obvious reasons why authors set out to get rid of either a god-like, omniscient narrator or a first person narration by a character is to weaken their own voice within their work. Ideally, this could give the reader more independence of thought; it could replace the single vision of the world (the author's, or the implied author's) with a more democratic representation of it; it could underline how the same event or character can be viewed from different perspectives, and it could also demonstrate how each or none of these viewpoints is valid. In other words, the technique of multiple narration (or multivoicedness) makes us reflect about 'the positioning of authorial discourse'[4] within a work of fiction and it is associated with a desire for more *objectivity* in the art of fiction, a more neutral authorial voice. Much has been written on this subject. Wayne C. Booth, for instance, writes in *The Rhetoric of Fiction* that the use of one technique rather than another does not necessarily mean that more objectivity is achieved. Gérard Genette echoes this conclusion and, refuting Henry James's argument in favour of showing (*mimesis*) over telling (*diegesis*), claims that 'the very idea of *showing* is [...] completely illusory: in contrast to dramatic representation, no narrative can "show" or "imitate" the story it tells' (Genette 1972: 163–4). These general observations – to the effect that it is not the technique itself, but how the technique is applied – are also reiterated in Bakhtin's *Problems of Dostoevsky's Poetics* (1963), the monograph in which the Russian critic famously coins the term *polyphony* and to which we shall return throughout this chapter. Bakhtin takes us a step further when he discusses the problem of the formal and artistic position of authorial discourse 'with regard to the hero's discourse':

> This problem lies deeper than the question of authorial discourse on the superficial level of composition, and deeper than any superficially compositional device for eliminating authorial discourse by means of the *Ich-Erzählung* form (first person narration), or by the introduction of a narrator, or by constructing the novel in scenes and thus reducing authorial discourse to the status of a stage direction. All these compositional devices for eliminating or weakening authorial discourse at the level of composition do not in themselves tackle the essence of the problem; their underlying artistic meaning can be profoundly different, depending on the different artistic tasks they perform.
>
> (Bakhtin 1963: 56–7)

The fact that Bakhtin does not include multiple narration in his list of 'compositional devices for eliminating authorial discourse' does not weaken his observations. Furthermore, the use of multiple narration is not in itself enough to give expression to a truly polyphonic novel (in the Bakhtinian sense): ᶜAbd al-Raḥmān Munīf's (1933–2004) novel *Sharq al-Mutawassiṭ* 'East of the Mediterranean' (1975) demonstrates how two different voices (Rajab's and his sister Anīsa's) can eventually merge into one conclusive voice totally controlled by the author's ideological viewpoint (the declaration of human rights quoted at the beginning of the novel makes this explicit, Munīf 1975: 5).[5] On the other hand, a novel narrated by the traditional third person omniscient narrator can genuinely express a plurality of equally independent voices (even if it focuses on one character as in Dostoevsky's *Crime and Punishment*).

Since we have referred to Bakhtin's pivotal work on novelistic polyphony, we now need to define better what he means by this term, which in the works of other critics sometimes seems to mean something else (in general, Bakhtin's concept of polyphony is much more complex).[6] In *Problems of Dostoevsky's Poetics*, the Russian critic praises Dostoevsky for having invented the polyphonic novel. According to Bakhtin, Dostoevsky's novels allow different voices to emerge – voices which are relatively independent from the author's. The various characters are treated by the author as autonomous consciousnesses expressing a point of view, an idea, a *word*, which is not entirely subordinated to the author's one, to his *dominant* ('the "leading value" in the hierarchical system of values inherent in any work of art' Bakhtin 1963: footnote c, p. 13).[7] In Bakhtin's own words: 'A plurality of independent and unmerged voices and consciousnesses, a genuine polyphony of fully valid voices is in fact the chief characteristic of Dostoevsky's novels' (Bakhtin 1963: 6). This innovative representation does not necessarily preclude the authors' ideas from being expressed in their novels, but means that they are placed on the same level as the ideas of others and do not possess any conclusive, judgmental value.

Meyer's discussion of the multivoiced Arabic novels mentioned earlier is only partly based on Bakhtin's ideas: other valid criteria are considered in evaluating the technique employed. For instance, the multiple narration can first of all provide the reader with an insight into how the characters' perspectives vary in perceiving the same event or person (Mahfouz's *Mīrāmār*, for example) and, by implication, how the reader's own perspective is altered. This alone could be regarded as a significant step forward compared to a narration from one perspective only: multiple narration offers a more complete picture of what is being represented. Admittedly, Bakhtin's reading of polyphony in Dostoevsky's works goes much beyond a purely formal discussion of the effect of a narrative technique, as Booth has pointed out:

> It should be clear [...] that what is at stake, in reading Bakhtin, is far more than the question of how we read, or even evaluate, fiction. The effort to transcend the author's voice in this book [*Problems of Dostoevsky's Poetics*] is not a handbook treatment of the technical means to specific artistic effects; it is rather part of a lifetime inquiry into profound questions about the entire enterprise of thinking about what human life means.
>
> (Booth 1984: xxiv)

Admittedly, our analysis will definitely be more of a 'handbook treatment of the technical means to specific artistic effects' than a philosophical inquiry *à la* Bakhtin. Nevertheless, we shall rely more on Bakhtin's observations about polyphony than Meyer does in his comprehensive discussion of early Arab experimentation with multiple narration. Meyer mainly refers to Bakhtin via other critics whom he quotes. For instance, in discussing Mahfouz's *Mīrāmār*, he quotes first Yumnā al-ᶜĪd's observation that the novel is dominated by one character's viewpoint (Meyer 2001: 23), then Walid Hamarneh writing about the author's control of the narrators (Meyer 2001: 26. Both comments reiterate one of Bakhtin's main concerns). He closes his discussion of Jabrā's *al-Baḥth* with a paragraph almost entirely dedicated to Mattityahu Peled's Bakhtinian reading of the novel (Meyer 2001: 54. Peled praises Jabrā's *al-Safīna* and especially *al-Baḥth*, see Peled 1995).

As already indicated, we will hereafter refer to the term polyphony only in a Bakhtinian sense (as defined earlier), employing terms such as multivoicedness or multiple narration to designate a narrative structure which simply has more than one perspective (and does not fulfil all of Bakhtin's criteria for genuine polyphony).

As we have already stressed, a truly polyphonic effect can be achieved even in novels which do not present a rigid structure whereby each perspective or voice is confined to one (or more) chapter(s) or section(s). We have seen that Bakhtin considers Dostoevsky the champion of novelistic polyphony even if the Russian writer usually employs one third person omniscient narrator only. Of course, other techniques too could tend to the same polyphonic effect, even if at a first reading they seem to be dominated by one voice only. This is the case with the novels of al-Kharrāṭ where, as we have noted earlier, everything is filtered and elaborated through the consciousness of a single character, Mīkhāʾīl. In her article on al-Kharrāt's novel *Yā banāt Iskandariyya*, Marlé Hammond shows how the Egyptian novelist allows mainly feminine voices to act as a counterpoint to and contrast with Mīkhāʾīl's male expressions (Hammond 2000). In a passage which can also be applied to the *Rāma* Trilogy she writes: 'Despite their intensely introspective tone, al-Kharrāṭ's narrators rarely narrate alone; rather they constantly invite other agents to participate in the narrative act, allowing those other narratives, perspectives, and voices to unfold and resonate within their own' (Hammond 2000: 38). In the *Rāma* cycle of novels, the feminine voice mainly belongs to the heroine Rāma and it is often an expression of stern opposition to Mīkhāʾīl's attitudes. But, as Hammond concludes in her article, the feminine voice is not there to be dominated by, or to dominate, that of the male narrator – rather it is part of the author's attempt at creating 'a communal voice, both personal and omniscient' (Hammond 2000: 57). Hammond explains that, in contrast to what some readers might think, the female voice in al-Kharrāṭ's works responds to the male 'narrator's expressions of carnal desire, tempering his libidinal postures and enabling him to transcend the limits of perspective' (Hammond 2000: 38). Meyer, on the other hand, underlines that, however successful al-Kharrāṭ's writing is (compared to Western 'high modernism'), his continuous descriptions focusing on women 'border on obsessional' (Meyer 2001: 210) and his 'lyricism is still used strictly for the purpose of masculine self-representation' (Meyer 2001: 213).[8] Musawi seems to echo Hammond's positive evaluation of al-Kharrāṭ, underscoring how the male postures and attitudes are exposed in the *Rāma* Trilogy rather than endorsed by the author. When Musawi analyses the Trilogy (focusing especially on *Yaqīn*), he concludes that '[w]hile giving full "vital space" to every voice, Idwār al-Kharrāṭ lays bare the problematic of gendered narratives', and that texts like these tend to deal frankly with 'obsessions, representations and preoccupations, and to problematize issues of sex, love and man-woman anxieties' (Musawi 2003: 253–4). It is nonetheless clear that all these valid arguments (including Meyer's sceptical ones) can be put into perspective by considering the symbolic and metaphoric value of Rāma.

As we will see in the following chapter, almost everything in al-Kharrāṭ's writing can be seen as an expression of his philosophical concept of the ambivalent, dualistic nature of human beings. Even in the novels dominated by Mīkhāʾīl's consciousness, we realize that a contrasting voice is emerging, that of the Other, in this case Rāma. This voice can be considered as another voice belonging to the same character, and we will see later in this chapter how more or less the same occurs in *al-Rajᶜ* when we deal with its hero's internal struggle and the emergence of the heroine's voice within him (we could say that al-Kharrāṭ's discourse is more oriented towards religious and philosophical – and increasingly political – issues, while al-Takarlī is more concerned with sociocultural changes).

In the *Rāma* Trilogy, Rāma also functions to contradict Mīkhāʾīl's non-erotic postures. For instance, the many registers and styles used by al-Kharrāṭ in *al-Zaman* include political argumentation. In the eleventh chapter of the novel we find a very long discussion (almost ten pages, Kharrāṭ 1985: 271–80) with Mīkhāʾīl on one side, and Rāma and their mutual friend Aḥmad on the other, passionately arguing about politics and social change. This argument, between people who clearly share a common leftist militant background, starts as an attempt by Mīkhāʾīl to refute his friends' willingness to use violence for political reasons,[9] and rapidly turns into a wider debate about absolute values and truths, ideologies, forms of government and terrorism.[10] Even if we think that the implied author is likely to share Mīkhāʾīl's point of view, the argument is not clearly resolved, and both Rāma and Mīkhāʾīl remain convinced that they are right: their ideas *dialogically* engage one another. In fact, Mīkhāʾīl states that this argument is closed (*munāqasha masdūdat al-bāb*, Kharrāṭ 1985: 271, 280) but, ironically, what is closed for the characters remains potentially open for the readers, who are left to ponder about the strengths and weaknesses of each argument. Elsewhere, we have noted how the couple's perceptions of the Egyptian nation and their ideological leanings differ palpably (Caiani 2005).

As we have pointed out, it is not always easy to see how much the character Mīkhāʾīl projects the ideas of the implied author, let alone those of al-Kharrāṭ himself. Al-Kharrāṭ, despite admitting that some autobiographical elements are undoubtedly present in his works, makes clear that it is not always correct to see him in Mīkhāʾīl. In fact, although we might assume that al-Kharrāṭ is likely to share some, maybe most, of his protagonist's ideas and thoughts, as expressed in the Trilogy, he seems to distance himself from Mīkhāʾīl's intransigent ideas on Egypt's non-Arab culture, saying in an interview with Hafez: 'I am an Arab–Egyptian–Copt; in the following order: Coptic, Egyptian and linguistically Arab. Arab culture has become one of the components of both my individual and collective lives' (Hafez 1994: 236).[11]

Even if we dismiss these clarifications from the author, the reader feels that the arguments between Mīkhāʾīl and Rāma could be seen as open-ended, especially if we see the two protagonists as two voices of the archetypal Egyptian, two tendencies within the same people. More generally, it is possible to observe a further development from *al-Zaman* to *Yaqīn*. In the latter novel, as has been observed by Musawi (Musawi 1999: 164–5),[12] Rāma's voice emerges more strongly as a prodigious source of storytelling, a sort of Scheherezade as Mīkhāʾīl calls her on more than one occasion (Kharrāṭ 1996a: 28, 76, 287). In one passage, we even have a conversation in which Mīkhāʾīl's voice is omitted and only what his beloved says is expressed (this follows Rāma's telling him about her inquiry into the sectarian violence in Upper Egypt, Kharrāṭ 1996a: 90–1).[13] More than once, Mīkhāʾīl's lengthy, romantically lyrical flights of fancy are abruptly brought down to earth by Rāma's brief, energetic, vernacular sentences (Kharrāṭ 1996a: 84, 128–9). More importantly, when it comes to dialogues, Rāma is aware of her partner's male posturing and is not afraid to speak her mind: she reproaches Mīkhāʾīl for having turned her into a sort of 'glorified whore' (Kharrāṭ 1996a: 71), for idealizing her when she is, she protests, only a normal woman (Kharrāṭ 1996a: 142).[14] She also comments on what she perceives as his feeling of superiority towards women (Kharrāṭ 1996a: 128). All this seems to point to an increasingly independent and challenging role for Rāma. She is not a mere object on which Mīkhāʾīl projects himself; she resists and subverts his efforts, at times merely with her matter-of-fact attitudes which, when juxtaposed with her partner's abstract, lofty, philosophical discourses, produce an ironic effect (Kharrāṭ 1996a: 128–9). Admittedly, this is not enough to make her emerge as the main consciousness subsuming Mīkhāʾīl's: in other words, despite Rāma's increasing independence and importance in storytelling and arguing, it is still Mīkhāʾīl who does most of the thinking (when al-Kharrāṭ has spent so many years reworking the themes and form of the Trilogy, some readers might wish he had experimented by giving Rāma the central role for once).[15]

As we have seen in the previous chapter, Barrāda's fiction is in some aspects similar to al-Kharrāṭ's. If we analyse the presence of different voices and perspectives within the narrative, however, we find that Barrāda operates in an altogether different fashion. In *Luᶜbat*, for example, although the dominating narrative voice clearly belongs to the protagonist al-Hādī, the writer includes other voices which appear more conventionally independent as compared to the feminine voice possibly emerging within Mīkhāʾīl's. As Issa J. Boullata has pointed out, the novel is based on the independence enjoyed by the various voices from the implied author's voice, which, as we will see in Chapter 5, clearly appears by virtue of the novel's metafictional nature (cf. Boullata 1996: 7). The first chapter, for example, is divided into three sections: the first (despite the self-referential 'false starts' analysed in Chapter 5) is a sort of conventional third person omniscient narrative (Barrāda 1987: 7–12/*16–20*); the second with the title 'Illumination' introduces a first person narrative from a secondary character, an unnamed woman (Barrāda 1987: 12–13/*20–1*); the third entitled 'Obscuration' is a first person narrative from the protagonist (Barrāda 1987: 13–16/*22–4*).[16] The presence of more than one narrator gives us more than one perspective on the main theme of the first chapter: al-Hādī's mother (the chapter bears the Gospel-like title 'In the Beginning Was the Mother'). The first part (following the two brief openings) functions as a general introduction to the setting (the traditional house in the old city of Fez which will always mean childhood to al-Hādī) and the characters of the novel, al-Hādī's family and neighbours. With the 'Illumination' sections we move closer to *Lālla* Ghālya (as al-Hādī's mother is respectfully called) with a personal assessment from a woman who knows her. The focus becomes even narrower with the following 'Obscuration' section from al-Hādī, who obviously offers us much more intimate observations: in his section we also have information about how al-Hādī is (while we do not get to know much about the unnamed woman). This is a very superficial account of how different perspectives can work, but later in the novel we will have other voices which carry out other more significant functions: for example, while al-Hādī's voice remains dominant (an 'Obscuration' section, always a first person account from him, is present in six of the seven chapters of the novel and takes up the whole of the last chapter), Barrāda allows contrasting and dissentive voices to emerge: for example, that of his brother al-Ṭāyi^{c}. In a section entitled 'al-Ṭāyi^{c} in the Circle of Adults' (Barrāda 1987: 76–82/*77–83*), we have a first person account from al-Ṭāyi^{c}, who was, like his brother, a fervent leftist activist and nationalist. Unlike al-Hādī though, he has now rejected the beliefs of his youth and retired completely from any sort of public commitment into a moderate, apolitical form of Islam. His voice also provides us with a new picture of al-Hādī, depicted as a cold, sarcastic and cynical person. Al-Ṭāyi^{c} has no time for his brother's reflections on their past and childhood: he dismisses all this as a useless activity. In shaping his narrative through different voices and perspectives, what Barrāda sets out to do is to give a depiction of post-Independence Morocco which is more heterogeneous and collective than one expressed through the experiences and views of one character only. Al-Hādī's leftist, secular voice is therefore paired with others which range from the traditional and religious to the official, passing through the rebellious and feminine. The latter is obviously significant in a novel which relies mostly on a male perspective: the women of the different households whose voices are present in the 'Illumination' passages tend to represent an ideal of good hearted pragmatism and domestic values. Al-Hādī, for example, becomes aware of how much he is privileged as compared to his sister Najiyya who has sacrificed her life in order to fulfil the roles society preordained for her: she is a good housewife and mother (al-Hādī himself, for all his striving to see her in other terms, comes to appreciate her as a sort of second mother after *Lālla* Ghālya's death).[17] Female characters are, however, not always so self-sacrificingly acquiescent, and we also have female voices which resolutely challenge this traditional order of things. Chapter 5 ends with the text of a letter written to al-Hādī by one of his lovers. F. B. (only her initials are given) is a Moroccan woman whom he had met in Paris and fell in love with. After five years they have a relationship in Rabat but she decides to leave her lover as, she explains in her letter, she rejects Moroccan society and refuses to wait for a change which she thinks will never happen. She voices a complete rejection of such a traditional society, a reaction which none of the male characters of the novel is ready to make, despite all their frustrations and disillusions.[18] Such a female perspective is also articulated in the character of

Fāṭima in the author's second novel, *al-Ḍawʾ*. Fāṭima is the daughter of Ghaylāna (the former companion of the protagonist, al-ʿAyshūnī). The young woman appears at the beginning of the novel to give back to the middle-aged painter some inspiration and *joie de vivre* (they have a short-lived and intense affair). Fāṭima embodies the process of disaffection and estrangement of an educated, committed and bright young woman whose traumatic personal experience nullifies all her education and ideological drive. At the moment she writes a letter from France (whence she escaped to seek refuge in sex and, eventually, in a loveless marriage) to al-ʿAyshūnī, she feels empty and is persuaded that all her past preoccupations with identity, homeland and history, and all her past militancy now amount to nothing. Barrāda does not stigmatize this rebellious attitude, but neither does he glorify it: both F. B. and Fāṭima reject Moroccan society but fail to find an alternative to it which would give them a sense of purpose in their lives. Al-Nowaihi underlines how in *Luʿbat* characters could be divided into two main groups: those who have a sense of purpose which derives from being connected to their community and 'those who have given up on society' who are 'prone to [. . .] self-doubt, loneliness, and despair' (Nowaihi 2000: 377). She ascribes this difference to a generational gulf: the old generation used to see France, the colonial power, as the source of all that was wrong with their society; the new generation, on the other hand, faces a much more complex picture in which Moroccans are both the victims and the perpetrators of injustice. As the text makes clear, the reaction to this increasingly complex postcolonial situation can differ: al-Nowaihi underlines how, for example, Najiyya and her husband (Sī Ibrāhīm) in their way of living still belong to the same generation as their parents since they conform to the traditional roles society gives them (Nowaihi 2000: 378). Al-Hādī and al-Ṭāyiʿ start from the common understanding that society should be changed and bettered, but, as we have seen, they end up taking different paths. In al-ʿAyshūnī, we have the quintessential apolitical character. He is, however, partly similar to the new al-Hādī, the self-doubting leftist militant: the former too is concerned about individual regeneration and an individual striving to make sense of life, but without the latter's ambition (or illusion) that personal regenerations like his would trigger a progressive transformation of society as a whole.

Khūrī, like Barrāda, is consciously committed to creating a novel which transcends the limits of a work characterized by a single perspective and consciousness:

> Khoury declares his intention to break with the tradition of the single narrator and embrace a variety of discourses. He rejects the oppressive and dictatorial stance of the single narrator who dominates the scene and insists on writing novels with a variety of discourses – in [*Riḥlat*'s] case, Gandhi's, Alice's, Rima's, the narrator's, and others'.
>
> (Aghacy 1996: 166)

The way Khūrī gives most of his novels a multivoiced structure differs significantly from the multivoicedness of, for example, Faulkner, Barrāda and al-Takarlī on the one hand, or Dostoevsky and al-Kharrāṭ on the other. The highly fragmented form of his texts (analysed earlier) continuously provides the author with chances to introduce into his narrative a new narrator and a new, often different point of view. Accordingly, Khūrī opens *Riḥlat* by quoting a verse by the Andalusian mystical poet Ibn ᶜArabī (1165–1240) which echoes his intentions as referred to in the passage cited earlier:

وما الوجه إلا واحد غير أنه

إذا أنت عدّدت المرايا تعددا

A face is only one, yet if you multiply the mirrors, it is multiple
(Khūrī 1989: 6; our translation)

In the course of the novel, Khūrī expands on Ibn ᶜArabī's image of the mirrors projecting many 'versions' of the same face and we find that Little Gāndī even turns the different shoes he polishes into different mirrors in which he can see the city of Beirut (Khūrī 1989: 162–4/*152–3*). However, drawing on Bakhtin in her article about *Riḥlat*, Aghacy dismisses the author's polyphonic plan, claiming that the novel remains dominated by the author's leftist ideology, according to which all the characters linked to the West, the church and the bourgeoisie are depicted in negative terms; the main characters of Ghāndī and Alice, who are Arab and belong to the lower strata of society, are favoured, idealized and function as mouthpieces for the narrator/author. In the critic's words: 'even though a diversity of voices and languages are [sic] presented, it is the narrator who controls and manipulates them by pulling them into his own frame of reference' (Aghacy 1996: 164). However, when we analyse the characters in the novel carefully we find it difficult to see that clear division between 'good' and 'bad' characters on which Aghacy bases her first attack. She claims that the narrator, whom she clearly associates with Khūrī (Aghacy 1996: 166), presents Ghāndī as the hero/martyr of the novel (which is in itself highly debatable). At the same time she states that the narrator's idealization is subverted by the text. Another example of Aghacy's contradictory argument is evident when she claims that the narrator says that the Israeli invasion is the cause of all the problems afflicting the characters, while the text shows that affliction was present well before the Israelis came (Aghacy 1996: 167–8). Again, Aghacy claims both that the narrator despises the church, and that the text reveals that it is the church which actually helps many of 'the poor and marginalized figures' of the novel (Aghacy 1996: 168). Aghacy's reading suggests a conflict between Khūrī as the narrator (according to Aghacy) and Khūrī as the author of the text. But why should the author subvert so clearly what his narrator (i.e. according to Aghacy, himself) believes? Why should he produce a text which in a way obviously subverts the clear-cut message it is supposed to convey (a leftist, simplistic criticism of the church, America, the West, and so on)? Aghacy could reply that he does this in order to hide his true intent, but we believe that the presence of such a clear-cut bias in Khūrī's fiction is debatable. Characters such as Ghāndī and Alice who, according to Aghacy, are painted as heroes (as opposed to the Western or Westernized characters who are painted as 'baddies') appear much more complex than she suggests. They can be seen with sympathy by the reader by virtue of their undeniable status as victims, but they are by no means idealized heroes whose actions are all justifiable and comprehensible (as Aghacy herself points out, when talking about Ghāndī's harsh reaction to his daughter's suspected rape; Aghacy 1996: 167). Similarly, the supposedly negative characters such as the Reverend and the American professor are hardly depicted as villains. As the Reverend, for instance, becomes mad and wets his pants, the depiction of his life's miserable final stage can evoke pity and sympathy in the reader (at least as much as the depiction of Ghāndī's death and the miserable final stages of Alice's life).[19]

Khūrī's ideological position is well-known and he himself is not shy about making it public. The thoughts of Khūrī the journalist are widely available through his articles. Our focus here is, however, on Khūrī the novelist. As far as the latter is concerned, all his works can be seen as governed by one dominant value, which he himself sees as literature's noblest goal[20]: to give voice to the marginalized, the Ghāndīs and the Alices of *Riḥlat*, and to those who are not the centre of social or political attention: the anti-heroes by definition, the Nahīlas, the Khalīls of *Bāb* and the Yālūs of his last novel (both analysed later). This is undeniable (and we could also add that Khūrī chooses to privilege this aspect of his *oeuvre* instead of creating a truly polyphonic novel as proposed by Bakhtin), but he does not do this in a simplistic way. As far as *Riḥlat* is concerned, the humble and marginalized are represented, not idealized. The author sympathizes with them, but their portrayal, it is fair to say, is usually realistic.[21] We will now consider two other novels by Khūrī, in an attempt to expand our argument.

Like *Riḥlat*, *Mamlakat* provides the reader with a comprehensive picture of various different groups of individuals, while at the same time depicting the tragic conflicts in their lives. Particularly in his portrayals of aspects of Lebanese life through diverse characters, *Mamlakat*'s author seems to underline the richness derived from the co-existence (once peaceful) of different ethnic and religious groups. It is important to notice how the author, who is clearly sympathetic towards the Palestinians, is also able to depict the complexity of the condition of the Jewish people in the Middle East, and their sufferings and expectations. In *Mamlakat*, we have three portraits of Jews. The narrator associates his friend Imīl (an Israeli living in New York) with Wadīᶜ, a Jew who left Beirut because of his son Mūsā's wish to go to Israel after 'Lebanon's little civil war' of 1958 (Khūrī 1993: 30–1/*24*, 109–10/*89*). In Israel the father becomes dumb before dying[22] (it is clear from the text that he feels alienated in Israel), but for his son, who takes the name Moshe, Israel means a new beginning and freedom: 'personal freedom, freedom with women, freedom from Beirut, freedom from the strict Jewish traditions that pervaded their home, and freedom from his father' (Khūrī 1993: 109/*89*). As for Imīl, he tells the narrator the story of his father who, by leaving Eastern Europe, escapes from the Holocaust to reach Palestine (Khūrī 1993: 31–2/*24–5*).

This shows that, while focusing mostly on the injustice and suffering caused by Israel to the Arabs (especially the Palestinians), Khūrī does not demonize Jews. This is also true in *Bāb* (even if, as we will see later, the author's sympathy towards the Jewish people is expressed in a less satisfying way as compared to *Mamlakat*, this is because of a formal flaw, not an ideological one). The lengthy novel can be considered a true 'Palestinian saga' in that it deals with several generations of Palestinians, following their drama from the creation of the state of Israel to the 1990s, and consists of an impressive number of stories and anecdotes. It is not an *epic* in the classical sense though, since it works to subvert heroic myths, rather than to create them.[23] But what concerns us most here is that *Bāb* is a novel which presents a large number of different voices. Before we analyse how these voices are introduced into the novel, we need to introduce the work itself, arguably Khūrī's most ambitious novel to date.

On Monday 20 November 1995 three months have already passed during which the narrator, Khalīl, has been with his beloved father figure, Yūnis, a middle-aged man in a coma, in a room of the Galilee Hospital in the Palestinian refugee camp of Shatila, Beirut. The narration, which is Khalīl's would-be dialogue with Yūnis (the man who years before had adopted him and whom he consequently calls 'father') is characterized by numerous flashbacks to key moments in modern Palestinian history: 1948 (the *nakba*), 1967 (the *naksa*), 1982 (the Sabra and Shatila massacre), 1985 (the Shatila siege and the massacre by *Amal*) and so on. The flashbacks refer specifically to events involving the narrator, his 'interlocutor' and their companions and lovers.[24] The locations of the anecdotes narrated by Khalīl are accordingly the following: Beirut, the south of Lebanon, the Palestinian countryside in Galilee where Bāb al-Shams is (a cave where Yūnis secretly meets his wife Nahīla). In many passages the time is connected to the place of the anecdote narrated. In fact, the time is often long past (mainly the period of the *nakba* and the early 1950s), and the place is often Palestine, since the narrators are all Palestinian refugees who live in Beirut (the present of the narration is 1995, hence many of the occasional narrators – not Khalīl – are women or elderly people who have not been expelled from, or murdered in, Beirut's camps). It is clear that the novel dramatizes how, for most of the Palestinian refugees, life has turned into nothing but a memory of a past and of a place which they will never regain, as if they have been deprived of a present and, most importantly, of a future.

Khalīl is talking to Yūnis who is in a coma, hence the latter is unconscious and unable to understand, or at least to reply.[25] Khalīl tells him a series of stories in order, he claims, to keep his 'father' alive.[26] Khūrī's frame-tale reminds us of *The Arabian Nights* in that storytelling is associated with life and survival (Khalīl tries to save bothYūnis's life and his own). The stories are at times those which Yūnis himself has once narrated to Khalīl. Sometimes, Khalīl gets lost in the stream of his narration and begins to talk about his own experiences. Even if Yūnis does not actively take part in the conversation with Khalīl, the latter's is not exactly a monologue. First of all, he is addressing somebody other than himself. Second, at times he guesses how his interlocutor might respond to what he is saying, so that a sort of imaginary dialogue occurs, as is evident in the following passage: 'Was Nada your way of escaping the incandescence of Naheeleh [Nahīla]? You don't want me to talk about Nada! Okay, suggest another subject. I know you don't like talking about these things' (Khūrī 1998: 47/*40*). This is a straightforward example where Khalīl makes clear he is taking into account his friend's possible reaction. However, even if this phenomenon is sometimes less explicit, we can generally claim that Khalīl's discourse corresponds to Bakhtin's 'microdialogue' (a monologue where a character imagines somebody else's reactions to what he is saying or thinking. These are included in the monologue to form a sort of imaginary dialogue; Bakhtin 1963: 74–5). In other words, Khalīl's discourse would not be possible without these other discourses: his is a discourse with a perennial 'sideward glance', as Bakhtin effectively describes that of *Poor Folk*'s Makar Devushkin (Bakhtin 1963: 210). Nonetheless, Yūnis's discourse (and that of other characters) is never fully formulated: Yūnis only speaks within Khalīl's consciousness;[27] his discourse is hinted at but it is mainly implied, rather than made explicit, even if the reader who knows Palestinian history will have no problems in defining it. It is through the main narrator's memories and considerations that the other's discourse is portrayed.[28] As we gradually come to realize, Khalīl's talking to Yūnis gives the former the possibility of speaking his mind (probably for the first time), expressing doubts about many of Yūnis's ideas and stories. His speaking frankly is maybe something he feared to do while Yūnis was conscious.

What hampers a truly genuine confrontation of different discourses in *Bāb* is not the division of characters into bad and good or the manipulation by Khūrī of other discourses to affirm his own, as Aghacy suggests when analysing *Riḥlat*. Admittedly, the reader can be justified in having a certain degree of suspicion when confronting Khalīl's handling of the other's discourse, since he is taking advantage of Yūnis's silence to voice his generation's doubts about the older generation. Still, his perpetually questioning attitude makes him generally fair, and he often questions himself too. *Bāb* is a novel which functions 'dialogically' on many levels (i.e. it develops through the confrontation of two, or more, different perspectives), but it can be hardly defined as polyphonic because Khalīl's point of view is privileged.

The novel promotes a reflection on some significant controversial aspects of Palestinian history, but it does so almost exclusively from within Khalīl's consciousness. For example, the obvious generational clash between Khalīl and Yūnis (which includes a confrontation between fighters of the *nakba*, Yūnis's older generation born in pre-1948 Palestine, and those of the Lebanese Civil War, Khalīl's new generation born in exile) fails to produce a true dialogue between the two. We could say that, in silencing the old generation, the author is ironically showing how the new generation of Palestinians can only confront the old when it is dying.

Another potential dialogue which is not fully formulated but is present in an embryonic form within Khalīl's consciousness addresses the perception of heroism. Apart from questioning heroism in general and showing how people can rewrite key events, the novel also depicts the hardship which relatives of heroes have to endure. Yāsīn, Khalīl's biological father, was a Palestinian 'hero' who was murdered when Khalīl was nine. The latter does not even know why he was killed and by whom. For him the fact that Yāsīn was seen as a fighting hero is of secondary importance. Most importantly for him, he was deprived of a normal childhood, and he indirectly challenges Yāsīn's responsibility as a father (he is so upset by people mistaking him for his father that he comes to hate him for this reason alone, Khūrī 1998: 369). The difficulties of Yāsīn's relatives are more fully mirrored in the relationship between Nahīla and her 'heroic' husband, Yūnis. Khalīl clearly blames Yūnis for all the difficulties his wife has to put up with: in 1948 Nahīla is left behind in occupied Palestine to take care of Yūnis's old parents in an abandoned house. From time to time she receives Yūnis, who comes secretly from Lebanon to the cave of Bāb al-Shams. In the cave, the couple make love and Nahīla regularly gets pregnant. Her life is characterized by daydreaming and waiting for her husband. Even before Yūnis loses consciousness, Nahīla is effectively a widow who suffers from acute loneliness and despair (on one level she can be seen as representing the Palestinians' condition under Israeli occupation, their status as foreigners in their own land). Nahīla dies at the end of the novel: the whole second section (Khūrī 1998: 237–527) is called 'Nahīla's Death'.

She is a pivotal character who, in a crucial passage of the novel, is poetically 'multiplied' by seven. (In *Mamlakat*, Jesus is said to have met seven Marys during his short life, Khūrī 1993: 57/*46*.)[29] The first six Nahīlas can be seen as six images/depictions of the heroine with alternatively positive and negative overtones. For example, the first Nahīla is the child bride who is scared by her unknown husband (negative overtone); the second is the beautiful woman who is married for the second time by Yūnis in the cave of Bāb al-Shams, this time following a private, intimate and much more meaningful ritual of love (positive overtone). The seventh Nahīla comes to life on the crucial night of what Khalīl believes to be the couple's last meeting. The seventh Nahīla is at last assertive, a woman in her early forties who looks back at her life and narrates its bitter story, voicing her disappointment. She effectively silences the hero and gives voice to what she represents: the quiet unglamorous suffering of a hero's relatives mentioned earlier, and the position of the Palestinians remaining in Israel. Khūrī deals with two different groups of Palestinians: 'the insiders' who did not leave in 1948 and now live in Israel, and 'the outsiders' who live in the refugee camps of the Middle East. This separation is depicted through the difficult relationship between the insider Nahīla and her husband Yūnis, the outsider and fighter. From the wife/insider's perspective, Yūnis is above all guilty of having told her a terrible lie: that one day he (and all those who left) would come back to Palestine. For the first time, Nahīla tells Yūnis her side of the story, how it is to live in occupied

Palestine and what she has to go through in her daily life. Against all odds, she is fighting to give her numerous children a future which is based on painful compromises (two of her children work for an Israeli mechanic). Yūnis is unaware of all this and Nahīla blames him for that. Both Yūnis and Nahīla's lives are harsh, but here the stress is on the less visible and glamorous experience of the woman/insider. Nahīla also rejects Yūnis's proposal that she should go to live with him in Lebanon. Indeed she rejects him, as if she knew, Yūnis reflects, that it would have been increasingly difficult for him to go back to Bāb al-Shams to see her: 'She wouldn't be an abandoned woman; she'd choose her new life deliberately' (Khūrī 1998: 404/*386*). The day after her rejection of him, Nahīla goes back to see her husband and apologizes for her words, but the importance of what she has said remains and her perspective has been voiced.[30]

Nahīla's strong personality, epitomized in her forcing her husband to make love to her after she has spoken tough words to him,[31] leads us to another significant theme of the novel: the perception of gender, mainly portrayed through the relationships between Yūnis and Khalīl, on one side, and Nahīla and Shams, on the other. We have just seen how Nahīla, in a pivotal scene of *Bāb*, emerges as a strong, brave and responsible character. Shams too is a strong character: she killed the man she loved because he refused to marry her and for this reason she was killed by his family. Not only is she sexually assertive, but she is also politically committed and fights in a militia. Other women characters are often shown as being more courageous and realistic than men (Umm Ḥasan, for instance, is another key character in the novel: she is the stalwart of the Shatila camp and the repository of its memory).[32] This positive depiction of women is also common in novels by Barrāda, al-Kharrāṭ and al-Takarlī. As we will see later in more detail, however, the portrayal of Munīra from al-Takarlī's *al-Raj*^{c} is more fully-rounded than that of Nahīla, who is excessively idealized.

A bigger flaw lies in the way the novel is narrated. Khalīl's narrative successfully reproduces an oral style which creates a beautifully simple language but this conversational style, despite its appeal, tends to create a stream of short, initially captivating sentences. These perhaps reproduce Khūrī's own ideas about relationships between writing, history and memory,[33] but they are at times only spelled out by a character and not put into a fictionalized context, that is, not dramatized in the narrative. As a consequence of this, the interesting concepts remain abstract and are easily forgotten. They lack a correlative image to expand them, and to which the reader can return.

For example, it is true that *Bāb* as a whole challenges myths of masculinity, but it does so in two different ways, one successful, the other less so. On the one hand, we have the two positive characters of Nahīla and Shams. The latter emerges only through Khalīl's random and casual observations – in other words, she is rarely allowed to express herself fully. The former expresses herself fully only in the passage mentioned earlier. The fact that this episode is parenthetic and that Nahīla is normally depicted by the narrator as a completely positive character make what she says to her husband sound like an uncharacteristic outburst, lacking in dramatic conviction. Khalīl, on the other hand, narrates a story (*ḥikāyat al-quṭna*) about a traditional early marriage, where the girl is the one who shows the boy how to consummate the relationship after instruction from the boy's mother (Khūrī 1998: 90–1).[34] Khalīl is convinced that Yūnis had the same experience with Nahīla but does not want to admit it. Here it is the myth of the hero's virility which is questioned. In this case though, the challenge is much more effective than in Nahīla's tirade against Yūnis or in Khalīl's random considerations about Shams. We do not simply have the dry formulation of a point of view: rather, the point of view is dramatized through a story, that of the piece of cotton, which is funny and bitter at the same time and involves the reader much more successfully. In addition, the reader can appreciate how Khalīl carries out a flamboyantly metafictional operation in referring the story to another character – Yūnis – thereby laying bare the mechanisms of writing fiction.

The writer, himself a fighter alongside the Palestinians at the very beginning of the long Lebanese Civil War,[35] questions some of the attitudes the Palestinians and their sympathizers, himself included, might find it natural to assume.[36] As a consequence of this, the debate promoted by the novel is within the Palestinian arena: it involves a supposedly mainstream Palestinian dominant discourse (Yūnis's self-righteous attitude, never fully formulated but represented by Khalīl) and Khalīl's all-questioning counter-discourse (the debate does not involve an Israeli voice). Khalīl, even if insecure and self-doubting, ends up having the upper hand, ultimately because his is the only consciousness fully present.

As we have noted earlier, the novel deals extensively with the perception of heroism. Within a Palestinian environment, the quintessential hero cannot be other than the *fidāʾī*, the fighter for the liberation of his occupied country. The hero of the novel is in fact represented by Yūnis, an old *fidāʾī*. It is, however, not incidental that Yūnis is now in a coma, unable to speak, abandoned in Shatila. Khūrī decides to silence the hero of the older generation of Palestinians and allows Khalīl, the representative of a new generation of Palestinian fighters who have never been in Palestine, to challenge many of the views of the old guard of *fidāʾiyyīn* and the process of mystification surrounding them.

One of the many examples of Khalīl's questioning of Yūnis is offered when he narrates the story his grandmother once told him. In 1948, the woman was in a group of people escaping from their village, now conquered by Israelis. In their escape to Lebanon, overwhelmed by fear, one night they reach a Druze village. The story tells how a desperate Palestinian woman in this group, unable to calm her crying child, ends up killing him. Khalīl comments:

> You won't believe [this] story [. . .] You believe, as I'd like to, that we don't kill our children and toss them under trees. You like things clear and simple. The murderer is a known quantity, likewise the person killed, and it's up to us to see that justice is done. Unfortunately, master, it wasn't as simple as 'them' and 'us'. It was something different that's hard to define.
> (Khūrī 1998: 211/*198–9*)

This is not to say that the old guard is dismissed as useless and incapable of self-criticism.[37] For example, it is clear that the novelist also dramatizes in the character of Yūnis (arguably sympathizing with him) an important shift in the politics of the Israeli–Palestinian conflict which occurred following the attempt to reach a peaceful solution, namely after the Oslo agreement of 1993. From this perspective, the *fidāʾī* is made speechless by the new political situation. In other words, in the 1990s the Palestinian National Authority of Yasser Arafat faced the big problem of dealing with old combatants, when it seemed that Palestine could have turned into an independent nation-state. The wider problem of the Palestinian refugees is also tackled by the author, as the very nature of the novel (its stories are about Palestinian dramas and are narrated by Palestinian refugees) makes us reflect about the future of the people living in the refugee camps of the Middle East.

Khalīl's attitude, it is true, is often critical even when it comes to his own ideas and experiences. However, to go back to the passage we have quoted, it appears as a didactic comment directing the reader towards the intended conclusion. Khalīl's point is made so clear that we might suspect that the author does not give much credit to his readers' interpreting abilities. Khūrī makes clear what his narrator's 'dominant value' is and he imposes it inspite of Khalīl's recriminations and doubts about heroes and their narrative of events. Yūnis has no chance to reply to Khalīl's questions and the reader has to accept them. Khalīl's saving grace is that what he wants to impose is fundamentally a healthy critical attitude. It is a pity that the promotion of such an attitude is sometimes carried out in a rather didactic way.

Another example of a dry, non-dramatized narration concerns the way Jews are portrayed by Khūrī. As we have seen earlier, in *Mamlakat* we find some sketches of Jewish characters. Even if these could have been more fully developed, they are nonetheless more successful in showing the author's tolerant stance and the complexity of the Middle Eastern situation than the passage where Khalīl in *Bāb* questions the attitude of Yūnis's generation towards the Holocaust. Once Khalīl makes it clear that he is not trying to give any kind of justification for what the Israelis did to the Palestinians ('the expulsion of an entire people from its country and the transformation of what remained of them into second-class citizens', Khūrī 1998: 291/*274*), he affirms that everyone, including the Palestinians, has a moral obligation to know what happened to the Jews during the Second World War and to speak against it, because the Holocaust not only killed Jews but also the human being within us all. Then Khalīl draws a parallel between the two victims: he asks Yūnis (and himself) if it would not be possible to find the faces of Palestinian refugees (like Umm Ḥasan, the woman who dies at the very beginning of *Bāb* in the Shatila camp) similar to the faces of the Jews on their way to the concentration camps. Before referring to the trains which carried the Jews to their death, he says: 'I see Umm Ḥasan in the midst of thousands of homeless in the fields [. . .] and I hear the whistle of the train' (Khūrī 1998: 291/*275*). But Khalīl wishes the Palestinians to avoid becoming enslaved by a single story (their tragedy as a dispossessed people), as he claims the Jews are by the Holocaust. He says:

> I'm scared by a history with only one version. History has many different versions. If it is frozen into one, it only leads to death. We shouldn't see ourselves in [the Jews'] mirrors only, because they are prisoners of only one story which seems to reduce and immobilize them.
>
> (Khūrī 1998: 292, our translation)

On a personal level too, Khalīl wishes his 'adopted father' to be freed from his love story with Nahīla, which is as idealized as it is unreal.[38] Khalīl would rather see him as a normal human being who, as well as loving, also betrays, repents, falls in love, feels afraid and is not an entirely positive hero. This is one of the central themes of the novel, as its conclusion emphasizes. Eventually, Khalīl himself is freed from his father figure thanks to the ghost of Nahīla. This conclusion can obviously be read on many levels, but it is beyond dispute that the novel expresses the wish for new generations of Palestinians to be able both to remember and to forget their heroes. They should be remembered for their sacrifice which was a necessary step in the creation of a national identity. At the same time, they should be forgotten as a necessary step towards progressing and moving on, to prevent Palestinians from becoming imprisoned by a single story.[39]

All these are powerful, brave political statements from Khūrī. The problem is that, as already stated earlier in the introduction, the content of a work of art has to be analysed and evaluated against the backdrop of its formal expression. In fact, *Bāb*'s 'historical' theme often remains only journalistically powerful: from a formal point of view, it is at times no more than a dry, documentary formulation of what the implied author thinks, expressed through Khalīl's questioning attitude, rather abruptly inserted into the text.[40]

From an ideological point of view, all these examples seem to confirm that by dealing with a series of controversial issues, the text chooses to give more space to the attitudes, or voices which are usually overlooked or under-represented, like those of women or of the younger generations. Admittedly, these monologues are complex ones ('microdialogues' or discourses with 'side glances'), but they remain monologues and maybe this (a novel limited by one consciousness only) is what the author meant to write. *Bāb* is not a polyphonic novel, and it is only partly multivoiced. It is very likely that Khūrī's flat, reportorial style in parts of the novel is adopted as a deliberate technique in place of more sophisticated (and maybe more conventional) dramatization and characterization.[41]

As we have seen, a crucial aspect of Khūrī's fiction is that its focus is on the marginalized, the 'little people', the anti-heroes (we should bear in mind that heroes like Yūnis who have been disgraced or questioned are also part of the wider picture of the Palestinians).[42] This is evident in the author's re-interpretation of heroism, and it can be related to what Linda Hutcheon says about writers whom she considers postmodern[43]:

> We may indeed get few postmodern narrative representations of the heroic victors who have traditionally defined who and what made it into History. Often we get instead both the story and the story-telling of the non-combatants or the losers: the Canadian Indians of Rudy Wiebe's *The Temptations of Big Bear* or Leonard Cohen's *Beautiful Losers*; the women of Troy in Christa Wolf's *Cassandra*; the blacks of South Africa or America in the work of J. M. Coetzee, André Brink, Toni Morrison, or Ishmael Reed.
>
> (Hutcheon 1989: 51)

We will now start to deal with *al-Raj^c* by contrasting Jabrā's approach to the formal structure of his novel *al-Baḥth* with al-Takarlī's. Peled tells us that Jabrā indeed meant his *al-Baḥth* 'to be a polyphonic novel, as defined by [. . .] Bakhtin in his book on the poetics of Dostoevsky' (Peled 1995: 140). Al-Takarlī, on the contrary, is keen to underline that, first of all, *al-Raj^c*'s multivoiced form 'imposed itself, was inevitable'[44] (in fact, we will see later how *al-Raj^c*, despite fulfilling some of Bakhtin's requisites for the genuine polyphonic novel, intends to achieve a different overall result. Of course, this does not mean that the author was unaware of Bakhtin's work before or during the writing of *al-Raj^c*). Second, as the author himself clarifies in the foreword to the French translation of *al-Raj^c*, the novel's multivoicedness is meant to involve the reader more than a less innovative form would.[45] In fact, the novel's most evident feature is that its narration is carried out through the perspectives (and in some cases through the voices) of different characters. This is something we find in all the Arabic novels quoted at the beginning of this chapter.[46] In *al-Raj^c* though, this kind of narration through multiple perspectives also involves some of the secondary characters who witness events rather than taking an active part in them. This is no trivial task for the novelist since the narration expresses the different age, sex and general attitude of the witness and contributes to shaping a comprehensive picture of what is taking place. It is possible to highlight various kinds of attitudes in the perspectives of the characters: the cynical tone of an egotist; the tormented tone of a hopeless, weak young man; the pure and innocent tone of a child; the materialistic, ever-complaining but comic tone of an elderly woman and so on. The novel also presents an impressive number of different language varieties (famously including the Baghdadī *^{c}āmmiyya* in the direct speech), registers, jargons and styles, mainly through what we could define as background characters (see later).[47] To shed more light on the complex cast of this novel, we could simplify matters by saying that *al-Raj^c*'s actors can be divided into four main groups (the following scheme is perforce a rough approximation of the novel's many characters and the situations in which they find themselves, and will mainly serve to introduce the main plot):

1 The main characters: the brothers Midḥat and ᶜAbd al-Karīm (hereafter Karīm, as he is also called throughout the novel). These are the protagonists of the main story, which gravitates around their cousin Munīra (Midḥat, as has already been pointed out,[48] has a prominent role: oversimplifying we could say that *al-Rajᶜ* is about him). Both brothers will end up falling in love with Munīra in their own different ways; both will fail to rescue her. In fact, the young schoolteacher is in need of help: she has been raped in the provincial town of Baᶜqūba by her nephew ᶜAdnān and now she has found refuge in her uncle's (Abū Midḥat's) house in Baghdad. Besides the obvious trauma suffered, her loss of virginity before marriage puts her in a very difficult situation, from both a psychological and a social point of view. Therefore, she decides to keep it a secret and tries to go on living in a sort of self-imposed isolation. This resolution will prove impossible to fulfil in her new temporary accommodation where she ends up attracting the two brothers, at last giving in to Midḥat's marriage proposal. As Meyer has pointed out in discussing other multivoiced novels (specifically, *Mīrāmār* and its alleged inspirational source, *The Sound and the Fury*), we notice that *al-Rajᶜ* also focuses on the central theme of woman's honour and the way this is perceived within a male-dominated society. Unlike Mahfouz's Zahra and Faulkner's Caddie, though, al-Takarlī's Munīra expresses herself directly.

2 There is another important story, but not as dominant as the main one: that of Ḥusayn and his wife Madīḥa (Midḥat and Karīm's sister). These, especially Ḥusayn, are important figures in the novel because their subplot interferes with and intertwines with the main one (Munīra/her cousins). At the beginning of the novel we already know that Ḥusayn has come back to Baghdad from Kuwait, having inexplicably fled there abandoning his wife and two daughters. Ḥusayn is now living in the Kurdish quarter with two elderly relatives. He lives in a small, dirty room which mirrors his new life as a penniless dropout who finds in alcohol a release from his responsibilities. In the second part of the novel the same room will welcome Midḥat who, shocked by having discovered on his wedding night that his beloved bride Munīra is not a virgin, decides to leave his home.

3 Secondary characters: all the remaining members of the family with which the novel deals. The extended family live in a traditional house built round a courtyard in the Bāb al-Shaykh area of Baghdad. This group includes the two youngest and oldest generations (the elderly: Umm Ḥasan and Ṣafiyya, also called ᶜAmmat Midḥat; the grandchildren Sanāᵓ and Suhā, daughters of Ḥusayn and Madīḥa) and the parents: Abū and Umm Midḥat (Nūriyya: The novel begins with 'her' chapter). Most of these secondary characters are given at least one chapter narrated from their perspective. Their chapters are also functional in moving the plot forward but this is not their only function. For instance, the little girl Sanāᵓ takes on the role of hidden witness of crucial events. This is curious, since she is not supposed to see most of the things happening in the adults' life,

but not incidental: her childish view is meant to be innocent and somehow neutral (she is not able to understand all the implications of what she witnesses).[49]

4 The background characters. These are only sketched briefly and they mainly serve as counterpoints to the main characters' thoughts or contribute to the general atmosphere. But this function, thematically peripheral perhaps, is usually executed with such artistry by al-Takarlī that it becomes an inextricable substratum of the narrative texture. For instance, the beginning of Midḥat's second section (Chapter 10) is a masterful interweaving of such voices in Midḥat's consciousness. For once, we fail to recognize right away by which character the chapter is narrated, until one of those background actors, Saᶜīd, enters the scene and, despite being subject to chronic loss of memory, finally manages to address Midḥat by his name. Saᶜīd's appearance, apart from being delicately comic, gives Midḥat the chance to reflect on his own story and he wishes he could lose his memories of what happened on his wedding night (let us remember that this chapter directly follows Munīra's, and by now we know about her rape although Midḥat does not). Thus we are gently introduced into Midḥat's mind and gradually work out how he has reacted to discovering that his young bride has lost her virginity before marrying him. Voices from other background characters appear at the beginning of the chapter and contribute to expanding on one of the general themes of the novel: that of family relationships in crisis (especially those between wife and husband).[50] Midḥat is sitting in the Murabbaᶜa café and before, during and after his meeting with Saᶜīd, he overhears the conversation of two men sitting at a nearby table: these are two Christians, Buṭrus and Abū Mīkhāᵓīl. The former, as we understand from chunks of their conversation, is in big trouble since his wife has abandoned him and converted to Islam, so that she is now forbidden to him. When a crying Buṭrus leaves the café with his friend, Midḥat reflects, obviously referring to Saᶜīd's amnesia: 'The tortured Boutros [has] no choice but to lose his memory and forget his wife's treachery' (Takarlī 1980: 294/*229*). We can already glimpse Midḥat's allusions to his own state and his misadventure with Munīra ('his wife's treachery'). His desire to forget what has happened to him becomes clearer soon after, when he refers openly to Munīra. The voices of his surroundings merge with his thoughts and revive his memories of Munīra (the flashbacks are numerous in this section and they all depict Munīra before and on their wedding night). This is how the background characters, at first glance insignificant, function: they unconsciously talk to Midḥat about his situation: at times they echo his thoughts, at times they guide them. When the scene changes and we find Midḥat sitting in the back room of Uwānīs's shop with Ḥusayn and some of his habitual drinking companions, another background actor reminds Midḥat of his situation as a fugitive from home. Abū ᶜAbᶜūb, Ḥusayn tells Midḥat, fell in love with the daughter of the estate manager for whom he was working and she, Ḥūriyya, got pregnant: her family arranged the marriage and sent the couple to Baghdad. Now the shepherd is singing a nostalgic song about his lost home and his family. The verses of his song are interspersed with Midḥat's interior monologue and make him wonder: 'Was this idiot really missing his family [. . .] and refusing

the life they had arranged for him with his erring sweetheart?' (Takarlī 1980: 318/*247*). Again, as with Buṭrus, Midḥat unconsciously makes the shepherd's song and situation relate to his own situation.[51] We will conclude this section by quoting Catherine Cobham who observes that '[l]ike Shakespeare's "rude mechanicals," these characters not only provide variety and cathartic humour, but put Midḥat's drama into perspective and give it depth and texture' (Cobham 2002: 189).

Having outlined the novel's content, let us now focus on its multivoiced structure. The first notable effect of *al-Raj*^{c}'s narration is roughly the same as that of other novels with a similar structure: the reader is introduced into the realm of characters and events gradually and through the characters' own perspectives. At this superficial level many of the observations made earlier on Barrāda's *Lu*^{c}*bat* and those made by Meyer about *Mīrāmār* can be related to *al-Raj*^{c} as well (despite the fact that in the former examples characters narrate in the first person). First of all, the reader is given 'a 360-degree view of events' and the writer 'concentrates on conveying the limitations of each character's range of awareness in order to build a composite picture of those events' (Meyer 2001: 26).[52] These novels are constructed as sorts of mystery stories: exploiting the partial awareness of the characters we gradually reach the truth. A mystery surrounds the relationship between Quentin and Caddie in *The Sound*; what happens in Sarḥān al-Buḥayrī's room between himself and Zahra in *Mīrāmār* is a mystery; Munīra's rape, as we have seen, is concealed from the reader up to her chapter (the ninth); the mysterious element is not present in *Lu*^{c}*bat*. Through this kind of narration the novelist evokes expectation in the reader. In *al-Raj*^{c} this is obvious when, after reading the first eight chapters, we, together with most of the characters, wonder about what happened to Munīra in Ba^{c}qūba, what lies behind ^{c}Adnān's strange behaviour, what there is between the two of them. Of course, this is not to say that suspense and expectation can never be achieved by means of a more traditional sort of narration – through one omniscient narrator only, for instance, or through a first person narrator. Genette shows us how a kind of narration with 'external focalization' (where the narrator says less than a character knows) at the beginning of many novels of intrigue and adventure (by Walter Scott, Alexandre Dumas, Jules Verne) is there to evoke an atmosphere of mystery and hence arouse the reader's interest. The same applies to the beginning of so many other novels that Genette claims that 'this initial "ignorance" has become a topos of novelistic beginning, even when the mystery is to be immediately dispelled' (Genette 1972: 190–1, n. 53, p. 191).[53] What we have stated earlier about *al-Raj*^{c}'s multiple narration and the type of suspense it creates echoes Genette's words regarding Balzac's *Une double famille* (1830; *A Double Life*, 1896 – part of *La comédie humaine*):

> in the first pages of *Une double famille*, where the narrative focalizes sometimes on Camille and her mother, sometimes on M. de Granville – each of these internal focalizations [serves] to isolate the other character [. . .] in

its mysterious externality: a rearrangement of curiosities that can only quicken the reader's own.

(Genette 1972: n. 57, p. 192)

In our case, 'the mysterious externality' is mainly Munīra's and it is the emergence of her voice which will dispel the 'enigmatic *introit*' (Genette 1972: 190), while in Genette's examples it is mainly a more direct intervention from the author (via the voice of the narrator) which does that. To go back to *al-Raj*ᶜ's multiple narration, this is not only a quantitative matter, it also has to do with a certain *quality* of the representation. For example, in the first part of the novel we all know that *something is wrong* with Munīra. This *something is wrong* is at first similarly depicted by all of the characters whose perspective is expressed (Genette's 'focal heroes'). For instance, Karīm: 'I noticed the pain in her eyes [. . .] Where had I seen that look of anguish before? I stared at her, drawn in by the aura of pain surrounding her. She was trapped in it, like me' (Takarlī 1980: 28/*20*); Ṣafiyya perceives that there is 'something broken, something abnormal in the girl's life' (Takarlī 1980: 65/*48*); Midḥat: 'her legs weren't quite straight, and he fancied that a slight weariness, an invisible spiritual weariness, was affecting her walk' (Takarlī 1980: 160/*123*). Of course, it is already clear that the characters express themselves in different ways; they see the world (Munīra is only an example) from their own angle; their language and their tone differ (even when they do not express themselves directly but through the narrator, as is the case with Ṣafiyya). Still, they all agree that there is something mysteriously wrong about Munīra which they are not able to define. But it is not long before their characteristic voices emerge (by voice here we mean 'tone'; we will see at the end of this chapter that the narrative method shifts according to who is the central character, the focal character). Hence, Ṣafiyya's gossipy, traditionally family-oriented voice emerges and it seems that we can hear it clearly saying: 'it is weird that such a clever and beautiful young woman is still unmarried. Granted she is troubled, but getting married will do her good – and, by the way,' continues our wise Ṣafiyya, 'she should definitely marry Midḥat who is the most suitable husband for her' (here and later we are paraphrazing and summarizing). Karīm, on the other hand, is less pragmatic than Ṣafiyya: we hear his sensitive but also over-sentimental and fundamentally self-obsessed voice saying: 'this beautiful creature is the only source of light in my life [*munīra* indeed], still she is suffering, like I am. Pity me, I can't help her, as I'm unable to help myself – poor Munīra, and poor me!' Midḥat's voice, at this early stage at least, expresses his desire to have everything under his control; he wants to plan his life rationally, with a cold emotionless mind. His voice would sound more or less like this: 'Munīra has a job, a mind and a beautiful body[54]: she might make a good wife. I have to study my position carefully and make a move.' Meyer observes in relation to *Mīrāmār* and *The Sound*: 'There is a central core of events about which our information is incomplete. Each narrator augments our information through the perspective from which they perceive the world, revealing their differing obsessions, motivations, and values' (Meyer 2001: 25). This effect is central as far as the superficial structure of multiple narration is concerned.

If the method of multiple narration is simply limited to giving the reader different perspectives, it is not enough to fulfil the true tasks of polyphony in Bakhtinian terms. These consist in: (1) a *fair* and *equal* representation of the characters' voices; (2) *dialogism* (as opposed to the monologism of the traditional novel), which, according to Bakhtin, is the only way to achieve this.

We have to make clear from the outset that *al-Raj*ᶜ, despite presenting some significant characteristics in common with Bakhtin's polyphonic novel, remains a fundamentally different sort of work with its own priorities and features. In other words, it is clear that al-Takarlī, unlike Jabrā in his *al-Baḥth*, did not begin the task of writing *al-Raj*ᶜ in order to reproduce a polyphonic novel *á la* Dostoevsky. Still, Bakhtin's reading of Dostoevsky can provide a deep insight into some aspects of *al-Raj*ᶜ.

Let us start by comparing *al-Raj*ᶜ with Mahfouz's *Mīrāmār* to underline the former's higher level of sophistication according to some of the criteria of Bakhtinian polyphony.

Despite being void of all the nuances and formal complexities of *al-Raj*ᶜ, *Mīrāmār* conveys one character's voice in each chapter (here, we are not concerned about the most evident difference in the narrative mode between *Mīrāmār*'s first person and *al-Raj*ᶜ's mainly third person narration).

Bakhtin's concept of a genuinely polyphonic novel as a fair and equal representation of different points of view does not seem to apply to *Mīrāmār*. As we have seen earlier, some critics have pointed out how the character of ᶜĀmir Wajdī, the old Wafdist journalist, now retired, is likely to convey the author's viewpoint. But, as we know by now, this is not the point: Bakhtin stresses that Dostoevsky's voice[55] is present and participates in the great dialogue of his novels: his innovation is the fact that it does not dominate and objectify the others' voices. The problem with Mahfouz's Alexandrian novel is not even the fact that the characters can be more or less easily divided into positive and negative, or more and less favoured, as al-ᶜĪd and Meyer have pointed out (Meyer 2001: 22–3). The crucial flaw (let us repeat: only if we observe the novel through Bakhtinian lenses) is that ᶜĀmir's voice seems to emerge at the end as the dominant one. The privileged position of this character is also evident in the fact that his voice has a conclusive, judging flavour, and not only because it literally concludes the novel (ᶜĀmir's voice is given both the first and the last chapter). In other words, ᶜĀmir is favoured by Maḥfuẓ.[56] Oversimplifying, we could affirm that the other characters' voices are there ultimately in order to highlight that ᶜĀmir's (Mahfouz's) voice is the most reasonable. At the end of the novel, we feel sympathy towards ᶜĀmir and we might even agree with Mahfouz about the overall picture he draws of post-revolutionary Egypt.

*Al-Raj*ᶜ, on the other hand, despite being so carefully set in a particular space (Baghdad) and time (the last part of ᶜAbd al-Karīm Qāsim's rule, i.e. 1962–1963), is very much an open-ended work with a universal breadth. The feeling of conclusiveness evoked at the end of both *Mīrāmār* and *Crime and Punishment*[57] is replaced by a feeling of uncertainty: after we finish reading it we are left with much to ponder over. In fact, the novel ends quite enigmatically as far as al-Takarlī's 'dominant value' is concerned.[58] Midḥat, shocked on his wedding night to discover that Munīra is not a virgin, leaves her and ends up living the last days of his life in Ḥusayn's dirty room in the Kurdish quarter. The last chapters focus on his enormous interior struggle to work out the meaning of what has happened to him and find out what he should do next. When he finally resolves to go back to Munīra because he realizes how ridiculous the traditional concepts of honour and innocence have become, he is killed by a stray bullet (the Kurdish quarter was the setting for the last stage of the violent clashes between ᶜAbd al-Karīm Qāsim's supporters and those who had deposed him).[59] Carefully avoiding any kind of naively happy ending (Munīra is not rescued by either Midḥat or Karīm; we are even left to wonder, as Karīm does, about the credibility of Ḥusayn's decision to change his way of living), al-Takarlī closes his novel in a way which leaves open where he really stands *vis-à-vis* his characters and their story: there is no resolution, no final judgement, no authorial conclusive tone.[60] All this is in line with what Bakhtin appreciates so much in Dostoevsky's polyphonic novels. The notable difference is that al-Takarlī's own voice in *al-Rajᶜ* is even weaker than Dostoevsky's in his novels, and than Mahfouz's in *Mīrāmār*. In fact, if we can agree that ᶜĀmir conveys Mahfouz's voice (and we could say that Sonya in *Crime and Punishment* mirrors Dostoevsky's religious ideal),[61] which of *al-Rajᶜ*'s characters represents al-Takarlī's? Is the writer more sympathetic towards any one of his characters? The Russian critic affirms that the author of a polyphonic novel is not passive: his voice engages that of his characters but it does so on an equal level, dialogically. The most likely answer to this question seems to be that al-Takarlī's point of view is to be found in an aspect of each of his main characters.[62] But there is another fundamental difference between *al-Rajᶜ* and the other two novels.

The symbolic nature of *Mīrāmār*, the fact that its characters clearly represent recognizable ideas or social types reminds us of one of the features in Dostoevsky's novels. To cite a few examples from *Mīrāmār*: the old journalist ᶜĀmir Wajdī is the symbol of the old Wafd party and the nationalist struggle of the 1919 Revolution;[63] Sarḥān al-Buḥayrī embodies the rising generation under Nasser; the young and frivolous playboy Ḥusnī ᶜAllām is the representative of the rich class of landowners; the complex and introvert Manṣūr Bāhī is the symbol of the radical left whose aspirations have been betrayed by the July Revolution, and who have betrayed their comrades, and so on.[64] All this is very distant from *al-Rajᶜ* and its characters, whom we do not consider to be symbols, despite some critics' tendency to do so[65]: even if they do possess some allegorical features, they do not embody social classes and political ideas as clearly as characters in the other two novels. Other contrasting examples: Munīra is idealized in *al-Rajᶜ*, especially through Midḥat and Karīm's eyes, but this ideal begins to be undermined with Munīra's own chapter (at the beginning of which she appears harsh towards her mother and more cerebral) and gradually collapses in the rest of the novel (this means that her character emerges as convincing and complex rather than negative). Zahra, on the contrary, remains an idealized character throughout *Mīrāmār* and, even if she makes a crucial error of judgement (perhaps because of that), she can easily be seen as a symbol for the Egyptian homeland.[66] Similarly, if on the one hand we can consider *al-Raj*^{c}'s Karīm and *Mīrāmār*'s Manṣūr Bāhī to be similar characters (they are both thoughtful, intellectual but weak and, despite their genuine feeling for the heroine, they tragically fail to understand and help her), it is difficult to associate the former with any specific political affiliation or idea.

Let us now consider a comparison between *Crime and Punishment* and *al-Raj*^{c}. In the former novel the battle of ideas is fundamental. The characters' ideological formulations are clear and, as Bakhtin highlights, they are placed on the same level and given equal weight, and they engage one another according to the criteria of dialogism: 'the ideas of Dostoevsky the thinker [. . .] are liberated from their monologic isolation and finalization, they become thoroughly dialogized and enter the great dialogue of the novel on *completely equal terms* with other idea-images (the ideas of Raskolnikov [. . .])' (Bakhtin 1963: 92).

If we apply Bakhtin's approach to *al-Raj*^{c}, we first find that, as we have noted earlier, the ideas of al-Takarlī are not as clearly stated as Dostoevsky's in his novels. In fact, we might well ask ourselves: is *al-Raj*^{c} a true novel of ideas? Is there a true 'great dialogue' as observed by Bakhtin in Dostoevsky's polyphonic novels?[67]

Midḥat's main idea of 'rational egotism' (*al-anāniyya al-munaẓẓama*, Takarlī 1980: 138/*105*) and his extremely rational attitude is as central in *al-Raj*^{c} as Raskolnikov's theory of the justifiable crime in *Crime and Punishment*. These ideas change and develop in different ways in the two novels. Notably, Midḥat's plan collapses more because of what happens to him than through continuous ideological clashes (dialogues) with contrasting ideas (Raskolnikov's idea against Sonya's, against Porfiry's, against Razumikhin's and so on.).[68] It is the fact that Munīra's world, with all its unsettling truths, enters Midḥat's that provokes the latter's crisis. We can, however, affirm that both authors are interested in showing how highly theoretical and abstract ideas can collapse when they have to confront actual circumstances. We can easily apply Bakhtin's observation about Dostoevsky to al-Takarlī's treatment of Midḥat's idea of rational egotism: 'As an artist Dostoevsky often divined how a given idea would develop and function under certain changed conditions, what unexpected directions it would take in its further development and transformation' (Bakhtin 1963: 91).

All this does not mean that in *al-Raj*^{c} Midḥat's ideas remain unchallenged (perhaps we could speak of embryonic and potential dialogues rather than fully formulated ones). The first insight into the characters' attitudes is provided through a conversation between Midḥat ('My life belongs to me. It's in my hands. Nobody's got the right to ask me to explain what I'm going to do with it'), Munīra (sympathizing with Midḥat's individualism but more pragmatic and more aware of social constraints: 'What you're saying wouldn't work here. Everyone questions you and interferes in your life, whether you want them to or not') and his father (voicing the traditional – 'There have to be questions and answers [...] I'm your father. Am I not allowed to ask you what you're doing with yourself [...]?' – and religious attitude: 'Our lives are in God's hands', Takarlī 1980: 77–8/*56–7*).[69] This embryonic ideological argument will have significant bearing on what happens in the rest of the novel and will be better expressed through the dialogue between Midḥat and Ḥusayn (his *alter ego*). When Midḥat explains his theory of extreme egotism, telling Ḥusayn 'ideas that he considered his personal secrets' (Takarlī 1980: 148/*114*), Ḥusayn reacts by reproaching him for promoting dangerous and irresponsible ideas (a criticism surprisingly voiced by a character like Ḥusayn who has so emphatically avoided his own important social and domestic duties). Midḥat replies, expressing the concept of the division of mankind between ordinary and special people, which seems to be a quotation from Raskolnikov's famous newspaper article:[70]

> These ideas aren't for everybody. [...] They're for a certain type of person, with clearly defined attributes and abilities. Such ideas exist separately from the world, history, evolution. Those are all circumstances, decor to round off the picture.
>
> (Takarlī 1980: 149/*115*)

Ḥusayn's surprising social common sense is matched by a revealing observation from Midḥat. After claiming that he does not have anything to do with the society in which he lives ('I'm attached to it by chance', Takarlī 1980: 150/*116*), Midḥat suggests to himself that Ḥusayn could have reached the situation in which he finds himself now (and which Midḥat considers foolishly suicidal) by following 'a vague idea close to his own'. In fact, Midḥat, unaware of his own future, goes on to say to himself:

> All things considered, was Ḥusayn not his mad twin? His double who had been formed by the same ideas, but then lacked the will, the determination, the sharpness of vision to put them into practice, and so had abandoned everything and let himself be carried along by the current, a bloated body floating on the surface of the water?
>
> (Takarlī 1980: 150/*116*)

And this is more or less what awaits Midḥat himself. The Midḥat/Ḥusayn pairing is one of the two main pairings on which *al-Raj*^{c} can be seen to be based (the other being Karīm/Munīra). This pairing is telling, and not only because Midḥat, in reflecting on it, unconsciously foresees his future.[71] More importantly, it shows us how Ḥusayn himself echoes a voice within Midḥat. The latter's internal struggle is the most important dialogue in the novel but, as the text makes clear, it is by no means a dialogue cut off from the external world, as Midḥat erroneously believes ('such ideas exist separately from the world').

The potential dialogue between Midḥat and what Munīra represents takes full shape only at the end of the novel and only within Midḥat's 'great dialogue' with himself. Midḥat's ruling idea (planned egotism) and dominant attitude (everything has to be under his constant control, every circumstance rationally evaluated) patently collapse when Munīra enters his life, as he admits to himself: 'Everything ran smoothly, easily, with no complications, as it always had done for him, until [...] Munīra came into his life' (Takarlī 1980: 473/*365*). The first unsettling element to creep into his plan is his unexpected love for Munīra. The unsettling power of Munīra is already hinted at in the terrace night scene when Midḥat simply sees her and offers her a glass of water in the darkness, and then questions his powers of rationality and ability to think lucidly: 'Such encounters with her were too much for him, especially in this lost time between night and day, moonlight and dawn, *when you couldn't predict what you might do next*' (Takarlī 1980: 183/*140*, emphasis ours).[72] The second even bigger blow is her not being a virgin. It is important to note how all these considerations are thought through by Midḥat in his long final interior monologue *a posteriori*, after he abandons Munīra. This is Midḥat's long and difficult process of becoming conscious of his circumstances and especially of himself, of what he really is as compared to what he thought he was before meeting Munīra. Again, in Bakhtin's words: 'Dostoevsky sought a hero who would be occupied primarily with the task of becoming conscious, the sort of hero whose life would be concentrated on the pure function of gaining consciousness of himself and the world' (Bakhtin 1963: 50). This struggle to gain self-awareness is even more evident in Tawfīq, the hero of al-Takarlī's novel *al-Masarrāt*.

To go back to *al-Raj^{c}*: why then is Munīra's loss of virginity before marriage so unsettling to Midḥat? It is an epiphany through which the hero gains consciousness of his true self. It is the cause initiating Midḥat's inner great dialogue. The battle dominating the last chapters of the novel is simply that taking place within Midḥat's complex mind, with its conflicting tendencies. As a consequence of this, the battle is always latent in him: before Munīra fully provokes it, it emerges in Midḥat's subconscious and is depicted in his dreams[73]: in his first chapter (the fifth) Midḥat cries out in his sleep because of an obscure dream (Takarlī 1980: 141/*108*). Al-Takarlī makes use of the dream again to shed light on the hero's subconscious where his strong ties with the backward side of his identity lie. In his confinement in the Kurdish quarter, he has a more telling dream in which he kills an unchallenging and tender Munīra who caresses his arm while he stabs her.[74] This vision terrifies Midḥat and the reflection caused by it leads him to discover that he is influenced by the society he so much rejects and despises.[75] What follows is the forefathers' monologue where Midḥat realizes that one of his inner voices is that of his forefathers, his ancestors who demand that he recovers his lost honour in the traditional way, by killing Munīra. The irrational side of Midḥat is made to emerge by Munīra's presence, her being what she is, rather than by what she says to him (which would be the Dostoevskyian way): indeed it is the absence of her voice which is efficiently dramatized in the pages of Midḥat's last monologue – at the outset of his monologue, Midḥat, unlike us, does not know the truth about Munīra and the crucial dialogue between them is always prevented: on the wedding night Munīra is silent; in the days preceding the wedding she has tried to say something to him and now he regrets not having listened to her; Munīra's letter to Midḥat (whose contents we do not know but can imagine) gets lost because of Ḥusayn's carelessness. However, through his inner struggle, Midḥat comes close to the truth: somehow he perceives that Munīra did not choose her status – she is the victim (Takarlī 1980: 474/*366*).[76] At the end, we could say that at last Munīra's voice emerges in Midḥat's mind and he reaches the truth (Takarlī 1980: 481/*371*). By truth, we do not mean the actual truth of Munīra's being raped by her nephew but the truth of Munīra's not choosing her present condition and a more profound truth about Midḥat's culture, society and his relationship to them.

The main difference between Dostoevsky's so-called novel of ideas and *al-Raj*ᶜ is that in this latter the ideological confrontation is not as clearly formulated (spelled out) as in the former. The political argument between Rāma and Mīkhāʾīl which we have analysed earlier (here, al-Kharrāṭ's *al-Zaman* conforms more closely to Bakhtin's interpretation of Dostoevsky than *al-Raj*ᶜ) provides us with an excellent example to shed light on this difference. In *al-Raj*ᶜ we do not have such long dialectic battles where two arguments are fully exposed: we rather have half dialogues, unexpressed truths, and its focus is more on the inner struggle of the characters.[77] Of course, this is not to say that in Dostoevsky and al-Kharrāṭ such struggles are not central: on the contrary they are, but *al-Raj*ᶜ's author is more discreet. More importantly than that, Midḥat's great dialogue is not often expressed out loud to another character for one fundamental reason, which becomes evident in the finale with its strangely arranged sequence of chapters: *al-Raj*ᶜ is a novel which also depicts a crisis in human relationships and communication. In a way, the same crisis is also present in *Bāb*, as it is depicted through the silences and misunderstandings between Yūnis and Nahīla and, especially, through the relationship between Khalīl and Yūnis and their unbalanced dialogue. Even if we refer to Barrāda's *Lu*ᶜ*bat*, the independence of its characters does not necessarily lead to a great dialogue as admired by Bakhtin in Dostoevsky: there are dialogues (such as the actual argument between the brothers al-Hādī and al-Ṭāyiᶜ; or the implicit contrast between different ways of living and identities), but even if al-Hādī's voice is dominant one feels that the novel is more about offering a pluralistic view of modern Morocco and its malaises than a clearly formulated ideological confrontation. Al-Hādī's voice, like that of most of the heroes of texts we are analysing, is not as coherently representative of an idea, a world vision (as those we might find in Dostoevsky's fiction): one of al-Hādī's most significant points concerns the power which the unconscious exercises over his being, his self. Al-Nowaihi writes about *Lu*ᶜ*bat* as a text which poses many questions without providing clear answers, and about al-Hādī's self as a process 'in a constant state of transformation and discovery', an 'inner dialogue of multiple forces' (Nowaihi 2000: 375). If we can imagine that al-Hādī mirrors Barrāda's ideas, like *Mīrāmār*'s ^{c}Āmir mirrors Mahfouz's, and if it is true that, like in Mahfouz's novel, even in *Lu^{c}bat* al-Hādī is given the last chapter, it is nonetheless difficult to affirm that al-Hādī's is a voice which has a judgmental flavour, which concludes.

We will now address the narrative methods (first and third person narrations) employed in *al-Raj^{c}* to shape its multivoicedness and also the upsetting of the chronological sequence in the final chapters, so central to its overall structure.

In *al-Raj^{c}*, the characters' independent ideas are expressed through the use of a third-person narration which focuses narrowly on one character at a time (one character only for each chapter). This is the same sort of third person narration we find in Dostoevsky's *Crime and Punishment*, for example. The difference is that in the Russian novel the narration is almost constantly focused on one character, Raskolnikov, while in *al-Raj^{c}* thirteen chapters are narrated from the point of view of eight characters. Bakhtin usefully describes this narration as follows:

> Narration in Dostoevsky is always narration without perspective [...] we could say that Dostoevsky had no 'distance perspective' on the hero and the event. The narrator finds himself in immediate proximity to the hero and to the ongoing event, and it is from this maximally close, aperspectival point of view that he structures their representation.
>
> (Bakhtin 1963: 225)

Within modern Arabic literature, an example of this type of narration combined with a similar structure (division into chapters/voices or perspectives) was used as early as 1963 by Kanafānī in his *Rijāl*. Meyer's comments on the significance of the novel are worth quoting.

> Although written in the third person, the narrative focus that Kanafani puts on each character in turn comes very close to a division of the text into different narrative voices [the same applies to *al-Raj^{c}*]. In this respect, Kanafani anticipates the polyphonic narrative technique that was to become a central feature of early experimentalism with the form of the Arabic novel.
>
> (Meyer 2001: 29)

The narrow focus on the character means that usually it takes us the first sentence of the chapter to understand through whose perspective it is going to be narrated (Midḥat's chapter ten is a notable exception – see earlier). In other words, if we apply Genette's definition of 'narrative mood' (i.e. the regulation of narrative information made up by 'perspective' and 'distance', Genette 1972: 162) to *al-Raj^{c}*'s main narrative technique, we could affirm that its perspective belongs to one character at a time and changes with each chapter, and that its distance never changes (not even with the shift from the third person to the first person): it is always extremely narrow.

The indirect free style representing the character's thoughts is typical of the main narrative technique of the novel. *Al-Raj*[c] is fundamentally based on inner struggles and dilemmas, the most important of which is Midḥat's in the finale. But it is also about the personal perspective of each character on another, which can prove to be wrong as is the case not only with the brothers' early over-idealization of their cousin but also with, say, Umm Midḥat's motherly, sympathetic evaluation of her eldest son's feelings. At the very beginning of the novel, she believes that her son truly loves his family, but he does it in his own way, silently. When Midḥat's section comes, we have a very different picture of his true feelings towards his family expressing his egotism and cynicism with sarcasm and harshness (cf. Takarlī 1980: 25/*17* with 141/*107*, 147/*113* and especially 145/*111* where he associates his family with the harshly dismissive phrase 'A world of blind, lachrymose sentiments'). All this is seen from the vantage point of the readers who alone, even if relatively late in the novel, will know what all characters think of each other and themselves, who is most mistaken, and who is most right. But this vantage point will not be instrumental in giving us a clear picture of what Genette defines 'the narrating instance' (see earlier and cf. Genette 1972: 212–15). For example, what do we conclude after we know that Midḥat's mother is misleading herself about her son's affection? Are we to disapprove of Midḥat's cruel disregard of his mother, or is she to blame for her naivety and unquestioning attitudes? Similarly, when focusing on Munīra, we the readers are left to decide whether her harshness in dealing with her mother and especially with Karīm at the end of the novel is justified by the difficult circumstances in which she finds herself, and whether this harshness is more strength of character or desperation or cruelty. Moreover, these can be considered only details in the overall characterization of the characters, but what about the very core of the novel: the crucial mutual ignorance of Munīra and Midḥat of each other's truth? Of course, we, unlike Munīra, know that Midḥat has at last resolved to go back to her; and of course we, unlike Midḥat, also know about Munīra's being mercilessly raped. What do we do with our 'surplus of knowledge' (as Bakhtin calls it)? Is it taking us to a clear-cut conclusion, a final judgement? On the contrary, the fact that we know crucial events of which the characters themselves are unaware, puts us in a grey position of doubt while the characters, by virtue of their ignorance, are in a situation of certainty (however painful and erroneous this might be): Munīra is certain that Midḥat betrayed her hopes and ended up being as bad and 'warped' as anybody else, as she shouts in Karīm's face. By virtue of what we have just noticed about the novel's structure, we can say that the author's plan to involve the reader in the events of his novel has been successful.[78]

Now that we have a clear picture of how al-Takarlī's third person narration works, we will deal with the reasons behind the writer's opting for this particular technique as his chosen means of narration. A third person omniscient narrator can register faithfully everything surrounding the character, but cannot influence the course of events (as might be the case with the first person narrator). He is a witness, as puzzled as each character (and reader) is by what happens in the novel.[79] In fact, the idea at the basis of the polyphonic novel is that a clash of ideas and perspectives is chronicled by the author and not solved. Bakhtin summarizes the function of this narration when he writes: 'The author does not insert into this material [the voiceless and accentless facts presented to the hero] any judgement or evaluation of his own. This is why the narrator has no surplus field of vision, no perspective' (Bakhtin 1963: 251). We have to appreciate that when al-Takarlī applies this third person, internally focalized narration (to use Genette's terminology), he does it with great rigour. When in Dostoevsky's *Crime and Punishment* the narrow focus on Raskolnikov is relaxed in order to follow the story of Svidrigailov (who in a way is the hero's double), we can feel this shift as a minor flaw in the author's plan.[80] In al-Takarlī's *al-Raj*^{c}, on the other hand, the shifts are part of the overall structure which, by virtue of its multiple narrations, aesthetically allows these shifts to happen without the readers (or more likely, the critics) raising their eyebrows.[81]

Another notable difference between Dostoevsky's techniques and those adopted by al-Takarlī is that in four of *al-Raj*^{c}'s thirteen chapters the narration shifts to the first person: the second, the seventh and the thirteenth narrated by Karīm; the ninth by Munīra (within which another very significant narration shift occurs).

As we have lamented in the introduction to the present work, non-Arab critics of contemporary Arabic fiction who decide to focus on its important themes deal only in passing with its formal aspects, usually limiting themselves to a descriptive commentary. In discussing the narrative shifts present in *al-Raj*^{c} we would like to show how a rigorous formal analysis is instrumental in expanding greatly a discussion of the themes treated. We are persuaded that this is the best way in which to put non-Western writers on an equal footing with their Western colleagues as not only *interesting* or *exotic* authors, but also skilful artists in their own right. Catherine Cobham's article on the theme of survival and renewal in *al-Raj*^{c} is an excellent example of a piece of literary criticism which, despite its focus on the subject matter of the text, is significantly enhanced by its treatment of technical aspects (Cobham 2002). Paying attention to the formal features of the novel, Cobham questions some of the most common assumptions made by other critics of *al-Raj*^{c}: notably its symbolic nature (i.e. the tendency to see Munīra as an idealized symbol (usually of Iraq) and ^{c}Adnān as representing, by virtue of his being 'the baddy', whichever political party the critic is hostile to).[82] When the narration at a very crucial moment in the novel, where we finally get to know about Munīra's rape, shifts from a first to a third person narrative (still from Munīra's perspective), Cobham unlike others (Walther 1995) sets out to explain why this happens or at least what could have justified this shift, and what could be its intended effect. This shift, she explains, 'is perhaps a way of dramatizing the taboo nature of the subject in Munīra's mind, the fact that she has never told anyone about it and cannot even find a way to tell her husband-to-be' (Cobham 2002: 185). Cobham goes on with her reading of the crucial passage, highlighting how Munīra seems to reflect not only on the destructive violence she has suffered from ᶜAdnān, but also on her utter inability to predict it:

> Within the logic of the narrative structure – that is, Munīra recounting the episode to herself in the third person some months after it happened – this must be taken as her crticizing her own inattentiveness and naivety in retrospect. [. . .] At the very least, the author must be suggesting here a lack of responsibility or maturity on the part of Iraq/Munīra, and unfocused, crude opportunism rather than evil intent on the part of ᶜAdnān/the Baath party.
>
> (Cobham 2002: 186)

Such an analysis may help us to avoid a facile symbolic reading of the novel and prevent us from jumping to simplistic conclusions. In other words, we can see how the author problematizes the central violent episode (the rape), and the way its victim (Munīra) recalls it. Of course, that does not mean that he justifies it.[83]

However, if we consider Munīra's chapter as a whole and analyse closely the form and significance of the third person passage within it, we believe that yet another reading of its function is possible. The first part of the chapter depicts a crucial moment which has become familiar to the reader through the other characters' depictions of it. Munīra is informed that somebody has come from Baᶜqūba with the official transfer papers she was waiting for. Munīra assumes this to be the school janitor, but, as we already know by now, she is shocked to find her nephew ᶜAdnān at the door. The episode has already been depicted in more detail from the child Sanāᵓ's perspective (Chapter 6, Takarlī 1980: 188–94/*146–9*). We already know that ᶜAdnān is complaining about Munīra's escape from Baᶜqūba and that Munīra is deeply affected by seeing him. We will learn from the third person passage, an extended flashback from the time when Munīra was living in the provincial town and established a special relationship with her nephew, the reason for her shock. Besides agreeing with Cobham's reading, we believe that this shift also emphasizes the dramatic presence of the past in Munīra's present, her effort to get rid of it, to forget it, as she says at the end of her chapter: 'I therefore excised several hours of my past and put them in parentheses, then began to think of the life ahead of me' (Takarlī 1980: 287/*224*). In fact the passage is very much put in parentheses by virtue of its formal divergence from the rest of Munīra's chapter, and, we could say, the rest of her life.[84] This is confirmed by the fact that the narration would flow perfectly even if we cut out the alien passage (as Munīra would like to be able to do, but fails). In the English translation of the novel, before the narration shift Munīra says: 'The slow pounding of my heart diminished as I squeezed Sana's hand and felt my reserves collapsing bit by bit' (Takarlī 1980: *197*); after the flashback she continues exactly from where she had interrupted: 'I sank down and down until I reached the bottom, then came the fluttering of the heart which separates life from death' (Takarlī 1980: *203*).

This perfect continuity between the part preceding the flashback and the one following is even more evident in the Arabic original:

وأنا أضغط على يد سناء وأتهاوى وأتهاوى ... [252] ... وأتهاوى

وأتهاوى أيضاً حتى أصل إلى القاع [259]

It is obvious that the memory of Munīra's rape (caused by ^{c}Adnān's unexpected visit) breaks through her present life as abruptly as the interruption occurs within the sentence just quoted. The sentence following the interruption depicts Munīra's feeling of recovering from death, and it is significant that this could be a reaction both to ^{c}Adnān's visit in the present and the rape episode of the past. In Munīra's mind, ^{c}Adnān is inevitably associated with the act of violence he had forced on her in Ba^{c}qūba. If it were not for the first person, the first part of Munīra's monologue after the interruption, until she finally perceives Sanā$^{\supset}$'s hand touching her, could have been related to her attempt to stay alive after the rape, and in a way this is what we are meant to feel[85]: her past/^{c}Adnān is still haunting her and, as we will learn in the rest of the novel, her courageous attempt to 'excise it and put it in parentheses' is destined to fail.

As we have noticed earlier, within *al-Raj*^{c} the major shifts in the narration mode (this time from a third to a first person) occur with the chapters narrated from Munīra and Karīm's perspectives. Obviously, these shifts make us reflect on the difference between a third person and a first person narration, a topic which has been much debated within modern criticism. Critics such as Norman Friedman and A. A. Mendilow have written about narrative techniques and their different effects. Both critics note that, contrary to what might be assumed, a third person narration is more successful in conveying a feeling of presentness and immediacy than a first person narration. This is due to the fact that an autobiographical first person narration is perforce retrospective: 'there is an avowed temporal distance between the fictional time – that of the events as they happened – and the narrator's actual time – his time of recording those events' (Mendilow quoted in Genette 1972: n. 10, p. 168).[86] In brief, these critics argue that with a third person narration the illusion that the action is taking place is stronger than in a first person one where the story is written, as it were, 'backward from the present'. In Munīra's chapter, we could appreciate the dramatization of the presence of the past (the third person narration of the flashback) in the heroine's present (the first person of the rest of the chapter). We could see how much would have been lost in immediacy and in the feeling of *becoming*, *happening now*, had al-Takarlī chosen to narrate the crucial episode of Munīra's rape in the first person, 'from the present backward'.[87] Genette refutes this theory, claiming that in Proust's masterpiece, probably by virtue of its famous 'rapture of reminiscence', there is '[e]xtreme mediation [the first person narration], and at the same time utmost immediacy' (Genette 1972: 168–9). But *al-Raj*^{c}, unlike *La recherche*, is not built on the 'rapture of reminiscence' and Friedman and Mendilow's observations on the different effects of the two narration modes are appropriate if we relate them to *al-Raj*^{c}. It is beyond dispute that the sections of the novel which are dominated by a first person narration depict characters (Munīra and Karīm) who are looking back at what has already happened or is happening without any chance of changing it.[88] The last chapters, narrated from Midḥat's perspective, dominated by a third person narration, depict a human mind striving to understand what has happened, but they also express a clear sense that the working out of the past is relevant to what happens next and could be followed by action. Unlike his brother and his cousin and wife, Midḥat, by virtue of his social and intellectual position, could bring about some sort of change. In other words, Midḥat's chapters convey a sense of presentness, of decision making, a possibility of change: with Midḥat we have the illusion that the action is taking place (life is happening), with Munīra and Karīm the action is perceived as having taken place (life is frozen). These diverse effects are amplified by the different narrative modes.[89]

The fact that Midḥat fails to make a change is part of the bleak drama which the novel manages so effectively to convey, thanks to the idiosyncratic arrangement of its last chapters – the twelfth and thirteenth. The twelfth chapter (narrated from Midḥat's perspective, and the only one with a title: 'Brief Shining and Survival') is divided into two sections by the thirteenth chapter (told from Karīm's point of view). Midḥat's long inner struggle (three chapters – 10 and 12, parts 1 and 2 – are mainly focused on his mental processes) is abruptly interrupted by Karīm's last section which in its characteristically self-centred style informs us of Midḥat's tragic death only in passing. The final page of the novel provides the reader with a lasting image of the hero's body lying on the asphalt, lifeless. This scene of death and silence is the most appropriate end to the novel: it dramatizes in a powerful image the fact that Midḥat's voice is silent, inasmuch as it never reaches its addressee, Munīra. *Al-Raj*^{c} dramatizes its characters' (Munīra's and Midḥat's) missed opportunities to communicate with one another. It is left to the reader to decide to what extent they are responsible for their failure, or if the circumstances in which they live are entirely to blame. The stress on Midḥat's painstaking efforts to reach the truth paradoxically dramatizes their practical uselessness. Paraphrasing the title of the chapter we could say that Midḥat's possible *survival* has turned into his moral *brief shining* before dying. In fact, we follow the hero's last efforts knowing that they cannot have a practical outcome and our satisfaction at his discovering the truth is inevitably diminished by the knowledge of his death.[90]

Why is Midḥat precluded from going back to Munīra and changing their situation? Why does al-Takarlī prevent him from giving practical application to the much suffered for, noble triumph over his forefathers' backward traditions? Many answers are possible and, again, we could assume that what seems to be a closed ending to the novel (the death of the hero) is on the contrary a very open ending for the reader who wants to make sense of the novel as a whole.[91]

In conclusion, borrowing again from Bakhtin, the following passage is a good example of the imposition of a monological vision on a work which is *not* monological. The German critic Wiebke Walther (who has so far been the most committed amongst non-Arab critics in studying al-Takarlī's works) concludes her mainly descriptive analysis of *al-Raj*^{c} as follows:

> The novel concludes that outdated social standards in connection with intolerable political conditions [. . .] can destroy the individual. As long as a society is unable to free itself from its obsolete social traditions, it will be unable to organize a life of political freedom.
>
> (Walther 1997: 22; 1995: 139)

In other words, Walther's ideological reading of *al-Raj*^{c} oversimplifies the novel's depth and nullifies its artistic treatment of complex issues. Of course, we can see that al-Takarlī expresses the need for Iraqi society to challenge and question its backward tendencies even if, in the short term, no apparent positive result will emerge (Cobham and Walther agree on this). But the key point here is that, contradicting Walther's words, the novel does *not* 'conclude', and in this inconclusiveness lies one of its strengths. What Joseph Conrad wrote about Henry James seems to be more appropriate to *al-Raj*^{c} and its author than Walther's observation:

> You remain with a sense of the life still going on; and even the subtle presence of the dead is felt in that silence that comes upon the artist-creation when the last word has been read. It is eminently satisfying, but it is not final.
>
> (Conrad 1924: 19)

And maybe it is eminently satisfying *because* it is not final.

In this chapter, we have tried to show how a rigorous formal analysis of fictional techniques can expand our reading of novels and their themes. It is clear that pure polyphony as conceived by Bakhtin might well be an unattainable utopia for novelists. Moreover, it is quite obvious that a novelist (if he or she is a skilful writer) who decides not to create a truly polyphonic novel is still able to give us a rich and significant work of art. The radical concept of polyphony was promoted by Bakhtin at least partly for ideological reasons: he was writing about Dostoevsky's fiction, but also about the lack of democracy in the Soviet Union (there is a natural parallel to be drawn between political democracy and literary polyphony).[92] Naturally, if we dismiss the crudest examples, all novels with the slightest artistic ambition are based on some polyphonic element, either through an inner dialogue within a character's many selves or through one or more dialogues between different characters. It is still to be demonstrated that Dostoevsky's method was more polyphonic than others'. Moreover, we referred earlier to the Russian critic's statement that the author of a polyphonic novel should not be passive, but engage his characters' ideas on an equal level, dialogically. If he fails to do that, Bakhtin goes on, he merely structures somebody else's points of view and truths, and gives up his own.[93] As our discussion has implicitly pointed out, Bakhtin's most practical observations (not the lofty philosophical ones) seem to be most poignant when applied to the so-called novels of ideas but, as seen in the introduction, fiction might well be about something other than ideological debates. We could well argue that, even if an author does not make explicit his or her own ideas, in the very way he or she decides to depict a certain debate there is a more subtle formulation of truths. But again, even if we concede that, all things considered, a writer always sets out to write in order to voice his or her own truths, could not these truths have to do with the depiction of a phenomenon or a situation (such as a highly fragmented one or an incoherent self), or 'an effort to know'?

All these limitations on Bakhtin's method notwithstanding, a concept as clearly formulated as that of polyphony can provide us with an effective critical tool through which we can both analyse a novel's structure, and deal with the very general problems of narrative voice and the author's 'dominant value' and presence in the text.

In dealing with such concepts, we have inevitably touched upon some of the most important themes of the innovative novels analysed here. Similarly, in the following chapter, we will again start by defining a general, technical aspect of these texts (intertextuality). The resulting analysis will enable us to deal with different subject matters and show how these come to life within a certain narrative structure.

4
INTERTEXTUALITY

At the beginning of al-Kharrāṭ's first novel, Mīkhāʾīl says in one of his imaginary dialogues with Rāma: 'What can one say about death, truth, or love? Everything has been said' (Kharrāṭ 1979: 8/5).[1] Apart from explaining soon afterwards his character's belief that mere talking about something is a betrayal, al-Kharrāṭ makes us think about one of the main issues raised by Western modernist writers and early postmodernist theorists alike: the consciousness that everything has already been said, everything has already been written (cf. Barth 1967: 69 ff.). The implications of this assumption are many: some even talk about the death of the author[2] and the death of the novel. Here, we are mainly concerned with the idea that a novelist is bound to rework and interact (more or less consciously) with the texts preceding his or hers: this process can be summarized in the term intertextuality. According to Bertrand Westphal, the concept of intertextuality seems to have been already present in an embryonic form as early as the 1930s in Bakhtin's work, but it is thanks to the French critic Julia Kristeva that the concept has become more widely known (Westphal 2001: 325). The term is open to wide interpretation and different Western scholars attach different meanings to it. For example, for Linda Hutcheon intertextuality in postmodernist terms is parody, pastiche, ironic quotation (Hutcheon 1989: 93–117); for Umberto Eco it is the assumption that every text (hence, every novel) is interconnected with other texts and this phenomenon reveals the cultural affiliation of the text;[3] Genette prefers transtextuality to refer to all forms of textual relations (while intertextuality is for him limited to an overt presence of one text in another in the form of quotation, plagiarism, allusion; Genette 1982: 1–7); Italo Calvino underlines how a writer needs other texts to write about his own experiences.[4] Calvino is a significant example since he gives a clear novelistic expression to this critical assumption in his novel *If On a Winter's Night a Traveller* (1979). In this novel the fictitious character of a writer, Silas Flannery, tries to overcome his writer's block by writing down the beginning of *Crime and Punishment*.

Even in the works of the authors discussed in this study, it is possible to track down the interaction (implicit or explicit, conscious or unconscious) between their novels and other texts of various natures. The search for these novels' 'sources' and references is not meant to be a mere academic exercise (to find out in which Dostoevskys our Flannerys seek inspiration). On the contrary, an intertextual analysis of the works of al-Kharrāṭ, Khūrī, al-Takarlī and Barrāda will help us to understand how and why these writers create literary texts. Before we begin to tackle the novels of these authors, we want to stress that our approach is based on a deliberately loose concept of intertextuality, encompassing both the evolving literary tradition to which the author belongs (he can rework religious or philosophical concepts and literary tropes to shape his original texts), and his *verbatim* quotation of other texts (as we will see later, there is a qualitative distinction between quotations which reinforce and expand the text's main themes and those which only contribute to forming the cultural profile of characters). It is reasonable to assume that the dividing line between the naturally evolving tradition and the more overt intertextual borrowing is the degree of awareness involved in using somebody else's texts. Obviously, every writer is influenced by authors and texts; here we will deal especially with writers who acknowledge such influences in their texts.

Let us begin our intertextual analysis with some observations on the formal aspect of al-Kharrāṭ's fiction. In the first chapter of this study, we quoted (and re-translated) an extensive passage from *Rāma* in which different techniques and styles alternate. Here, we will only focus on one of the paragraphs quoted earlier:

> I am still calling you Rāma . . . *Anima* . . . *Mandala* . . . my woman . . . my harbour . . . my cave . . . *Kemi* . . . my dream, merciful Ment, Mut wife of Amun, Ma'at my mirror . . . my blessing . . . Mary full of grace . . . buried Demeter, her wet mouth raining blessing and mercy . . . her womb greedy for sperm, destined to the cycle of death and blazing pleasures . . . mother of the hawk . . . mother of patience . . . mother of the golden jasmine trembling on the waters . . . Rāma.
>
> (Kharrāṭ 1979: 105)

This passage is only one of the relatively numerous sections of the *Rāma* Trilogy where the author allows himself a virtuoso exercise: almost every word appearing in the passage contains the same letter (in this case the *mīm*). Unfortunately, the translated passage can hardly reproduce the assonance of the original, which is typical of poetic alliteration[5]:

مـــــا زلت أناديك رامة.. أنيما.. ماندالا.. امرأتي.. مينائي.. مغارتي.. كيمي.. منامي يامنت الرؤوم يا مؤوت زوجة آمون.. يا معت مرآتي.. كرامتي.. مريم المملؤة بالنعمة.. ديميتير المدفونة يمطر فمها المبلول بالمنّ والرحمة.. رحمها المنهوم إلى المنـــيّ والمحكوم عليه بمدار الموت مباهج الاحتدام.. يا أم الصقر.. أم الصبر.. أم الياسمينة الذهبية المهتزة على المياه.. رامة.

These insertions where the author consistently uses alliteration, quite unusual in prose writing (albeit present in Western modernist writers such as Virginia Woolf and Joyce), amplify the effect of his habitual lyrical flights. These are evident, for example, when the author uses vivid metaphors and powerful images in order to describe situations (e.g. the numerous erotic ones, cf. Kharrāṭ 1979: 76–7) and sensations (such as feelings of frustration and alienation, mirrored also in the physical environment, cf. Kharrāṭ 1979: 219–20). It is not incidental that the writer himself defines his first novel as a 'poem–novel' (Kharrāṭ 1994b: 21). Al-Kharrāṭ seems to allude to this when, in *al-Zaman*, Mīkhāʾīl confesses to Rāma that during his university years he used to write *shiᶜr manthūr* 'poetry in prose', or 'lyrical prose' (Kharrāṭ 1985: 168). But the alliteration passages, we are warned by the author, are not only exercises displaying his skills *per se*, or a suitable space for literary jesting, reminiscent of similar exercises by ancient Arab and Persian poets (M. M. Badawi claims that the writer's verbal skill 'is in fact a modernist development of the medieval verbal games of al-Ḥarīrī's *maqamas*' Badawi 1993: 175). Not only does al-Kharrāṭ claim that in these sections the recurrent sound is meant to evoke a sensation, an emotion (for instance the sound of the Arabic letter *ḥāʾ*, Kharrāṭ 1979: 100, corresponds to 'a moment of heat, incandescence'), he also insists that writing in such an extreme style came to him quite spontaneously (Hafez 1994: 242–3).[6]

The mixture of different literary techniques and languages is further developed in *al-Zaman* and *Yaqīn*, where the proliferation of the alliterative passages and the intertextual nature of the novel are evident. While there are only two alliterative passages in *Rāma*, there are seven in *al-Zaman* and six in *Yaqīn*.[7] This stylistic device could be considered both fascinating (the author's attempt to reproduce a feeling and a sensation through the repetition of a sound) and innovative (in modern Arabic literature alliteration is mainly confined to poetry). Sometimes, however, when these experiments are overdone, they make the text less readable and fluid. The alliterative passages can be considered as exercises in which form is overwhelmingly dominant over content and meaning.[8] The aforementioned *mīm* section taken from *Rāma*, which clearly refers to Rāma's femininity (she is associated with the Virgin Mary and goddesses like Demeter and Mut), is paralleled by a similar section in *Turābu-hā zaᶜfarān* (1986) where the letter *mīm* is a symbol of masculinity, while the *nūn* section praises femininity (as Frances Liardet, the English translator of the novel, points out, Liardet 1989: ix–x). This may confirm that these passages are meant to evoke abstract feelings or vague sensations more than conveying precise, well defined meanings.

Reviewing the novel *al-ᶜĀshiq wa-'l-maᶜshūq* 'The Lover and the Beloved' (1994) by the Egyptian writer Khayrī ᶜAbd al-Jawwād, al-Kharrāṭ explains the meaning of the Arabic letter *mīm* in authors such as the mystic poet Ibn ᶜArabī, the grammarians al-Khalīl ibn Aḥmad (d. 791) and Aḥmad ibn Muḥammad al-Rāzī (d. ca. 1232) (Kharrāṭ 1999: 213–32).[9] Moreover, we could easily relate what Annemarie Schimmel writes about the style of mystical writing to these virtuoso passages present in the *Rāma* Trilogy: 'Indeed, one aspect of mystical language in Sufism that should never be overlooked is the tendency [. . .] to play with words' (Schimmel 1975: 13).[10] The fact that al-Kharrāṭ is obviously familiar with the *ṣūfī* writers of the past and the symbolism they attached to letters might suggest that he has been inspired by them to adopt a similar style. However, we have to stress that, if the letters used by al-Kharrāṭ in his alliteration are indeed symbols, this symbolism is not the same as the symbolism found in the *ṣūfī* tradition.

Following the formal development of the *Rāma* Trilogy, we notice that these alliterative passages become longer and more complex: in *Yaqīn*, we have the *bā*ᵓ passage extending over four paragraphs (almost a whole page, Kharrāṭ 1996a: 93–4) and passages including French words in Latin characters (one in the *bā*ᵓ passage – Kharrāṭ 1996a: 93 – and four in the *fā*ᵓ section – *ibid.* 226). It is clear that such wordplay, at least in this latest, extreme form, becomes little more than a display of stylistic virtuosity.[11]

We have referred earlier to a similar feature in the fiction of Virginia Woolf and Joyce. There is, however, a striking difference between the use of alliteration in, for example, Joyce's *Ulysses* and al-Kharrāṭ's Trilogy. In *Ulysses*, Joyce's alliterations can be imitative of ancient styles (as in the imitation of Anglo-Saxon English in the chapter *The Oxen of the Sun*, Joyce 1922: 502–3), or they can be an onomatopoeic use of language with no particular source of inspiration. In both cases, the effect is ironic (at the end of the *Ithaca* chapter, for example, by manipulating the phrase 'Sinbad the sailor' Joyce depicts a human mind overcome by sleep; Joyce 1922: 871). As we have seen earlier, al-Kharrāṭ's use of alliteration is not ironic (not, at least, by intention – in his interview with Hafez he seems to dismiss the element of play in alliterations; Hafez 1982: 242–3). In the first chapter of the present work, we observed that these passages may also be inspired by Arabic indigenous forms: alliteration, assonance and rhyme characterize the *saj*ᶜ of both the *maqāmāt* and the Koran. Besides the alliteration observed earlier, we also have in al-Kharrāṭ's fiction passages which are reminiscent of the formally sophisticated *saj*ᶜ (see, for example, Kharrāṭ 1996a: 46, 67).

Whether al-Kharrāṭ's alliteration is inspired by Joyce or by Arabic literary forms is difficult to say (even if the author seems to privilege the indigenous affiliation, cf. Hafez 1982: 242–3, 245). In some passages of the *Rāma* Trilogy where dialogue is predominant, we believe that the author goes back (probably not without some irony) to using speech more as it is used by certain classical Arabic prose writers. Beside some lively dialogues between Mīkhāᵓīl and Rāma (in contrast with those passages where the author employs a highly lyrical and sophisticated language), we often find what the narrator himself defines as Mīkhāᵓīl's 'inner and silent talk to her' (Kharrāṭ 1979: 75). If, on the one hand, these imaginary dialogues and non-articulated sentences convey Mīkhāᵓīl's tragic inability to express himself *vis-à-vis* his beloved (the protagonist's silence is the symbol of his weakness and inability to achieve perfect communication with Rāma), they could also be interpreted as a parody of the classical style mentioned earlier. In the Trilogy as a whole we often find speech systematically introduced by the verb *qāla* as in classical Arabic prose, where the reader comes to know the characters' feelings and psychological state mainly by means of direct speech.[12] In other words, they tend to express what they think orally.[13] Similarly, al-Kharrāṭ, besides using the usual modern techniques of interior monologue (couched in both free direct and indirect discourse), often feels the urge to stress that Mīkhāʾīl is actually articulating his thoughts, usually to himself (*qāla li-nafsi-hi*, or simply *qāla*). In fact, the author indulges in the repetition of the verb *qāla*[14] and often writes that Mīkhāʾīl did not (or will not) say such and such to Rāma. Obviously, in both cases al-Kharrāṭ is dealing with his character's thoughts.[15] Whether this is a radical adoption of a classical style or a parody of it is debatable.[16] From a formal point of view, this sometimes obtrusive way of inserting the verb 'to say' provides the narrative with a certain rhythm (similar to that obtained in poetry by the repetition of the same word).[17] If we focus on the content of these passages, as we have seen in Chapter 2, regarding denials and questionings of narrated episodes, these imaginary sentences are also as important as those actually uttered by the protagonist. All this makes us focus on the fact that al-Kharrāṭ is indeed committed to expressing both what his characters do not do and what they do not say. This is because in what we might define as the '*lam yaqul la-hā* sessions', Mīkhāʾīl expresses his most sincere and important ideas and feelings which he has clearly been unable to tell his beloved.[18] In these sections of the narrative a strong sense of frustration and regret is conveyed.

This peculiar use of the verb *qāla*, along with the highly sophisticated language in which the alliterative passages are couched, and the use of rare and archaic words, has some connections with Arab authors of the past. Moreover, if we consider the themes treated in his novels, it is clear that al-Kharrāṭ uses precise references which are related to his own culture (which he defines as Coptic–Egyptian–Arab, cf. al-Kharrāṭ quoted in both Hafez 1982: 236 and Halim 1994: 18). Of course, these cultural references are likely to appear obscure to a readership (e.g. the Western) which is not entirely familiar with the Arab–Islamic literary heritage. In addition, some of these references are so sophisticated and complex that an Arab audience may also have difficulty in appreciating al-Kharrāṭ's techniques. The fact that the dense network of cultural references and textual allusions which al-Kharrāṭ uses can pass unnoticed (or is inaccessible to a high proportion of the readership), does not mean that his work cannot be appreciated and enjoyed.[19] A more important factor which perhaps prevents many readers from easily understanding and appreciating his work is the continuous shift of time and place, and of linguistic registers.

To return to our intertextual approach to al-Kharrāṭ's Trilogy, its connection with past texts is twofold: on one hand there is a conscious revival of ancient forms (both popular, such as the 'chain stories' structure of *The Arabian Nights* mentioned in Chapter 2, and literary, such as the alliteration sections with their lyrical classical tone); on the other, the themes treated in the Kharrāṭian text are expanded by references to the *ṣūfī* and other aspects of their cultural background. Before we discuss this latter aspect it is useful to compare and contrast al-Kharrāṭ's attempt to recover some narrative techniques from the past with that of other Arab writers. As far as the formal aspect of his works is concerned, al-Kharrāṭ's ambitious plan to revive some past literary forms seems to link him to that 'generation [of Arab writers] which sought to refashion the novel on the basis of distinctly Arab cultural, linguistic or historical characteristics' (Meyer 2001: 3, 117). In his work on the experimental Arabic novel, Meyer points to three successive stages, roughly corresponding to three generations of writers, in the development of the innovative novel. According to him, in the 1950s and especially in the 1960s, writers like the Egyptians Mahfouz and Ṣun[c]allāh Ibrāhīm, and the Palestinians Kanafānī and Jabrā are more 'artistically self-conscious' in their new way of writing. In the following decades the Palestinian Imīl Ḥabībī (1922–1996), the Syrian Salīm Barakāt (b. 1951) and [c]Abd al-Raḥmān Munīf, amongst others, represent an attempt to renew the Arabic novel through the revival or discovery of typical Arabic forms. Despite the over schematic nature of Meyer's characterization, we will tentatively include al-Kharrāṭ in this, Meyer's 'second generation'. The indigenous revival promoted by this generation, still according to Meyer's reading, is contrasted in the late 1980s and in the 1990s by novelists such as the Lebanese Khūrī and Rashīd al-Ḍa[c]īf (b. 1945) who are not interested in 'the "Arabizing" tendencies of their immediate predecessors' (Meyer 2001: 3). Leaving aside this later generation for the moment and focusing on the 'Arabizing' authors, it is useful to compare al-Kharrāṭ's Trilogy to two highly significant examples of the revival of narratives of the past analysed by Meyer: Munīf's *al-Nihāyāt* (1977; *Endings*, 1988) and al-Ghīṭānī's *al-Zaynī Barakāt* (1971; *Zayni Barakat*, 1988).

Munīf structures his work in an original way: the first part of his novel is a conventional third person narrative from an omniscient narrator who introduces the reader to the setting of the novel (the fictitious village of Ṭība, the Arabic for Thebes, and especially the desert surrounding it) and the way of living of its people, and gradually focuses entirely on its hunter hero, [c]Assāf. This narrative conveying [c]Assāf's story and ending with his death provides a sort of frame-tale in which the writer inserts the fourteen stories narrated during [c]Assāf's funeral vigil (the novel's second part, entitled *Ba[c]ḍ ḥikāyāt al-layla al-[c]ajība* 'Some Stories of the Exceptional Night', Munīf 1977: 93). Formally, the switch between the conventional narration of the events concerning the life and death of the hero and the series of short stories is very striking. These stories are united thematically, all dealing with animals and nature (*al-Nihāyāt* could be defined as an environmentalist novel) but they form a separate section. They very much resemble classical *ḥikāyāt* (two are actually taken from al-Jāḥīẓ's *Kitāb al-Ḥayawān*) or *asmār* (tales traditionally narrated at night) and the whole structure of the novel, frame-tale and thematically-connected stories, has its roots in the indigenous narrative heritage.

In al-Kharrāṭ's *Rāma* novels, as in Munīf's *al-Nihāyāt*, there is no significant use of irony as a technique to make political attacks (these, as we will see later, are made, but not in ironical terms). In other words, the formal revival of ancient techniques and styles does not function as a veil for criticizing the problems of the present, which is an important aspect of al-Ghīṭānī's *al-Zaynī* (and also Ḥabībī's *al-Waqā'iᶜ al-gharība fī ikhtifā' Saᶜīd Abī al-naḥs al-mutashā'il* – 1974; *The Secret Life of Saeed the Ill-fated Pessoptimist*, 1982).[20] *Al-Zaynī* relates the events which shook Egypt in the years 1516–1517. While the book evokes that particular historical period in detail, it is clear that the author is using these events from the past to confront controversial issues concerning Nasser's rule and the 1967 *naksa*.[21]

As far as the use of the *turāth* is concerned, we could say that Munīf, al-Ghīṭānī and al-Kharrāṭ all see in formal innovation an artistic value *per se* and not a means to convey political ideas.[22] However, one difference separating al-Kharrāṭ from both Munīf and al-Ghīṭānī is that he is not as consistent as either of them: for example, his use of classical narrative methods concerns only his works' overall structure. His linguistic exercises, as well as being reminiscent of, rather than actually modelled on, classical examples, are limited to some striking passages and, more importantly, are his own invention. Here we allude to the fact that Munīf's *al-Nihāyāt* presents two episodes which are a reproduction of two stories from al-Jāḥiẓ's *Kitāb al-ḥayawān* 'The Book of Animals' (Munīf 1977: 121–6, 132; this seems to have been ignored by Meyer despite the novelist's acknowledgement of his sources in the very text of his novel). Similarly, in *al-Zaynī*, al-Ghīṭānī allows himself to quote from the Egyptian historian Muḥammad Aḥmad Ibn Iyās's (1448–1522) *Badāiᶜ al-zuhūr fī waqāiᶜ al-duhūr* 'The Choicest Blooms Concerning the Events of Fate'.[23] This difference shows us how al-Kharrāṭ is more creative in adopting his own style, although it may be influenced by classical Arabic texts as well as by Western writers. This influence is not acknowledged explicitly by the author, even if his way of portraying Mīkhā'īl's inner dialogues and thoughts in the *Rāma* novels is reminiscent of the stream of consciousness technique used by many Western writers. The very strength of al-Kharrāṭ's style rests to some extent on its heterogeneity and fluent changes of pace and register. While Munīf and al-Ghīṭānī, at least in *al-Nihāyāt* and *al-Zaynī*, might be bolder in their experiments, they decide to reproduce somebody else's style, if not actual words. Al-Kharrāṭ's attitude towards the Arabic *turāth* is in some ways similar to, and in others different from, that of al-Ghīṭānī. The latter too is concerned with a revival of the *turāth* (as he makes clear: Ghīṭānī 1984) and some of his *ṣūfī* sources are the same as al-Kharrāṭ's. It seems, however, that the revival of indigenous forms is the main goal for al-Ghīṭānī (no matter whether his main reason is political or artistic), while it is important but not central for al-Kharrāṭ.

Whatever our aesthetic response to these more or less radical experiments might be, today it is difficult to reiterate in an acritical way what Charles Pellat wrote some decades ago about modern Arabic literature:

> To be fair, it must be said that some modern Arabic authors are trying hesitantly to revive the ancient themes in order to make of them truly literary works, but it is quite certain that, on the whole, folklore hardly inspires contemporary writers, who are more interested in imitating the

> West, neglecting this traditional material [the tales of *The Arabian Nights* and the myths and legends of the past]. The choice would not in fact be an easy one, for the world of today is more attracted by the *ḥikāya* in the sense in which Abu 'l-Muṭahhar al-Azdī understood it [realistic depiction of contemporary life] than by the myths of antiquity, and one even has the impression that the ordinary people have less and less the time to listen to the stories and tales which delighted their ancestors – at least when they did not consider it beneath their dignity to be interested in them.
>
> (Pellat 1966: 371)

One of the recent trends in Arabic fiction is to be increasingly concerned with the traditional ways of narrating, especially within the genre of the novel. R. Allen writes about an 'ever-increasing interest among Arab littérateurs in the [*Arabian Nights*] and other collections of popular narrative.' He then concludes: 'This trend is, of course, part of a larger process whereby Arab writers are searching back into the history of their narrative tradition for inspiration on both form and content' (Allen 1982: 164). This was written in the early 1980s and we can now say that the revival of the *turāth* has been characterizing Arabic literature for several decades. What we have been describing in the *Rāma* Trilogy is, however, a more sophisticated experiment.

The content of classical literature has perhaps had an even greater influence on al-Kharrāṭ than its form.[24] In his work the association with particular texts is expanded by allusions to more general cultural and religious concepts. Intertextuality here is not limited to texts, it includes interdisciplinary excursuses into culture at large: popular beliefs and folklore, myths and legends, and so on. These cultural interconnections shape the characterization of Rāma.

The figure of Rāma,[25] herself a Muslim woman, is elaborated by Mīkhāʾīl, who refers to her with images taken from various cultural and religious traditions: Christian (the Virgin Mary); Pharaonic (Isis, Nut, Hathor); ancient Greek (the swan, Circe, a siren, Demeter); Semitic (Astarte, the Phoenix) and Assyrian (Ishtar). Throughout the Trilogy, the figure that is most often associated with Rāma is the ancient Egyptian queen–goddess Isis.[26] At the beginning of *Rāma* this association leads the reader to see Isis as a symbol for Rāma's desire to be completely free, and hence, despite the painful anguish this causes Mīkhāʾīl, free also from him. However, in Mīkhāʾīl's vision, Isis is also characterized by her classical, mythological significance: she is the goddess of harvest and thus the mistress of life, strongly associated with the Nile flood and the concept of birth and rebirth.[27] Not only this: it is also clear that the Pharaonic myth of Isis has an even deeper meaning for Mīkhāʾīl:

> Isis was not a legend of the ancients. On one level in his life, it was a guiding value which could be neither denied nor proved . . . his acceptance of it – should he say his faith in it – was primordial; it was not a matter for discussion. This faith was like a precedent to him, a condition of his

> existence, something that had to exist before he could exist, and was greater than he was.
>
> (Kharrāṭ 1979: 173)

As a result of this stress on the mythical Rāma, the character loses her individuality and particularity and can be regarded not as a woman any longer but as the embodiment of a concept, as its allegorical projection. It is important to underline that besides the usual ideas and concepts that the myth of Isis evokes, in Mīkhāᵓīl's mind Isis stands for the archetypal goddess or the archetypal feminine divine character. In fact, he considers Isis 'the ancient, first and everlasting goddess of love. The Virgin, mother of Horus, mother of Jesus, our Immaculate Lady.[28] Astarte, Persephone, Hera, Demeter, Aphrodite, every Madonna' (Kharrāṭ 1979: 171). At the same time, Rāma stands for the archetypal woman in Mīkhāᵓīl's life, since she 'has in herself something of all the women of his life' (Kharrāṭ 1979: 224).[29] The pairing Rāma–Isis gradually emerges as a clear symbol of Egypt, or more precisely, the eternal idea of a female Egypt, often (but not always) expressing an extremely positive image of female sexuality. This female entity is not only capable of giving birth but also eternal like the phoenix (often associated with Rāma), the legendary bird (worshipped in ancient Egypt) which was believed to burn itself and rise rejuvenated from its ashes.[30]

This return to a past which is perceived as glorious is a constant feature of the Trilogy: the very fact that Rāma and Mīkhāᵓīl are archaeologists is not incidental. Some metaphors used in these novels are expanded through explicit cultural references: an excellent example of this is the depiction of the mystical search for the self in *al-Zaman*.

The metaphor of this search for the self (i.e. Mīkhāᵓīl's pursuit of an ideal relationship with Rāma) is expanded through extensive references to a passage from a Coptic Gnostic text, *The Apocalypse of Adam* (*Ruᵓyā Ādam*; Kharrāṭ 1985: 78–9). This text 'is the last treaty of Code V of the Coptic library discovered at Nag Hammadi [Najᶜ Ḥammādī], Upper Egypt, December 1945' (Morard 1985: 1).

A mystical reading of the *Rāma* novels relies also on the Christian belief according to which Christ's two natures (one divine and one human) co-exist in one unity. This belief is alluded to in the novels of the *Rāma* cycle in the very relationship between the heroine and the hero. Mīkhāᵓīl's perennial search for the perfect union with Rāma is the search for the absolute, eternal, divine nature of the self, whereas Mīkhāᵓīl himself is the symbol of the contingent, ephemeral nature of every human being. The never-ending, at times desperate and hopeless, search for oneness depicted in these novels mirrors what the author maintains to be the true Coptic orthodoxy. He says:

> The core of Egyptian orthodoxy is specifically the incarnation and the fusion of the absolute in man. The absolute is man, and man is the absolute without division: not even for one moment or a blink of the eye;[31] it is the communion of the human and the divine. This is the [...]

> creed of Egyptian orthodoxy, and the essence of being a Copt. I claim that this also is basically the essence of being Egyptian.
>
> (al-Kharrāṭ quoted in Hafez 1982: 236)

Here we should make it clear that the dragon of the title, as well as Rāma, can also be a symbol for the divine element in man, and it is actually the dragon that al-Kharrāṭ is talking about in the passage quoted earlier. The image of the dragon appears in each of the novels of the Trilogy.[32] Its meaning is obscure and many critics have ventured to explain its significance. The range of interpretation is extremely wide.[33] It seems, however, that the appearance of the dragon generally evokes negative feelings of fear, evil, and a force perennially hostile to the hero (as happens in the fairy tales of the European folk tradition). As al-Kharrāt himself argues, the mythical animal might be associated with the satanic element of the absolute, which is eternal like the divine.[34] Again, the image of the dragon is also borrowed from the *ṣūfī* tradition, as al-Kharrāṭ seems to tell us at the very end of *Rāma*, when he quotes a passage from a poem by the famous mystical poet, al-Ḥusayn ibn al-Manṣūr al-Ḥallāj (857–922), which seems to confirm a close proximity between good and evil:

> My intimate companion, not known for betrayal,
> Invited me to drink as a host would his guest.
> As the cup went around,
> He called for the execution mat and the sword.
> Such is the lot of him who drinks wine
> In midsummer with the dragon.
>
> (Kharrāṭ 1979: 348/*1*)

It is a distinctive feature of al-Kharrāṭ's writing that intertextual references are not limited to references to other writers: he frequently alludes to other works of his own.[35] Here, it will suffice to refer to one of these autorefential allusions: a paraphrase by al-Kharrāṭ of al-Ḥallāj's lines quoted earlier in the opening of one of his novels: *Ḥarīq al-akhyila* 'Fire of Fantasies' (1994):

> No time for nostalgia
> The passions of the soul [cannot be] arranged
> And the infinite meaning is a dragon with whom I drank wine.
>
> (Kharrāṭ 1994a: 5)

This last passage does not clarify the significance of the dragon, but it confirms the association between the mythical animal and the ambivalent 'infinite meaning' in al-Kharrāṭ's writing. In the Trilogy, the dragon comes to acquire the same rich and ambivalent symbolism which the mythical animal (often associated with the serpent) has acquired as one of the most ancient symbols found in most cultures of the world (Cirlot 1958: 81). In the Book of Revelation, the Archangel Michael

(Mīkhā°īl in Arabic) is depicted fighting a many-headed red dragon, which in the Bible is usually associated with the serpent and clearly symbolizes Satan (Revelation 12 and 13 *passim*).[36] The battle, which is fought in the presence of a woman who is about to give birth, is evoked in a scene rich with obscure symbolism at the end of *Rāma*'s eighth chapter (Kharrāṭ 1979: 202–4/*186–8*), in which Mīkhā°īl calls out for his homonymous Archangel. If in the Bible the dragon/serpent is a negative, satanic symbol, St George (in Coptic Egypt the venerated *Māri Jirjis*) slaying the dragon in Christian mysticism is read as the triumph of reason or mind over emotion or desire (Gaskell 1960: 307).[37] The dragon symbolism can, however, be much more ambivalent: the universal dragon of the Gnostics is 'the way through all things' (Cirlot 1958: 84), and, still in Gnostic circles, 'the primal idea of this dual, Janus-like character', the dragon/serpent, is good and bad at the same time (Blavatsky 1888: 404).

With this Gnostic depiction of the dragon, we go back to see how al-Kharrāṭ makes use of *The Apocalypse of Adam* in *al-Zaman*. Mīkhā°īl reads the beginning of the Coptic Gnostic text[38]:

> The revelation [*ru°yā*] which Adam taught his son Seth in the seven hundredth year, saying: 'Listen to my words, my son Seth. When the lord [*al-rabb*][39] had created me out of the earth, along with Eve, your mother, I went about with her in glory [*majd*] which I[40] had seen in the aeon from which we had come forth. She taught me the word of knowledge of the eternal God [*al-rabb al-abadī*]. And we resembled the great eternal angels, for we were above the light of the god [*al-rabb*] who had created us and higher than the powers with him.
>
> (Kharrāṭ 1985: 78)

This reference to Gnosticism serves to expand al-Kharrāṭ's characterization of Mīkhā°īl's dualistic nature which, according to him, is quintessential to Egyptian religious belief. Hence, the belief present since Pharaonic antiquity of one, united entity in which two natures merge is mirrored in the Rāma–Mīkhā°īl pairing, which also relies on Coptic orthodoxy.[41] At the beginning of *The Apocalypse of Adam*, the couple Adam–Eve are depicted in their initial glory, which is derived from their knowledge of God (Gnosis, *ma^c^rifat al-rabb al-abadī*) which Eve taught Adam.[42] Here the two are united in one being and, according to Gnosticism, by Eve we have to understand the spiritual Eve (and not the corporeal), Eve as the intelligence-light of the primordial being.[43]

Let us go back to Mīkhā°īl's reading of Adam's words in the Coptic text: 'And the glory which was in our hearts left us, me and your mother Eve, along with the first breath of knowledge that breathed within us. And after that God became darkness in our hearts'[44] (Kharrāṭ 1985: 78). Mīkhā°īl explains the book's words to Rāma by saying: 'The glory [*majd*] which is in our two bodies, the light of our two hearts is the knowledge [*ma^c^rifa*], Rāma, a different knowledge, primordial. Through this glory we will achieve all of the powers of the eternal angels'

(Kharrāt 1985: 79). Again the key word is knowledge (ma^crifa): the descendant of primordial man (Adam–Eve), who lived in the glory of Gnosis, is now bound to this imperfect earth ('confrontée ici-bas à une situation dramatique et conflictuelle où se mélangent le pur et l'impur', Morard 1985: 11) where he is separated into two beings.

In the Hafez interview, Hafez and al-Kharrāṭ argue that true self-knowledge can be achieved only through knowledge of the Other and of the world (Hafez 1982: 237), which ultimately is the knowledge of God. In a critical article quoted earlier, al-Kharrāṭ makes some observations about a novel by Khayrī ᶜAbd al-Jawwād, who appears to have been highly influenced by him. His critical comments could usefully be taken to refer to his own works. For instance, when he comes to analyse the relationship between the lover and the beloved in ᶜAbd al-Jawwād's novel, al-Kharrāṭ explains first of all that they are to be considered as two parts of the same whole, and that the beloved can be seen as the absolute (Kharrāṭ 1999: 214–15). Second, even more significantly for the topic we are treating, he says that one of the main features of this connection – unity between lover and beloved – is 'the infatuation with knowledge or, more precisely, the struggle towards knowledge' (Kharrāṭ 1999: 219). Then (Kharrāṭ 1999: 220–1) he goes on to say three important things about the nature of this maᶜrifa which both confirm what we have seen earlier and add new elements:

1 the search for knowledge can be fatal to man (al-Kharrāṭ here refers to the tree of knowledge as depicted in the Book of Genesis and the expulsion of Adam and Eve from Eden), but it is in man's nature to search for knowledge regardless of the price he has to pay to achieve it;
2 this kind of knowledge is mystical: it is already present in man and it is there because of God; hence man might be able to discover it within himself, but he does not create it from nothing;
3 the search for knowledge cannot be carried out successfully except through love.

All of these points are relevant to the *Rāma* novels and the depiction of the relationship between Rāma and Mīkhāʾīl. In fact, regarding the connection between love and knowledge, to draw a parallel between the deity and Rāma is to express the belief that love (both spiritual and physical love are very much at the centre of these novels) is a means to acquire knowledge, or better, knowledge can only be achieved through true, total love.[45] And it is indisputable that Mīkhāʾīl often associates Rāma with the divine side of himself.

This association with the spiritual, superior Eve of Gnosticism will become even clearer when Mīkhāʾīl goes back to other fascinating stories of Adam and Eve, Lilith and Naamah[46] which are clear allusions to early Christian or Jewish exegeses of the Old Testament (such as the Jewish *midrash*). Again the creation and origins of human kind are the topic of the passages to which Mīkhāʾīl refers. From a formal point of view the source text is not clearly mentioned in this case, but the images of the characters in those texts enter Mīkhāᵓīl's thoughts and daydreams. Here, the distinction between a spiritual and a corporeal Eve is clear. We are told: 'the first Eve, perfect and shining, not that of the apple and the snake, Eve the rebellious, more than that[47]: the other face, one and double, of the first Adam, one twofold being' (Kharrāṭ 1985: 297). Here, al-Kharrāṭ's concern with this duality within man is clearly expressed within his reference to Biblical exegetic texts. Hence, Mīkhāᵓīl asks himself shortly afterwards: 'When did separation take place? Why did the sin of schism occur? When will it be forgiven? When will the one who will carry the cross come so that I can collapse under its rejuvenating and deadly weight?' (Kharrāṭ 1985: 297).

The idea of going back to a divine origin of man, that is to God, is reiterated in al-Kharrāṭ's allusions to Islamic mysticism. In these novels, he shows an obviously syncretic approach: in his philosophical concept of man, he relies on a religious belief (the unity in Christ of two natures), which we have defined earlier as typically Christian; he alludes to Gnostic concepts (including those which contain Jewish elements); and he also includes mythological, especially Pharaonic imagery. It is in this ecumenical context that the allusions to Muslim mystical writers occur.

Rāma, and probably even more clearly *al-Zaman*, are characterized by allusions to mystical beliefs. Let us take as an example a beautifully evocative passage from chapter VIII of *al-Zaman* (whose title, 'The Hidden Beacon [*al-manār*] on the Path', is enough to indicate a reference to a well-known *ṣūfī* belief which sees human life as a difficult and uncertain journey on the path towards reunion with God):

> The one essence carries in itself diversity and [at the same time] allows only oneness. The two connected opposites cannot exist without one another, while the billows of the raging waves knock over my extremely fragile boat but her shell is very solid and what makes my heart flow copiously with tenderness are higher and mightier waves; no shore is for her, she has no anchor. Do not tell me: land! For what can I do if this boat with her broken belly neither sinks, nor reaches [the land], she cannot resist, still she does not break into pieces.
>
> [...] *I cried*: Show me a light on the way.
> *He said*: There are no lights on our way.
> *I said*: It is in darkness, despite all its clarity.
> *He said*: And, although it is concealed, you can see it as clearly as day.
> O Farīd al-dīn, how cruel you are!
>
> (Kharrāṭ 1985: 195–6)

The last part of this passage is nothing short of a quatrain (*rubāᶜī*, rhyming in *-ār*) in the form of a duet between Mīkhāᶜīl and, presumably, the great Persian mystical poet Farīd al-Dīn al-ᶜAṭṭār (who died in the early decades of the thirteenth century).

This duet, which is formally reminiscent of the *guftugū-ī* (in classical Persian poetry, the alternate sequence of questions and answers), is thematically related to mystical feelings. The symbolic way Mīkhāᵓīl has to travel towards his beloved is like the difficult path the mystic has to travel towards his creator.[48] As we have seen earlier, this journey towards Rāma can also be seen as the mystical journey towards the self, hence all the references to ᶜAṭṭār, Ibn ᶜArabī, al-Ḥallāj and the like seem to be appropriate. It is clear that more important than these explicit allusions, where the name of a mystic is mentioned, or a verse from one of his poems is quoted (as often happens in *Yaqīn*), is the overall allusion transcending the details of the text. As the author himself signals in a note at the end of *Yaqīn*, he does not feel the need to relate those quotations to their exact sources, because 'they have merged in the text of [the] novel and become a part of its special texture' (Kharrāṭ 1996a: 309). In addition to these indigenous sources we should also consider his references to Western poets, such as the English Romantics, who, Musawi tells us, inform some of the major themes of *Yaqīn*. Musawi underlines how al-Kharrāṭ is willing to use the connections he sees between the Islamic mystics and poets such as Shelley, Byron, Keats and Coleridge.[49]

When analysing al-Kharrāṭ's experimental attempts to introduce techniques borrowed from the literary heritage into the hybrid literary genre of the novel (which is, according to certain definitions, modern – having its origins in nineteenth century European thought – and according to others more specifically connected to a sense of contemporaneity),[50] a number of relevant questions inevitably arises. Does this indulgence towards the *turāth* betray a certain conservative, if not reactionary, intellectual attitude on the part of the author? In dealing with the issue of culture in the Arab world in the early 1970s (but the topic is still relevant today), the Syrian poet Adonis speaks about the desirability of an Arab cultural revolution which would initiate change and progress. What is most interesting for us here is his discourse on the *turāth*, felt by the poet to be a sort of burden (at least as long as it is considered sacred and unreachable). For example, he writes:

> It is impossible to generate consciousness by reading the cultural legacy (*al-turath*) or by studying it, for such reading transmits a culture external to actual life and from above, that is, it transmits a culture which is both didactic and abstract.
>
> (Adonis 1972: 28)

Maybe the Syrian poet himself provides us with an answer: the crucial problem here is not to get rid of the *turāth*, it is rather to change the way in which an author uses it:

> the meaning of the relation between the revolutionary intelligentsia and that which is inherited changes. It is not a relation or revival or glorification. It is, rather, a relation of criticism, analysis, and transcendence. In this way, we realize that the role of innovation does not lie in the

> preservation, but rather, in the explosion and development of the inherited cultural system. Every intellectual who does not do this remains below the revolutionary standard: he does not create, but rearranges what has become unfastened from the chains of words preserved in the books and memory.
>
> (Adonis 1972: 28)

We wonder if all the references to the *turāth*, but also to other non-Arab–Islamic texts, which we find in al-Kharrāṭ are, using Adonis's expression, a creative 'explosion and development' of his manifold cultural heritage. It would be difficult to explain al-Kharrāṭ's revival of the literary past as a mere gratuitous display of knowledge or an exercise *per se* because the themes treated in his first novels are expanded through his use of ancient forms of expression and through his references to other similar concepts found in mystical or religious texts. In his critical works, al-Kharrāṭ explains that the use of the *turāth* (by writers such as ᶜAbd al-Jawwād, and himself of course) is much more than the mere imitation of past styles and themes (e.g. the background for historical novels such as Raḍwā ᶜĀshūr's *Thulāthiyat Gharnāṭa* 'Granada Trilogy', 1994–1995, which he clearly considers an inferior genre), and more than a means to express political attacks through metaphors (is he alluding here to al-Ghīṭānī's *al-Zaynī*?). According to al-Kharrāṭ, the *turāth* serves as a stimulating inspiration and a valid constituent of the novel, but at the same time remains secondary to the author's creative ability (cf. Kharrāṭ 1999: 211–12, 222; Kharrāṭ 1993: 245). Only when exploited by the writer using innovative literary techniques can the *turāth* function in a significant way.

The concern about a writer's relationship with his cultural heritage has been at the core of literary criticism in the West since the advent of modernism and the new literary criticism accompanying it (as well as being obviously related to theories of intertextuality). For instance, al-Kharrāṭ's attitude is reminiscent of T. S. Eliot's ideas about the new poets and their use of tradition, expressed in his famous essay 'Tradition and the Individual Talent' (1919). Louis Menand, in his essay on Eliot, explains the poet's self-conscious resuscitation of English verse drama as a sort of natural outcome of his critical theory about the poet and his literary tradition (Menand 2000: 34).[51] This is reminiscent of the exercise carried out by al-Kharrāṭ with the *Arabian Nights* narrative structure (see al-Kharrāṭ quoted in Hafez 1982: 242, discussed earlier).

In these attempts to revive literary tradition the key term seems to be the adverb *consciously*, since Eliot, and others (e.g. Calvino) argue that the intertextual nature of literary works is a fact (even if the author is unaware of it).[52] But here we are dealing with authors (Eliot and al-Kharrāṭ) who consciously go back to their literary heritage and try to revive it. We have to stress that while it is possible to relate Eliot's observations to al-Kharrāṭ, it is also true that, since the *nahḍa*, Arab authors have been driven by two main inspirational forces: their own tradition and the influence of non-Arabic literatures, mainly Western. The second source for inspiration is all the more active today when writers around the world can read and influence each other much more easily than in Eliot's time. It is sometimes difficult to establish whether a writer is borrowing from his own tradition or from an author in another tradition (as we will see more clearly later when analysing Khūrī's fiction). In al-Kharrāt's writing, we find a serious attempt to recover a literary past in a non-ironic fashion, unlike the way Eco and other critics tell us happens in postmodern fiction (Eco 1983: 67 *passim*). The crucial point seems to be that al-Kharrāṭ combines this non-ironic return to his literary past with techniques which are typically modernist (disruption of plot, fragmentation of narration). As we have noted in the introduction to this study, a writer can return to his own literary tradition as a natural reaction against Western culture in a postcolonial environment (the same phenomenon is easily discernible in South American and African literatures).

The intertextual nature of al-Kharrāṭ's fiction is not limited to literary texts. In many novels by contemporary Arab authors the allusions to sociopolitical issues are veiled (in the form of the historical novel, for instance, as in al-Ghīṭānī's *al-Zaynī*). In al-Kharrāṭ's works, despite their formal and thematic allusions to the past, the references to today's problems are explicit and visible. The treatment of socio-political problems is also carried out through what Hutcheon considers 'a formal mode of overt intertextuality' (1989: 89): paratextuality, or the insertion into the narrative of metafictional texts (not only footnotes, titles, chapter headings, but also imported external texts such as newspaper clippings or passages from other texts).

As we have seen in Chapter 2, al-Kharrāṭ's novels are characterized by an unusual mixture of narrative techniques. In *al-Zaman*, a novel notable for its high number of intertextual references, we find epistolary texts and brief journalistic anecdotes, or even genuine pieces of news, inserted into the narrative. If the repetition of the same letter can correspond to certain sensations in the alliterative passages which we have analysed earlier, the use of these epistolary and journalistic texts serves the writer's desire to place his novel in a well defined socio-political context. In *al-Zaman* political and social issues are treated more explicitly than in *Rāma*. The main characters often discuss political and social topics. An important element in the novel is a vehement criticism of the social malaise caused by the so-called *Infitāḥ*, the 'Open Door Policy', inaugurated in the 1970s by the late President Sadat.[53] The alien texts inserted in the narrative function as a sort of frame within which Mīkhāʾīl and Rāma's arguments take place. The epistolary texts (and the journalistic, reportorial information provided in the couple's dialogues) can be divided into two categories: letters sent to Egyptian newspapers, generally the leading daily *al-Ahrām* (ten public letters),[54] and the personal correspondence of Mīkhāʾīl's family (seven private letters). Usually the public letters appear in the newspapers in the late 1970s and early 1980s and, along with the journalistic accounts of the facts, depict the appalling conditions in which some Egyptians are forced to live: schoolchildren who have no place to be taught, a widow who is forced to sell her kidney in order to support her children, poor quarters of Alexandria invaded by packs of dogs, and so on. The journalistic texts, along with what the characters say, also highlight a moral decadence which they perceive as a typical feature of the time in which the novel is set (the 1970s) and hint at Egypt's total submission to foreign powers, even if their main themes remain the complete failure of public services and sheer poverty.[55]

The function of the personal letters is more complex than that of the public ones. They contribute to characterizing Mīkhāʾīl, providing the reader with biographical information. They also function in the same way as the public ones in that they depict the material difficulties which Mīkhāʾīl's family had to undergo in the 1930s and 1940s, but here the stress is on the members of the family more than on the socio-political context.

From a formal point of view the text of the letter is usually inserted abruptly into the narrative. The following passage taken from *al-Zaman* is another good example of this juxtaposition and also of the switch from one register (both stylistic and thematic) to another:

> It was that closeness which could never be stronger, deeper, in that high, luminous room of that Alexandrine hotel on the sea, there was the one dual body whose never-ending extremes and moving roots touched embraced rolled raised became firm became like waves and the stone flowed in the fluttering [wings] of divinity itself.
>
> Once she said to him, on the verge of falling asleep, in that house which she said was his:
>
> – Mīkhāʾīl, lock the door…
>
> He said with amazement, mixed with affection:
>
> – Why? Does the open door spoil some aesthetic convention or norm?
>
> She said seriously: So that devils won't come in after I fall asleep…
>
> He stood up at her side, straightened the light cover on her shoulders as she was about to fall asleep, and locked the door carefully and quietly after she was already sleeping.
>
> Fuʾād Fawwāz wrote to *al-Jumhūriyya* the 7th November 1979: 'The tax inspectors went down through the *Imām* al-Shāfiʿī cemetery to make sure that there was no tax-evading activity. At first, the gravediggers welcomed the tax inspectors, taking them to be medical students in search of corpses. Then some fell silent and others tried to mislead them. Some women began to scream from within the tombs to frighten the inspectors. The tax office discovered in the inhabited areas of the cemetery joiners and tailors evading taxes.'
>
> As for the village of Dast al-Ashrāf, Kūm Ḥamāda, the rice crop was flooded, and the water was diverged into the cemetery so that the dead floated…
>
> He said to her that a statue of the driver of Ramses II's chariot was discovered in an abandoned tram station in New York. He said that a statue of the imperial driver Merneptah disappeared from the British Museum

> in London. He said that he saw the picture of the statue in an archaeology magazine and that its face reminded him of the face of Ḥusayn *Effendī* who used to live below them in Gheit al-ᶜEnab. He was the director of the bridge over the Maḥmūdiyya [canal], had a rounded face with swollen eyes and was a good man. He said to her that *Sett* Wahība, his wife, was fond of him when he was a child and he loved her tenderness and her pleasant body.
>
> He said to her that a strange thing was happening to him, the relation between inside and outside was changing.
>
> (Kharrāṭ 1985: 192–3)

Again, it is useful to compare and contrast al-Kharrāt's experimentation with the insertion of documents into his narrative, with the Egyptian writer who has made this technique his unmistakable trademark: Ṣunᶜallāh Ibrāhīm. Since 1974, with the publication of his second novel *Najmat aghusṭus* 'August Star', Ibrāhīm has been inserting documents (mainly newspaper clippings) into his narratives. The imported documents in novels like *Dhāt* (1992; *Zaat*, 2001) are, however, fundamentally different in nature from al-Kharrāṭ's insertions. First of all, the texts employed by the latter mainly provide the characters' (and the author's) concerns with a backdrop and reinforce their social criticism. In Ibrāhīm, on the contrary, the imported texts usually present the version of reality provided by the political and economic establishment which is then contradicted by that of the political opposition, and ultimately ridiculed by the events of the narrative. Second, the difference is also a quantitative one, since in *al-Zaman* the imported texts are not as prominent as in *Dhāt*, which can be considered a true narrative collage. Moreover, in Ibrāhīm there is an implicit fundamental discourse, absent in al-Kharrāṭ, on the way in which the media produce their version of reality (cf. Mehrez 1994: 140–1). Similarly, in Barrāda's *Luᶜbat*, we have an implicit discussion on the use and misuse of language. In a highly metafictional passage, the author of the novel is said to have given his narrator-in-chief a bunch of documents from which the latter has selected three texts to include in the novel. The journalistic texts (extracts from newspapers or transcripts of radio broadcasts from the late 1970s) draw the reader's attention to how language can be misused to falsify, to hide truth behind empty rhetoric and pointless verbosity: the first two articles are crass examples of hyperbolic praise of the authorities of the day (the first generally hails the beauty of the land, the happiness of its citizens and the wisdom of their leaders, whereas the second is even more comically improbable as it exploits a beauty contest to make similar points!). The third excerpt is from an article which sharply contrasts with the first two as it denounces a case of abuse of power in a simple and effective way (the sort of article, we guess, the leftist journalist al-Hādī might write; Barrāda 1987: 89–92/*90–3*). Al-Nowaihi reflects on how, apart from these examples, the novel as a whole expresses Barrāda's preoccupation with language: what it can and cannot achieve, how it can be used (Nowaihi 2000: 380–2).

Another effect which Ibrāhīm's and Barrāda's use of documents is also intended to achieve is an ironic, parodic one (as to the former, see Mehrez 1994: 126). It is also possible to perceive some dark irony in al-Kharrāṭ's use of the same technique in *al-Zaman*. Irony, in Ibrāhīm's and Barrāda's case, is achieved through the juxtaposition of two contrasting versions of reality or rather through ridiculing the official version of reality. In al-Kharrāṭ, the contrast is between the often dramatic content of the public letters and the scenes of Rāma and Mīkhā᾽īl's domestic life, which depict a bohemian, stylish way of living, as is evident in the following passage:

> When he went back to Cairo he said to her:
>
> – Listen my lady, aren't you an historian also? Take note of what's in today's *al-Ahrām*: 'I used to live some years ago with my father and mother in our village, district of Abū Qurqāṣ, province of al-Minyā, in a dark rented room with no water, no electricity, no furniture but the mattress we slept on. My father who worked as a hired peasant [day labourer or farmhand] died and left my mother and me 'with the earth as a bed and the skies as a cover.' I worked in the village as a baker so that we could get something to keep us alive. I gained the high school diploma and joined the Faculty of Medicine at the *al-Azhar* University where I couldn't find anybody to support me, couldn't find food, or clothes, or books and all the rest . . . I reside in a room built on a terrace in a quarter of Cairo with the roof covered by reed and the ground just as God made it! I've got nothing but a cover I wrap myself in to sleep.
>
> Shaḥāta Ḥasan al-Manzilāwī, student
>
> al-Amīriyya, Firdaws City, Abū Bakr al-Ṣiddīq St., Quarter Wahba Ḥasan, House n. 7
>
> After they had made love several times, they were having dinner, eating off the concave brass table, on the left side of the big salon, which was on a lower level than the rest of the room, beside the huge hi-fi, which she had named 'the music monster', from which flowed Bach's abstract rhythms with their precise emotions played on a piano pure as crystal. The light descending from the Mameluke lamp was falling on the latticework of the *mashrabiyya*, darkened by the dark, warm-breathing leaves of the plants.
>
> (Kharrāt 1985: 96)

The characteristic juxtaposition of the two passages expresses in an ironic fashion the gap between the poor and the privileged class to which the protagonists belong. Here, the author ridicules Mīkhā᾽īl's radical-chic attitude: Mīkhā᾽īl finds it disgusting that the majority of his fellow citizens live in poverty, but at the same time he finds himself distant from the people he would like to help. The gap dividing the intellectuals (represented by Mīkhā᾽īl's character) from the rest of the people within Egyptian society is one of the main themes of the *Rāma* novels, and it obviously refers to al-Kharrāṭ's own status. Here, the difference between the two passages is also stylistic: on the one hand, we have the prosaic and matter-of-fact tone of the letter; on the other, a style precise in its description and lyrical in its evocative overtones ('the dark, warm-breathing leaves of the plants').

In another passage of *al-Zaman* al-Kharrāṭ makes fun of Mīkhāʾīl's proud but, in the context, inappropriate display of *shiʿr manthūr*. Rāma has just read one of the letters from the press (from the young widow who is offering to sell her kidney because she cannot afford to pay for her children's education). Mīkhāʾīl, who does not seem to be particularly affected by the dramatic content of the letter, proceeds to read one of his own letters, dated 1942, his first year at university. He introduces it by saying that at that time he used to write lyrical prose. After the formal and ornate language of the letter, the narrative is resumed with the following short sentence: 'She was asleep beside him, while he was wide awake, smoking tensely' (Kharrāṭ 1985: 168). It is probably not Mīkhāʾīl's letter which has sent Rāma to sleep: we know that the sudden continuous shift from one situation to another is typical of al-Kharrāṭ's narrative. However, the juxtaposition of these two passages, even if they depict two different moments, produces an ironic effect (this example also adds to the ironic effect caused by the different passages, a depiction of Rāma's dismissive tone towards Mīkhāʾīl's pompous attitude).[56] Obviously, here the irony is self-directed and devoid of the political edge which we have observed earlier in Ibrāhīm's and Barrāda's intertextual pastiches.

One of the main functions of the experimental technique of inserting alien texts into the narrative is also achieved in *al-Zaman*: as Mehrez points out in her article on Ibrāhīm, 'such juxtaposition [of documents within the narrative] transforms the documents into "docu-fictions" and helps generate a crucial level of awareness in the reader' (Mehrez 1994: 126). While we will deal with these issues (including the characteristically autorefential tone of Khūrī's and Barrāda's fiction – metafiction) in the next chapter, we will now stress some features common to al-Kharrāṭ and Khūrī's intertextual allusions. Khūrī, like al-Kharrāṭ relies on allusions to, and quotations from, literary and non-literary material: the novel *Mamlakat al-ghurabāʾ* (1993) is an excellent example of this phenomenon. The main theme of the novel is based on the concept of being a stranger, or alienated, in one's own country. As well as dealing with the theme at an individual level, the author clearly refers to the status of the Palestinian people who have been expelled from their own country or turned into refugees all over the Middle East by the creation of the Israeli state. Like al-Kharrāṭ, Khūrī too relies on references to religious texts to expand his work's content in a powerful manner. In *Mamlakat*, the references to the Bible are numerous and easily recognizable.[57] The central concept of being a stranger in one's own land is rendered through allusions to Jesus Christ as the archetypal stranger in his own land. The main intertextual allusion regarding Christ as a stranger is a Christian Orthodox hymn, traditionally sung during the funeral procession of Christ on Good Friday and depicting Joseph asking Pilate for the dead body of Christ. The almost complete text of the hymn is quoted at the end of the novel:

> Joseph,
> When he saw that the sun had hidden its rays,
> And the veil of the Temple was rent at the death of the Saviour,
> Approaching Pilate, pleading with him, crying out and saying:
> Give me this Stranger,
> Who from his youth has wandered like a stranger,
> Give me this Stranger,
> Whom his kinsmen killed in hatred like a stranger,
> Give me this Stranger,
> At whom I wonder, beholding him as a Guest of death,
> Give me this Stranger,
> Whom the Jews in envy estranged from the world,
> Give me this Stranger,
> That I may bury him in a tomb,
> Give me this Stranger,
> Who being a Stranger,
> Hath no place whereon to lay his head,
> Give me this Stranger,
> To whom his Mother, beholding him dead,
> Cried, My Son and my God,
> Give me this Stranger,
>
> In these words the honourable Joseph pleaded with Pilate,
> Took the Saviour's body,
> And with fear wrapped it in linen and balm,
> And placed it in a tomb.
>
> (Khūrī 1993: 125–6/*102–3*)

This quotation provides the central image of the novel, that of the Palestinian people as strangers in their own land, with a lyrical and religious/cultural dimension.[58] Some references in the text of the hymn are clearly highly evocative within the framework of Middle Eastern contemporary history: the stranger is said to have been 'estranged from the world' by 'the envy of the Jews', but he is also said to have been 'killed in hatred' by 'his kinsmen'.

Some of the many intertextual references of *Mamlakat* serve also to depict the historical and geographical background of the novel. The focus here is on a place, the Jordan Valley and the Dead Sea, where the narrator remembers his past. Within Khūrī's often ill-defined spatio-temporal frame, we somehow understand that the narrator (probably a Palestinian fighter or someone who, like Khūrī himself, has fought with Palestinian militias) finds himself in this place in 1991 on his way to Beirut, and recalls when he went for the first time from Amman to the river for his 'baptism with water, with the Holy Spirit, and with blood' (Khūrī 1993: 29/*22*). But the place is much more than a geographical space for the narrator: it is a sort of ideal state of mind in which the narrator recalls his past and has visions. At the beginning of the third chapter an encyclopaedic style text describing the Dead Sea's physical features ends with this remark: 'Ezekiel mentions that the restoration of the Dead Sea and the proliferation of many kinds of fish in it will be among the signs of life in God's New Kingdom' (Khūrī 1993: 37/*29*). This is the prelude to another quotation, this time from the Old Testament (which Khūrī acknowledges: Ezekiel 47: 6–12), which depicts Ezekiel's vision of the future Temple and its utopian surroundings:

> 6 He asked me, 'Son of man, do you see this?'
> Then he led me back to the bank of the river.7 When I arrived there, I saw
> a great number of trees on each side of the river.8 He said to me, 'This
> water flows toward the eastern region and goes down into the Arabah,
> where it enters the Sea. When it empties into the Sea, the water there
> becomes fresh.9 Swarms of living creatures will live wherever the river
> flows. There will be large numbers of fish, because this water flows
> there and makes the salt water fresh; so where the river flows everything
> will live.10 Fishermen will stand along the shore; from En Gedi to En
> Eglaim there will be places for spreading nets. The fish will be of many
> kinds – like the fish of the Great Sea.11 But the swamps and marshes will
> not become fresh; they will be left for salt.12 Fruit trees of all kinds
> will grow on both banks of the river. Their leaves will not wither, nor
> will their fruit fail. Every month they will bear, because the water from
> the sanctuary flows to them. Their fruit will serve for food and their
> leaves for healing.'
>
> (Bible, Ezekiel 47: Verses 6–12;[59] Khūrī 1993: 56/*45–6*)

This is one of the prophetic passages which describe Israel as promised by God to the Jews, and therefore it is relevant to the topic of Khūrī's novel. The depiction of the Promised Land as such a blissful place in the biblical passage could serve to establish an idealized setting which will be undermined in the novel's portrayal of the same place, now devastated, indeed profaned, by war, deprived of its sacred status by injustice.

The quotation from Ezekiel is preceded by a passage where the narrator reports a fascinating and mysterious myth regarding the creation of salt. In Khūrī's fiction, as in the Bible, salt is an important symbol whose meaning can change significantly. In *Mamlakat*, when the narrator talks about its creation as depicted in the obscure myth quoted earlier, salt is a synonym for life and is associated with woman (Mary, maybe 'the sister of Moses and Aaron and daughter of Umran, or maybe [. . .] another Mary'; Khūrī 1993: 55/*45*), and lack of salt means death. In *Riḥlat*, on the other hand, salt is associated with death: 15 September 1982, the day the Israeli army enters Beirut, is the day the protagonist Little

Ghāndī dies, killed by a stray bullet. That day, the narrator tells us, the city streets are covered by salt, salt is everywhere (Khūrī 1989: 13–14/*9*).[60] Throughout the same novel, salt is also central in the shape of allusions to the Sermon on the Mount (especially Matthew 5: 1–8, where salt is positive, that which gives the earth its flavour).[61]

Here the author uses the Gospel text ironically, contextualizing it in the Reverend Amīn's attempts to convince Little Ghāndī (who is Muslim) to go to church.[62] The irony lies in the fact that Little Ghāndī is left unaffected by the Reverend's rhetoric and all his erudite quotations are lost on, or easily dismissed by, him. Ghandour, in analysing the same dialogues between the Reverend and Little Ghāndī, observes: '[l]anguage, instead of being a means of communication and understanding, becomes an obstacle to its intended purpose' (Ghandour 2000: 192).[63] Little Ghāndī's reactions to Reverend Amīn's religious quotations also form comic sketches: when Reverend Amīn explains to Little Ghāndī the biblical tale of Abraham's sacrificing the lamb instead of his son Ishaq (Ishmael, according to the Koran, as the Reverend himself promptly reminds a probably unaware Little Ghāndī), the latter replies in a dismissive way: 'I get it, I get it, without the lamb it doesn't work!' (Khūrī 1989: 29/*24*).[64] It should be noticed that the stress is not on a religious misunderstanding but rather on a cultural one. In fact, the Reverend Amīn even quotes the Koran to Little Ghāndī to show him that going to church cannot be that bad after all ('And nearest among them in love to the Believers wilt thou find those who say "We are Christians" '; Khūrī 1989: 102/*97*; Koran, V: 82), but the latter finally gives in to the Reverend's invitations simply out of curiosity and because he is a 'cool guy' (*akhū al-shaḥṭa*, 'a son of a gun' according to Paula Haydar's English translation).

The misunderstanding between those who self-indulgently portray themselves as loving the simple-minded, 'the meek', and wanting to help them, and the simple-minded themselves, is further exposed when the character of the young Reverend George comes on the scene (Khūrī 1989: 130/*123*). In his encounter with Little Ghāndī his hypocritical attitude is clear: his good will has a hidden agenda, the conversion of Little Ghāndī, or at least it is not wholly altruistic, as Reverend Amīn himself concedes: 'This guy [George] had just come from America. He studied philosophy and wants to prove how smart he [is]' (Khūrī 1989: 133/*126*). However, the parody is not directed at the biblical text itself, but at the way the Reverend George exploits it: at every 'blessed' he points Ghāndī out to the congregation, who turn to look at him, making Ghāndī feel uneasy if not humiliated. Furthermore, Ghāndī does not understand much of the standard Arabic in which the young Reverend speaks! But the whole encounter shows how the young American does not understand how to speak to 'the meek' and 'the poor in spirit' – like Ghāndī – whom he claims to love so much.

Khūrī, like al-Kharrāṭ, relies on religious image patterns. The fact that they are both from Christian traditions probably explains why they mainly refer to Christian figures and beliefs (Gnosticism and Coptic doctrine in al-Kharrāṭ, Eastern Orthodox in Khūrī). However, both novelists also employ Islamic imagery (cf. al-Kharrāṭ's use of the symbolic power of al-Ḥusayn ibn ᶜAlī ibn Abī Ṭālib and *al-Sayyida* Zaynab in *al-Zaman*; Khūrī's quoting of the Koran, for example, in *Riḥlat*; Khūrī 1989: 207/*194*), and both rely on the same cultural Arab–Islamic background of the *turāth*. As Khūrī himself clarifies: 'I have never felt that being a Christian and not a Muslim means that I am not part of the Arabic Islamic [sic] culture. Islam is part of my cultural background' (Mejcher 2001: 13).[65] Accordingly, Khūrī, like al-Kharrāṭ, makes references to *ṣūfī* literature. He does this in a rather more conventional way by quoting prose passages or verses which function as brief introductions, and not through insertions in the text. The use of this paratextual device has become very common in modern Arabic literature. The importance of the content of these usually brief texts cannot be overlooked, as they sometimes express or summarize one of the strands of meaning in the novel. For example, as we have seen in the previous chapter, Ibn ᶜArabī's verses prefacing *Riḥlat* convey Khūrī's multivoiced intent: 'A face is only one, yet if you multiply the mirrors, it is multiple' (Khūrī 1989: 6).

The purpose of opening a novel with a quotation from another author's text is, however, not always as clear as in *Riḥlat*. *Bāb*, for instance, is introduced by an extract taken from a *ḥadīth*, probably referring to another *ṣūfī* icon, *al-Shaykh* al-Junayyid (d. 910), whose verses also open al-Kharrāṭ's *Yaqīn*.[66] The passage quoted at the beginning of *Bāb* depicts the encounter between the *Shaykh* and a dervish who will unexpectedly reveal himself as one of his disciples (Khūrī 1998: 5). This could be taken to refer to the complex relationship between the two main characters of the novel: Khalīl and his mentor or father-figure, Yūnis.

These quotations and allusions can fulfil more than one function: we have just seen how they can relate to one of the main themes of the work. They automatically hint at the concept of literature as systems of texts which interact with each other (the theory of intertextuality), and at the exhaustion of literature (what one is writing has already been written, maybe in another form, by somebody else). The reference to another author, generally an illustrious man of letters of the past, can also simply fulfil the author's need to acknowledge his intellectual sources of inspiration. It seems that this whole range of functions can apply to al-Takarlī's radical use of quotations in *al-Masarrāt* (this is unusual for the Iraqi writer, who does not insert quotations in any of his other novels). In fact, this lengthy novel ends with some eleven quotations of prose and poetry, from mainly European scholars and writers: Blaise Pascal (2 quotations), Weil (2), William Carlos Williams, William Shakespeare, Paul Verlaine, Umberto Eco, Emile Cioran (the Romanian writer who spent most of his life in France), an anonymous Bedouin and Freud. As in Khūrī's novels, all this material refers in some way to the main themes treated in the novel. In brief, *al-Masarrāt* depicts through an original use of different narrative techniques (see Chapter 2) the life of Tawfīq, an Iraqi who initially goes through his normal middle-class life (a combination of work, wife and poker games), only to witness its sudden, disastrous end: he is sacked, divorced, abandoned and his romantic love story with Adele is ended by external, historical circumstances (this is a recurrent motif in al-Takarlī's fiction: in *al-Raj*ᶜ too individual life is inevitably influenced by the external world and by history despite the characters' attempts to ignore them).[67] In recounting Tawfīq's misfortunes and eventual radical change of lifestyle, al-Takarlī explores the extent to which people can control their future and become aware of what is happening in their lives. This is a work which, despite being carefully set against events of modern Iraqi history and a specific social environment, discusses universal issues of human experience, typical of every latitude and culture: its final quotations confirm this. The themes of both the novel and the quotations are: morality, pleasure, happiness, love and, above all, the workings of the human consciousness (*al-wa*ᶜ*ī*).[68] Whether the fact that a human being reflects on and is deliberately aware of what is happening in his life helps him to live a better life or not is a question implicit in the text. Tawfīq reflects on his life's misfortunes extensively and becomes increasingly aware of the reasons for his miserable condition. This does not make his life easier: unaware, even silly, characters whom Tawfīq encounters, both harmless (Jāsim al-Ramaḍānī, the new husband of Tawfīq's ex-wife) and harmful (the villain Sulaymān Fatḥallāh), seem to live better than him, the *thinking* character who tries consistently to be aware of what surrounds him and of who he is. Drawing heavily on Pascal, however, al-Takarlī suggests that this is what he, as a human being, is morally obliged to do: constantly working at being aware of one's condition is what makes a man different from an animal.[69] Pascal's *pensée* n. 347 which opens the eleven quotations at the end of the novel tells us:

> Man is but a reed, the most feeble thing in nature, but he is a thinking reed. The entire universe need not arm itself to crush him, a single drop of water suffices to kill him. But, even if the universe were to crush him, man would still be more noble than that which killed him, because he knows that he is killed while the universe knows nothing of the advantage it has over him.
>
> (Takarlī 1998: 465)

As for the remaining quotations, they combine in an apparently impressionistic and random way to convey the novel's general themes. For example, a beautiful poem by Paul Verlaine (*Mon rêve familier*, loosely translated into Arabic) about an imaginary, ideal woman, is followed by a short sentence by Eco, 'In order for the world to have a mirror, it needs a shape' (Takarlī 1998: 467).

More important than these quotations, which come after the end of the narrative of *al-Masarrāt*, are Tawfīq's ideas about literature and his inclinations towards Western fiction (well reflected in al-Takarlī's decision to quote predominantly Western thinkers). This is, however, a topic which will be discussed in the next chapter. In contrast to Tawfīq's often critical attitude towards Arab *literati*,[70] in *Mamlakat* we find another reference by Khūrī to the well-known champion of the pre-Islamic *qaṣīda*: Imrū°-'l-Qays (d. ca 550). This time the quotation is inserted in the main body of the novel. It goes without saying that the effect and purpose of these two kinds of quotation are very different: in those placed at the boundaries of the novel itself the reader sees the evident intervention of the writer/creator (Genette's *paratext*: the novel's title, subtitles, preface, and so on. Genette 1982: 3); those inserted in the main body of the novel are perforce fictionalized, at least in the texts we are studying, and are part of what the characters (including Khūrī's possibly autobiographical narrator/author) think and say.[71] These quotations, rather than being a gratuitous display of knowledge, function by associating the novels' themes with cultural items (whether religious beliefs or literary figures) to which the majority of educated Arab readers would relate. For instance, Khūrī reinforces his treatment of the concept of the stranger with lyrical echoes provided by Imrūᵓ-'l-Qays's allegedly last verses:[72]

أجارتنا إنَّ المزار قريبُ   وإنّي مقيمٌ ما أقامَ عسيبُ
أجارتنا إنَّا غريبان ها هنا   وكلٌّ غريبٍ للغريبِ نسيبُ

O my neighbour, the shrine is close
And I will stay [here] as long as mount ᶜAsīb
O my neighbour, we are two strangers here
And every stranger to a stranger is kin
(Khūrī 1993: 41; our translation)

These two verses are obviously related to the novel's general theme of being a stranger. More than this, they add another, more lyrical dimension to one of the main stories narrated in *Mamlakat*, that of the white Circassian, Widād, and her husband, Iskandar, and are an important element in their characterization. The lines are favourites of Iskandar, and his young wife Widād recites them to him at the very moment of his death. Eventually they are recited again by Iskandar's son George to the widow Widād when she is ill. Widād, who comes from Azerbaijan, is obviously a stranger in Beirut (see how at the end of her life she forgets how to speak Arabic and speaks her own language). As for Iskandar, he becomes a stranger to his family when he converts to Islam to marry Widād and goes to live with her, abandoning his wife and children. This story helps us to address one of the main concerns in Khūrī's works (tied in with the concept of being a stranger), that of the cosmopolitan nature of Beirut and Lebanon, places where people of many different racial and religious origins meet and mix (*Mamlakat*'s Widād somehow reminds us of *Riḥlat*'s Vitsky, the White Russian, another woman from the East – Eastern Europe – who is forced into exile in Lebanon and eventually dies in Beirut). Khūrī deliberately chooses to underline this cosmopolitan character of the city's inhabitants, whether they be Lebanese, Palestinian, Syrian or Egyptian; Arab, Circassian, Armenian, Syriac; Muslim (Shiite and Sunni), Christian (Greek Orthodox, Maronite, Protestant, Catholic) or, in one instance, Jewish. Moreover, in *Riḥlat* this cosmopolitan aspect of the city is evoked with a certain nostalgia for a past of co-existence, now obliterated by the violence of the war.

Obviously all these characters could be considered strangers in Beirut, which is a place where, according to Khūrī's texts, people get stuck and do not belong. In *Riḥlat* we read that 'the real story is the one about those who couldn't escape' (Khūrī 1989: 25/*20*) from the war and the city, although most have originally come from outside. This is important since it is a concept which the author obviously develops in order to undermine the fierce tribal, racial, sectarian and ideological divisions which maybe did not cause, but definitely aggravated the Lebanese Civil War. This is another reason why the concept of the stranger is regarded with sympathy, if not idealized, in Khūrī's works: it is Widād, one of the most obvious strangers in *Mamlakat*, who gives the novel its title: the white Circassian who movingly sings the 'Hymn of the Stranger' claims that the 'kingdom of strangers' is what the archetypal stranger, Christ, intended to build, that is a country for the deprived, the victims, the poor, the rejected (like himself).

In his novel *Yālū* (2002), Khūrī focuses on a family belonging to the Syriac Orthodox Church who live in Beirut: Yālū (the protagonist's nickname) criticizes his grandfather's rejection of his daughter's husband on the basis that this is Arab and not Syriac (Khūrī 2002: 302). The novel (in which the massacres of Armenians and Syriacs at the hands of the Ottoman Turks and Kurds are mentioned, along with the latter's suffering under the Turkish Republic) makes it clear that Lebanon and the wider Middle Eastern region is inhabited by different peoples whose culture is often heterogeneous. The main characters in the novel, who are Syriac, are culturally polychromatic: it is not incidental that the character of Yālū's grandfather (Father Afrām), who is the one who laments the demise of the Syriac language and seems very protective of his Syriac roots, was raised by Muslim Kurds and is able to speak Syriac, Kurdish and Arabic. The issue of language is central in Khūrī's works: Yālū's mother, Ghābī, does not share her father's anxieties regarding the disappearance of the ancient Syriac language – she depicts the assimilation of their mother tongue into spoken Lebanese Arabic as the blossoming of a rose (Khūrī 2002: 289). The same concept of peaceful assimilation is reiterated when Yālū, having become disillusioned with the Civil War,[73] recalls with sadness his mother's words echoing his grandfather's ideas: the Syriacs are like the leaven which penetrates the dough to become bread – this is why they do not have to fight (Khūrī 2002: 154). Another recurrent feature of his novels is the fact that characters are given more than one name: this could point at the characters' crisis of identity but also at their rich and heterogeneous culture.

There are other intertextual connections in Khūrī's texts as many other literary figures, not necessarily of the Arab past, are mentioned. Contemporary Arab writers such as the Palestinian poet Maḥmūd Darwīsh (b. 1941), the Jordanian Ghālib Halasā (1932–1989) and Jabrā are mentioned along with Rushdie and the Russian Formalist Vladimir Propp among others. We should notice in passing that, unlike Western modernist writers who tended to refer to an illustrious literary past (the classics), authors like Khūrī refer to their contemporary colleagues too. However, many of these references are not as significantly integrated into the overall structure of the novels as those analysed earlier: in other words, they do not significantly expand the meaning of the text. These are meant to be passing references, which the narrators occasionally make to reinforce their point, and the author employs them to build up a certain picture of a character or evoke familiar ideas and concepts for the readers.[74] For instance, when *Mamlakat*'s narrator voices the Palestinians' sense of loss, he refers to Darwīsh's poetry, familiar to most Palestinians (Khūrī 1993: 34–5/*27–8*).[75] When, in *Bāb*, Khalīl says that he wants to bring his unconscious friend back to life, he recites verses from other familiar texts as diverse as the lyrics of Fayrūz's songs, Aḥmad Shawqī's verses and the beginning of *Sūrat al-nās* (Khūrī 1998: 51). The difference between these quotations and those studied earlier from Imr'ū-'l-Qays is a qualitative one: the latter expand a theme of *Mamlakat*, the former do not inform the main themes of *Bāb*, but merely contribute to the cultural profile of the characters.

A curious example of another reference to a contemporary author is found in Barrāda's *al-Ḍaw'*. In this novel, Fāṭima is inspired by the heroine of the French novelist Jacques Laurent's novel *Les dimanches de Mademoiselle Beaunon* (1982). This is a more subtle reference than the passing mention of a writer or an extract from his or her work, because the fictional material of another text is partly re-worked and re-fictionalized.[76] However, ultimately, this reference too is only significant to the characterization of Fāṭima, and does not bear upon the overall structure of the novel. It lacks the extensive re-working of referential texts observed earlier in our discussions of Gnosticism in al-Kharrāṭ's Trilogy, or religious texts in Khūrī's *Mamlakat*.[77]

In conclusion, Khūrī's approach to the Arabic literary heritage is different to al-Kharrāṭ's. The Lebanese author, as we have already stated, is not concerned about reviving ancient narrative techniques. Nevertheless, he is aware that he too is heir to the Arabic 'literary history [which goes] from Imrū'-'l-Qays to al-Sayyāb' (Khūrī 1999: 14). In other words, Khūrī and al-Kharrāṭ, despite producing two kinds of fiction which could hardly be more different, have what Eliot defined in his essay 'Tradition and the Individual Talent' as 'historical sense'. But apart from being aware of their cultural belonging to the Arabic heritage, they are also committed to using their fiction lessons learned elsewhere: for example, from Western and other literatures,[78] from the Arabic popular and folk tradition, and from within other disciplines (poetry, music, journalism).

We can already point to one of the possible effects achieved by the use of intertextual references in the fiction of Khūrī and al-Kharrāṭ. A conscious use of intertextual connections in their novels serves the literary function of employing images in order to expand ideas and concepts (cf. the use of the image of Eve in al-Kharrāṭ's *Rāma* Trilogy and that of Christ in Khūrī's *Mamlakat*). It also indicates the authors' consciousness of the fact that all their novels are somehow naturally connected to the texts of their cultural past (and also to other literatures). The allusions to other texts and writers are not limited to this artistic goal and we will see in the next chapter how they play an important role within the self-referential discussions of fiction which are presented in some of the novels under discussion.

We will end this chapter, as we started it, with a reference to Calvino's *If On A Winter's Night a Traveller*. Published the same year as *Rāma*, this novel could also be regarded as a literary exercise (reminiscent of Raymond Queneau's *Exercices de style*, 1947) in reproducing various styles and registers (the beginnings of ten different novels). In *Rāma* and his other novels, al-Kharrāṭ too reproduces different styles and registers, and so, in a different way, does Khūrī. Surely, as Calvino tells us, one of the reasons for this mixture of different languages and styles is mere entertainment. The reader is also supposed to enjoy this virtuoso exercise while reading the novel. As for the question of whether these exercises are carried out purely for their own sake in the novels of Khūrī and al-Kharrāṭ, we hope to have given at least a partial answer to this in the present chapter.

5

METAFICTION

This chapter will analyse the extent to which the novels under scrutiny here deal with fiction itself (and more generally with the acts of writing and reading), highlighting the purpose and effects of such a phenomenon.

This autoreferential element (metafiction) is linked to the foregoing analysis of both polyphony and intertextuality through the figure of the author. The author disappears, or at least weakens his position, in an ideal polyphonic novel where his point of view seems to be absent or is made equal to that of various other characters. In addition, according to Barthes, the intertextual nature of the novel confines the author to the mere function of organizer of somebody else's texts.[1] With metafictional experiments, the figure of the author is to be clearly reinstalled within the text. Using the logic of paradox, Brian McHale explains how modernist writers in the West tried to conceal the author in their texts through different devices, only to have their readers increasingly thinking of 'the strategist' behind such devices (such as the dialogue-dominated text, free indirect discourse, first person narration, the interior monologue, the montage text).[2] On the other hand, according to McHale, postmodernist writers indulging in self-advertisement in their texts achieve self-effacement more successfully: again, Barthes claims that the author is not merely absent from his or her text (as the modernists wished it to be), he or she is simply dead (McHale 1987: 199–200).[3]

As noted in the previous chapter, one of the effects of introducing extracts from other texts in fiction is to increase the reader's awareness of the novel as an artefact: the readers are invited to reflect on literature itself rather than the external world which it is supposed to portray. This effect is also and more directly achieved by other metafictional devices such as more or less explicit discourses on fiction which are included in the novel itself. There are two main methods by which the novelists under discussion here introduce this self-reflexive element into their novels:

1 The writer/reader *topos*. At least one of the novel's characters is involved in the act of writing and/or reading (e.g. in al-Takarlī's *al-Masarrāt*, the protagonist Tawfīq writes his own diary, he is an avid reader of fiction and, more importantly, he reflects on both activities; similarly, in Barrāda's *al-Ḍawʾ* and in Khūrī's *Yālū*, the protagonists engage with the activity of writing).

2 The authorial persona. This character implicitly promotes, or explicitly provides reflections on, narrating/writing/storytelling within the fictional text (e.g. the character of the narrator in most of Khūrī's novels). It is clear that the dividing line between these first two categories can quite easily become blurred. The crucial distinction is that the character of the narrator in method 2 is a writer (as in some of Khūrī's novels; al-Takarlī's Tawfīq, on the other hand, is not a writer).

These self-referred reflections can also be expressed in an overt way (e.g. through the introduction of the 'narrators' narrator' and his arguments with the implied author in Barrāda's *Lu*ᶜ*bat*).

Khūrī is undoubtedly one of the Arab authors most involved in using metafictional techniques.[4] In his novels the stress is often on ways of writing and storytelling[5]: up to *Yālū*, Khūrī has been the champion of what we have defined as method 2. In fact, this self-referential discourse is usually expressed in his novels (e.g. in *Riḥlat* and *Mamlakat*) by the character of the narrator who, like Khūrī himself, carries out field-work and interviews many people in order to write his fiction. In the acknowledgements which appear at the end of *Bāb* he writes that the novel would not have been possible without the contribution of women and men from the refugee camps of Lebanon who 'opened the door of their stories' to him (Khūrī 1998: 528). A good example of Khūrī's metafiction is the novel *Mamlakat*. First of all, in this work Khūrī shows himself to be aware of the intertextual connections which we have identified in the previous chapter. *Mamlakat* can be seen as a text which includes a novel and also passages related to literary criticism. For example, al-Kharrāṭ's stressing in *Rāma* that everything has already been written (see earlier, beginning of Chapter 4) is here echoed by the narrator who reports his imaginary encounter with Christ at the Dead Sea:

'[I'm] just the one writing this story.'
Jesus turned to look. The water was up to His knees, as He was standing as though listening to mysterious voices we couldn't hear.
He turned and asked: 'What story?'
'Your story, my Master,' I said.
'But it is written,' He said.
'I am writing it because it is written,' I said. 'We always write what has been written. If it were not written, we would not write it.'
And a man [from] there asked Him, 'Are you the Messiah?'
'It is as you say,' He answered. He didn't say He was. He let them say it. He said only what had already been said before.

(Khūrī 1993: 29–30/*23*)

It is worth noting how in this passage the character of Khūrī's novel 'enters' the Gospel text and interacts with Christ (the same thing does not happen with al-Kharrāṭ because the character Mīkhāʾīl tends to witness his visions of various divine figures more passively or ecstatically). In *Mamlakat*, the acts of writing and narrating are central to what the characters think and discuss. The character of the narrator gives the reader much food for thought as to how and why stories are narrated, and the passage we have just quoted is only one of the many possible examples. Khūrī's narrator addresses many asides to his readers such as 'I forgot to tell you that' (Khūrī 1993: 10/*8*). In *Mamlakat*, the question 'What am I writing?' occurs throughout the text (Khūrī 1993: 12/*9*, 21/*16*, 37/*29 passim*). To repeat the same passage at the start of every section, as happens with the simple question in *Mamlakat*, 'is another method of making the reader aware of the narrative presence and the process of telling a story' as Meyer rightly points out (Meyer 2001: 253).[6] The same characteristic is more difficult to ignore in *Riḥlat* where nearly a whole page is repeated as an opening formula for most chapters (from the 2nd to the 6th). The Brechtian effect of the passage is enriched by the narrator's admission to being unreliable: 'I recall Alice's words and try to imagine what happened, but I keep finding holes. All stories are full of holes. We no longer know how to tell stories' (Khūrī 1989: 12/*7*, 24/*19*, 46/*43*, 88/*83*, 199/*185*). Obviously, the reader is invited to reflect on how fiction is composed, how a writer works: trying to imagine what happened is different from telling what happened, telling the truth.

The many asides addressed to the reader work in the same fashion (apart from adding an ironic tinge): they establish the narrator as unreliable (a strategy familiar to Western modernists) and this has significant implications for the reader.[7] Khūrī makes us ponder on how fiction works but this *mise en abîme* of his own craft underlines that the narrator is fallible: we are not dealing with the authoritative omniscient narrator of *realistic* fiction, the one who tells us: 'this is what happened'. To shed more light on this phenomenon Khūrī's method will be compared to the asides to the reader found in the first chapter of al-Takarlī's *al-Masarrāt*. The following is the most important one: 'These pages, the preceding ones and those that follow, are an attempt to discover the wrongs we have done in our personal lives, which have shackled us, and those which we have not done, which have shackled us more' (al-Takarlī 1998: 104; Cobham 2004: 31).[8] Despite the fact that this aside is self-reflexive, it is fundamentally different from those of Khūrī's narrator. In the first chapter of al-Takarlī's novel, the narrator directly addresses the reader but he does it from his privileged, omniscient position. As in the passage quoted earlier, he tells us what the book is about, what he is doing: the reader is apparently told what to expect from the pages he is reading by an authoritative voice (obviously, the reader has to understand what such a voice means and this might not be as easy as it seems: an authoritative voice can be deliberately obscure).[9] In Khūrī's novels such a voice is generally undermined: the reader is dealing with a subversion of the traditional narrator. It is as if Shklovsky's formalist concept of *defamiliarization*[10] is here applied to the figure of the narrator. The narrating voice cannot be considered as a given which is perceived automatically (hence, ignored), because it is represented in an unfamiliar way: it questions itself, contradicts itself or dwells on what it is doing. The American novelist Ronald Sukenik underlines how the inclusion of the authorial character in a work of fiction should terminate that 'illusion of reality' so admired by Henry James and force the reader 'to recognize the reality of the reading situation as the writer points to the reality of the writing situation' (Sukenik quoted in McHale 1987: 198). What is generally aimed at here is the replacement of a passive and escapist reading with a much more active and creative one. As Frank Kermode states in reviewing a novel by Rose Tremain:

> Good novelists claim as a traditional entitlement that their readers should make a substantial contribution to their enterprises. If what they are doing calls from them a large exercise of imagination, displaying the full powers of their minds in a happy delineation of the varieties of human nature – then we must accept that the demand their performances make on us is one of the criteria by which we distinguish the real thing from the easy substitute.
>
> (Kermode 1992: 14)[11]

What are the devices an author has at his or her disposal to stimulate such a contribution from the reader? Is method 2 on the list proposed earlier the only or most efficient method? The effect of disorienting the readers and stimulating them to take on a more creative role is also achieved in *al-Masarrāt* by a different method. In *al-Masarrāt* it is based on the manipulation of narrative voices and techniques and the writer/reader *topos* (method 1). Al-Takarlī's narrator, unlike Khūrī's, will never say: 'Beware, reader, I am telling you a story' or 'I am not sure what I am writing about'. His method is probably more traditional, less overt, but at the same time more subtle and effective. Obviously, the moment the narrator states that he does not remember clearly what happened, that he recognizes that his story is 'full of holes' (as in *Riḥlat*), that he is reporting a story narrated by someone whose reliability he himself questions (as Khalīl does with Yūnis and most of his sources in *Bāb*), the reader's role becomes much more important: he or she is forced to be creative, to reflect on and make sense of the story. However, the same thing happens in al-Takarlī's *al-Masarrāt*. Tawfīq's contradictory feelings about the importance of writing and reading and, perhaps more importantly, the final metaphorical riddle[12] he has to be able to interpret prompts the reader's 'contribution to making the text' (as Cobham explains, Cobham 2004: 25) more implicitly, but perhaps more effectively, than Khūrī's overt techniques (referred to as method 2). Maybe what the reader of postmodernist fiction is asked to do in an overt way had already been understood by Tawfīq, the reader of non-metafictional twentieth and nineteenth century fiction.[13] He writes in his diary:

> It's not only what's written that's important. You have to read what's not written as well, and that's different from reading between the lines, as they say. [. . .] I think reading what's not written means reading another writing which isn't there
>
> (al-Takarlī 1998: 108; Cobham 2004: 33)

Saleem Sinai, the narrator of Salman Rushdie's *Midnight's Children* (a novel with the authorial persona of method 2, similar in some aspects to Khūrī's works), says that he is writing his story because he wants to end up meaning something (Rushdie 1981: 9). Similarly, you read 'to end up meaning something', al-Takarlī implicitly tells us.

In theory an unreliable narrator is better placed than an authoritative one to challenge us to reflect on what we are reading. But appearances can be deceptive. Aghacy claims that Khūrī's narrator in *Riḥlat*, despite hiding himself behind 'an "I don't know" attitude [. . .] dominates the narrative and dictates it' (Aghacy 1996: 172). As shown earlier, this criticism is unfair as far as *Riḥlat* is concerned. Nevertheless, the point made by Aghacy is valid: assuming an 'I don't know' attitude does not necessarily mean that the writer's ideology is not imposed. At the same time, a seemingly assertive and authoritative tone from an omniscient voice can still draw the reader's attention to metafictional issues. As far as these are concerned, Khūrī is certainly also willing to push his readers to reflect on the nature of fiction, and by extension, on the ways in which stories, and histories, are constructed. It could be argued that he spells out these concerns in a straightforward fashion. It could also be argued that his style is less sophisticated and successful than al-Takarlī's, but Aghacy misses the point when she claims that Khūrī is guilty of '[sliding] into metafiction' (Aghacy 1996: 171). Here, Aghacy considers metafiction as a shortcoming, failing to understand that the authors she quotes to back up her point are not likely to share her disapproval of such self-referential writing (even Meyer, who supports Aghacy's critical reading – Meyer 2001: 209 – fails to understand this). Quoting Linda Hutcheon, Seymour Chatman and Peter Currie, Aghacy affirms: 'The novel [. . .] "begins to reflect upon [its] own genesis and growth," and the narrative begins to expose "its own condition of artifice," referring to its own "devices and strategies"' (Aghacy 1996: 171). These are precisely the effects Khūrī and others are seeking to achieve in their writing.[14] However, even if metafiction were regarded as a negative element in contemporary fiction and its consequences were not understood by Khūrī, the strength of Aghacy's discourse remains in doubt. She should either attack Khūrī for being too focused on the form of his novel, betraying his 'self-effacement' (as Meyer writes in support of Aghacy's point, Meyer 2001: 209) or attack him for being too ideologically driven ('the narrator's ideology is everywhere [. . .] [he] dominates the narrative and dictates it', Aghacy 1996: 172).

Aghacy's analysis of Khūrī's metafiction is not based on enough evidence; the latter's writing is, however, not always successful. For instance, the many self-reflective asides voiced by the unreliable narrator of *Bāb*, Khalīl, eventually convey a didactic tone which is the opposite of disorienting and stimulating to the reader. This negative feature is absent from Khūrī's shorter novels such as *Mamlakat* and especially *Riḥlat* where the asides are less frequent and the unreliability of the narrator is more successful in frustrating our expectations. But in *Bāb* the reader seems to be told what the novel is and what to expect from all its stories: its metafictional implications too are spelled out. Some of the many possible examples: Khalīl makes clear from the beginning of the novel that, in order to put together Yūnis's story, he has had to gather details from the latter's real words and the ones Khalīl has imagined (Khūrī 1998: 34/*28*; he is therefore unreliable and what he says might be untrue); he claims to be unable to focus on one story only and jumps from one to another (Khūrī 1998: 35/*29*; this is a comment on his narrating style); on the importance of remembering and forgetting, Khalīl says to Yūnis: 'what we're doing now, you and I, is [...] [to] remember in order to forget' (Khūrī 1998: 160/*149–50*). This last comment very much spells out to the reader what *Bāb* is trying to achieve. The problem with these self-referential passages is the same as the one observed earlier about Khalīl's style: they explain what some of the themes are without really dramatizing them. If the many stories narrated do indeed provide such a dramatization (drawing the reader into an imaginative understanding of the importance of memory and forgetfulness for Palestinians, for example), then Khūrī does not need to spell out these concepts so overtly: he is more successful when he relates them to the stories in an inventive and less didactic way. A novel in which Khūrī provides a more successful fictional framework for his metafictional discourse will now be analysed at length.

Yālū, published in 2002, represents a turning point in Khūrī's fictional production.[15] This novel, despite presenting most of the characteristic features of his writing,[16] is the first in which the key metafictional character of the narrator/writer (that of Yālū) is not played by an authorial persona but by somebody extraneous to the activity of writing, somebody who does not even intend to write but is eventually forced to. In typical metafictional fashion, the third person narrator comments on Yālū's inability to write as follows:

> Had Yālū been a poet, he would have written that he had drowned in a well of words, had embraced the night and his ink had become blacker than the night.
>
> Had he been a novelist, he would have written his memories all in the same tone, calling them '[c]Ayn Ward'. He would have begun his story with the young man that his grandfather once was [...]
>
> Had he been a *ḥakawātī*, he would have sat in the prison and told stories about how he had fought like no other, and how he was bold and brave [...]
>
> Had he been.
>
> But he wasn't.
>
> Yālū was a young man who was trying to read into the whiteness of the page his story which he didn't know how to tell, his language which he didn't know how to write, his memory which he didn't know how to interrogate.
>
> (Khūrī 2002: 177)

Yālū is neither the authorial persona, nor does he voice his intentions (and what might well be Khūrī's own concerns and ideas) as clearly and openly as Khalīl often does in *Bāb*. In fact, in *Yālū* there is more distance between the author and the main character. Khūrī is presumably not the macho yet awkward and puritanical character that Yālū is, who has always struggled to express himself.[17] If the character of the writer is replaced in *Bāb* by Khalīl, *Yālū* constitutes a step further in Khūrī's attempt at doing away with the authorial persona as a sort of medium through which other consciousnesses are presented to the reader.

In order to fully appreciate *Yālū* as a metafictional text which portrays a man gaining self-awareness through writing, it is appropriate to focus on the shifts in the narrative, which occur less randomly here than in Khūrī's other texts. One of the most noticeable differences between this novel and the preceding ones is that this begins with a third person and not a first person narrative. The lengthy first two chapters of the novel (Khūrī 2002: 9–118; 119–78) introduce the main characters through a third person narrative which is, however, mainly focused on Yālū's perceptions of events and people (while in novels like *Bāb*, *Mamlakat* and *Riḥlat* we have a first person narrative).[18] Subsequently a first person narrative of the protagonist's life (the actual confessions which Yālū is ordered by the police to write in prison) is added. As a consequence of this narrative method the novel never attempts to offer an objective or judgmental point of view.

The reader meets Yālū as he is being interrogated in a police station. The reasons behind his arrest and more general information about his life are gradually revealed: he was born into a family whose oldest living member, Yālū's grandfather, is a priest in the Syriac Orthodox Church. A series of flashbacks, either narrated in the third person or written by Yālū himself in prison, depict his childhood, which was spent with his mother (Ghābriyāl, usually called Ghābī) and his grandfather priest (Hābīl Jibrāʾīl Abyaḍ, usually called Father *-al-Kūhnū*, in Syriac-Afrām); Yālū's participation in the Lebanese Civil War; his subsequent migration to France; his return to Lebanon, thanks to solicitor and arms dealer Mīshāl Sallūm; his affair with Sallūm's wife, Randa; his work as a night watchman in Sallūm's villa in Ballūna (close to Beirut); the way he turns into a petty thief and rapist; and, finally, how he falls in love with one of his victims, Shīrīn. The latter has reported him to the police and accused him of raping and stalking her, which is why he is being interrogated at the beginning of the novel.

In the earlier part of the novel, Yālū emerges as a character who has little inclination to reflect on the situations in which he finds himself. He seems overwhelmed by them and assumes a largely passive attitude towards external challenges. Withdrawn, obsessed by details and unable to empathize with others' points of view, Yālū falls victim to his own unorthodox and naïve behaviour (for example, he foolishly tries to impress Shīrīn, whose more modern outlook is distant from his traditional way of thinking, by behaving like the hero of one of the Egyptian movies he admires). By presenting his thoughts and feelings as they are, however, and not mediated through an omniscient or judgmental narrator, the text helps its readers relate to Yālū, possibly sympathize with him or possibly even dislike him. On the other hand, later on in the novel, the activity of writing will eventually lead Yālū to comprehend better the causes of the misunderstandings between himself and others.

Starting with the third chapter (Khūrī 2002: 179–87), most of the remaining chapters of the novel are taken from the confessions Yālū himself has been forced to write in prison (these are alternated with chapters narrated in the third person, more similar to the first two).[19] In fact, after he has failed to defend himself from the accusations of having raped and stalked Shīrīn, the police force him to write the story of his life as a kind of confession of his crimes, those which he has committed and, especially, those which he has not committed. It becomes clear that Yālū has indeed been guilty of criminal activities while working as a night watchman at Mīshāl Sallūm's villa,[20] but after being tortured he agrees to confess to having worked for a terrorist group which had planted bombs in Beirut, and this is clearly untrue. Thanks to writing and the reflection which writing initiates in his mind, however, Yālū becomes aware not only of his past but also of his present circumstances, and he begins to resist the police attempts to make him a scapegoat. He starts questioning the police version of the facts and also that of the other characters involved (Shīrīn and her fiancé Imīl).

As he struggles to write the story of his life, he starts reflecting on his past more critically and imaginatively, remembering telling details, asking himself uncomfortable questions. As a consequence, Yālū constructs his own narrative of obscure episodes in the lives of his relatives. For instance, the vagueness surrounding aspects of his grandfather's life is eventually dispelled by Yālū's linear narrative, which sharply contrasts with Khūrī's usual fragmented style (Khūrī 2002: 352–60).[21] Such a switch in style can be interpreted in contrasting ways. The unusually orderly passage could be seen as an ironic dramatization of a writer's need to impose a clear narrative through which he or she can make sense of the past. On the other hand, this linear narrative could also be seen as a superfluous element which jars with the surrounding text, as if Khūrī eventually gave in to a more conventional form of expression in order to shed light on fragmented and obscure parts of the narrative. The following passage is more in line with Khūrī's convictions about writing, as it shows how Yālū learns that words can sometimes lead their writer to follow their logic, rather than his own:

> war taught Yālū to believe his eyes and not the words' eyes, and he would only become reconciled with words in prison, when the police interrogator would force him to write the story of his whole life, from beginning to end, several times. Then he would discover that his grandfather had been right, that words, when written, look at their author and conduct a dialogue with him and impose on him what he has to write.
>
> (Khūrī 2002: 93)

There is another turning point in Yālū's learning process which occurs later in the novel, when he realizes that what he has written so far will not convince anyone, let alone satisfy the authorities. He therefore engages in two acts of rebellion: he protests his innocence for the first time and, more importantly, new ideas come to him which he likes and, again for the first time, he sets out to write them down of his own free will (Khūrī 2002: 258).

Writing is a gradual and painful process which is hardly ever idealized by Khūrī. It can be a double edged sword: at the end of the first chapter Yālū compares himself to a squid which uses its ink to try to hide from its enemies but at the same time is aware that, if it fails to do so, it will end up being fried in its own ink (Khūrī 2002: 112–13). Apart from the ironic image of the dangerous-living writer/squid, it is not incidental that the activity of writing is coupled with the (graphically described) physical tortures Yālū suffers at the hands of the police;[22] in other words, despite the many differences between the two characters, he is, like Mitya Karamazov, 'a soul that has suffered and has become conscious of its humanity' (Dostoevsky 1881: 694). Yālū, unlike Mitya, becomes aware of his humanity through the 'torture' of writing.

While both *The Brothers Karamazov* and *Yālū* can be said to deal with 'a miscarriage of justice', in the latter such a miscarriage is blatant. In his depiction of the workings of the legal system in Sicily (and more generally in the whole of Italy), Leonardo Sciascia (1921–1989) suggests that the system can so easily become unjust that one should be sceptical about its ever delivering justice. In the novel *Equal Danger* (1971; originally entitled *Il contesto. Una parodia*, set in an imaginary country), the legal system is so badly run, even when not completely in the hands of corrupt individuals, that one of its victims is forced to ask: 'What does it mean to be innocent when you get caught in the wheels of the system?' He then concludes that, because of the way the system works, the people who get caught in it could all be innocent (Sciascia 1971: 18). Sciascia thus focuses on the faults of a system which often punishes the vulnerable and leaves the powerful untouched. The parallel to Yālū is easily drawn despite the many clear differences[23]: Khūrī does not focus on Yālū's faults as much as on those of the judiciary for, however guilty Yālū is, he does not deserve the systematic torture he is forced to undergo. It seems that, as in the passage from Sciascia's novel referred to earlier, whether the accused is guilty or innocent is almost irrelevant because of how the law works. It is not incidental that Yālū's crimes are depicted through his own consciousness and perception (or, earlier in the novel, lack of consciousness and perception).[24]

Even if *Yālū* implies a discourse on the abuse of power which is similar to that promoted by Sciascia, Khūrī's main discourse in this novel remains focused on the transformation of an individual's consciousness. The focus on this internal change is one of the differences which separate Yālū's characterization from that of Khūrī's other protagonists. Khalīl's questioning attitude is a given in *Bāb*. Indeed, it is his main characteristic, and it is part of his personality from the very beginning of the novel. At times, it seems that he is speaking *ex cathedra*, as it were. This is never the case with Yālū even if Khūrī's voice increasingly emerges in what Yālū is writing.[25] However, even if Yālū's voice eventually comes to resemble his creator's and this can be seen as an implausible development, we are at least shown the process through which Yālū gradually assumes this voice, which here works as Yālū's inner voice of consciousness.[26] In other words, a critical, questioning and more self-aware voice is not a given, it is something the character acquires gradually, something he has to strive for. The tone and style of the third person narrator (with Khūrī's characteristic lyrical moments and switching of topics through the association of ideas) gradually subsumes and merges with Yālū's own voice: what he writes at the end is different from what he wrote at the beginning of his ordeal with pen and paper. It resembles the free indirect discourse in which the character's language mixes with the author's.[27] As noted earlier, the switches in the narrative methods are significant in this novel. They are the formal outcome of the split in Yālū's personality which occurs when he is subjected to torture. This split is a survival technique: Yālū is said to abandon his body to his torturers and watch the scenes of torture from the outside. In other words, he is trying to put a distance between himself and the unbearable physical pain.

Reflecting this split in Yālū, the narration is split into the first person and the third person narratives. Starting from the ninth chapter, the protagonist is both Dānyāl (Yālū's full name), the body which is writing the story of his life, and Yālū, the soul which is dying. Such a separation of Yālū's body and soul, as well as dramatizing the distance Yālū requires to write about himself, also reinforces the depiction of Yālū as a sort of contemporary Christ (we have seen earlier how Khūrī relies on a similar allusion in *Mamlakat*). Yālū dies, at least spiritually (he loses all hopes for a better future), when his soul leaves his body but, unlike Christ, his body and soul are not reunited and therefore he is not resurrected. Yālū recalls being told as a child that his family is like the Holy Trinity: his grandfather Afrām is the Father, he is the Son and his mother Ghābī is the Holy Ghost. However, the grandfather, who is generally angered and disappointed by him, starts calling him Yālū instead of Barrū ('son' in Syriac; Khūrī 2002: 38). It is as if injustice and violence deprive this present day Middle Eastern Christ of the divine possibility of resurrection: Yālū/Christ remains all too human in his suffering and ultimate demise.[28] The novel is cyclical in more ways than one. Above all, the fact that Yālū's potential for resurrection is ultimately wiped out by the sheer violence of the police is an echo of the novel's opening quotation of Maḥmūd Darwīsh's verses:

> As the Messiah walked on the lake
> I walked in my vision
> But I came down from the cross
> Because I'm afraid of heights
> And I don't preach the Resurrection
> (Darwīsh quoted in
> Khūrī 2002: 7)[29]

Yālū's increasing self-awareness, like that of the protagonists of al-Takarlī's novels, is an intellectual triumph and a victory *per se*. The birth of a new Yālū (i.e. the reunion between body and soul) will remain hypothetical and will never materialize in the course of the novel. The finale of *Yālū* is unmistakably bitter and gloomy: the protagonist is left asking for more paper on which he now desperately wants to write his mother's story. He concedes, however, that in order to write a new, better story for his mother he needs to imagine a different finale (the actual ending of Ghābī's life is grim and Yālū is well aware of this), but he is unable to imagine any alternative.[30]

If Khūrī expands the metafictional content in *Yālū* through a more efficient use of fictional tropes as compared to the sometimes dry formulations of *Bāb*, which position do *Mamlakat*'s overtly metafictional passages occupy? At times metafiction seems to make *Mamlakat* more like 'a reflective essay than a novel' (Meyer 2001: 113). Khūrī's direct observations on other writers' works (like Rushdie's, for instance) or his criticism of magical realism are a case in point. The overall structure of the novel can, however, be seen to justify these vagaries of literary discussion. In fact, what the narrator says about Rushdie at the end of the novel can be applied to himself as well: Rushdie has become the character of one of his novels when Khomeini's *fatwa* is issued (Khūrī 1993: 102/*83*). Likewise, in *Mamlakat* Khūrī sometimes turns into the character of his narrator: since the very structure of the novel is based on the narrator's freedom to narrate whatever crosses his mind, making references to secondary stories like a person talking informally, he can presumably also tell his readers about his ideas on literature and his encounters with writers. Thus, the form imposed by the writer on his narrative allows him even to include literary criticism in his fiction (it has to be said that Khūrī's fictionalized criticism is at times ironic). Obviously in a novel like *Yālū* the author does not have the same freedom, which is why *Yālū* has to be considered a more engaging metafictional text, where Khūrī displays more discipline and inventiveness.

Another important implication of the strategy of the unreliable narrator (on which Khūrī relies in all his novels)[31] is the questioning of the way history is written: this is one of the main preoccupations of contemporary, so-called postmodernist writing throughout the world (Hutcheon 1989: 62–92).[32] To draw another parallel between Khūrī and Salman Rushdie has now become inevitable. In typical postmodernist fashion, the parallel between these writers has been suggested by Khūrī himself: in *Mamlakat*, the authorial persona tells about his meeting Rushdie and adds his observations about him and his work (Khūrī 1993: 96–8/*78–80*). In Rushdie's *Midnight's Children* the writer/reader relationship is fictionalized in the Saleem/Padma relationship. Through the depiction of such a relationship, Rushdie makes us reflect on how his text is created, and his ambitions as an author of fiction are exposed. This depiction is highly ironic and narrated with much gusto: at times Padma, the amateur reader, complains about the way Saleem writes his story, Saleem has to explain why he chooses to write the way he does, but sometimes it is Padma who helps him to get back on track and move his story on in a more conventional fashion. Writing is ironically depicted as a sort of compromise between the high (but also pretentious) ambitions of the professional writer and the more basic requirements (but also the common sense) of the common reader. Do Khūrī's narrators operate in the same way as Rushdie's? The irony and humour with which the relationship between Saleem and Padma, and most situations in Rushdie's novel, are related are usually missing in Khūrī's *Bāb*, where the narrator on the whole takes himself very seriously. Khūrī's *Riḥlat*, however, is more ironic and humorous, and closer in tone to Rushdie's works.[33]

It is possible to draw other parallels between Rushdie's novels and Khūrī's. The verses by Ibn ᶜArabī which open *Riḥlat* ('A face is only one, yet if you multiply the mirrors, it is multiple', which, we have seen earlier, can be considered as the author's declaration of polyphonic intent) could be applied to historiography, or historical truths as they are conceived of in *Bāb*: they could be nothing more than the version of history according to a particular historian. This concept, considered by many to be typical of postmodern literature (cf. Hutcheon 1989: 47–92), is fundamental in *Midnight's Children* as well as in *Bāb*, where Khūrī's narrator introduces his critical view of a particular official version of Palestinian history. More than that, the author confronts the question of how history is interpreted and re-interpreted to suit a particular individual or faction, as is evident in the hypothetical dialogue between Khalīl and Yūnis. Hutcheon, in a passage describing postmodern novels (especially *Midnight's Children*), writes:

> The narrativization of past events is not hidden; the events no longer seem to speak for themselves but are shown to be consciously composed into a narrative, whose constructed – not found – order is imposed upon them, often overtly by the narrating figure. The process of making stories out of chronicles, of constructing plots out of sequences, is what postmodern fiction underlines. This does not in any way deny the existence of the past real, but it focuses attention on the act of imposing order on the past, of encoding strategies of meaning-making through representation.
>
> (Hutcheon 1989: 67)

In *Mamlakat*, the victims of political and military defeats are said to tell each other stories which they believe to be true, but truth, the official version at least, somehow eludes them because it belongs to the victors (the Israelis). Accordingly, Maryam (Mary in the English translation of the novel), one of the main characters of the novel and one of the women the narrator has loved, says to the narrator: 'You believe your own stories, and you forget the truth' (Khūrī 1993: 17/*14*). This bitter remark is expanded further in *Bāb*, which deals more extensively with the Palestinian odyssey. Khalīl, for example, offers two endings of ᶜAdnān's story. First he narrates what seems to be the standard version of the story (Khūrī 1998: 136–7/*127–8*): ᶜAdnān, one of Yūnis's friends, is the Palestinian fighter at first defiant of Israeli institutions, then humiliated and destroyed by years of prison. Yūnis refuses to see his friend after it is clear he is sliding into madness. It is said that Yūnis intends to kill him but eventually the disgraced hero ends up in a mental hospital. Khalīl then narrates an ending he considers much better: Yūnis (referred to in the third person) kills ᶜAdnān, proclaiming him 'a martyr', and a memorable funeral procession accompanies him to his grave.

This metafictional episode draws the reader's attention to how a writer/narrator can easily falsify reality according to his or her wishes. This tale with two endings is all the more significant because it is placed in a narrative where stories are told and retold according to different versions and the reader is constantly left wondering which might be the most reliable story. With ᶜAdnān's story it is clear which version is dictated by the narrator's wishes, whereas Khalīl rearranges other tales in order to expose how a version of a story (History) might turn out to be the canonical version because it is the one its narrators prefer. There are many other examples of more than one version of events being told, or instances where Khalīl takes advantage of his monopoly on Yūnis's (and anybody else's) version of reality to question it, to insinuate doubts into the reader's mind.

For example, the story of ᶜAzīz Ayyūb, the guardian of the mosque, graveyard and Christ's-thorn tree of al-Ghābisiyya (one of the villages abandoned after the *nakba*) is told and retold throughout the second part of the novel. When ᶜAzīz is found dead at the foot of the Christ's-thorn, a rope tied around his neck, he is at first believed to have committed suicide but then the *shaykh* of a neighbouring village officially proclaims him a martyr gratuitously assassinated by the Israelis. Consequently, ᶜAzīz becomes a venerated saint figure with a shrine visited by devotees (Khūrī 1998: 342/*325*). Umm Ḥasan (one of the narrators of the story), who was not present when ᶜAzīz was found dead, comes up with her own version of the story which is a compromise between the two other versions (suicide, murder): ᶜAzīz, who was living alone, abandoned by his wife and children, went mad and decided to kill himself but, thanks to divine intervention and a weak tree branch, fell from the tree and died, thus avoiding sinning and deserving his sainthood ('the tree proclaimed him a saint', Khūrī 1998: 343–4/*326*). All the different versions of ᶜAzīz's death contradict one another (even Umm Ḥasan seems to change her own version), but the stress here is on how easily myths can be fabricated to serve a purpose.[34] At the same time the onus on Khalīl to work out what really happened is immense: the narrator, like the writer, has to arrange and rearrange his material, edit it and imagine what he does not know.

Nuhā is a young woman (from the same generation as Khalīl) who talks about the fall of the village of al-Barwa and implies that the older generation was partly responsible for it (because they were naïve in believing what the Arab Legion commanders told them). After Khalīl relates Nuhā's critical version of the fall of the village (which she learned from her grandmother), he admits to editing her story and making her say, for instance, that her grandmother was like a tree without branches. Obviously, adding imagery is a different kind of rewriting from changing causes and effects of events. Nonetheless, even in a mere embellishing activity, it is possible to see the intervention of the narrator/writer. The gap between writing and reality is already clear. Khalīl invites Yūnis, and all of us, to imagine what really happened when the old woman returned to the ruined village where a kibbutz had been built and met a group of Yemeni Jewish children. Nobody knows what really happened; the only information we are given is that the kids start throwing stones at her. Why? 'Anything's possible' says Khalīl (Khūrī 1998: 207/*194*).

The kind of imaginative effort which the reader is asked to make here mirrors the author's own effort in writing the novel (we have a similar phenomenon with the pairing al-Takarlī/Tawfīq in *al-Masarrāt*), although *Bāb* is admittedly built on real people's memories: those of the Palestinian refugees whom Khūrī met in the Lebanese camps. But *Bāb* is not a history book or a collection of memoirs, it is a novel. The stories are fictionalized and much has been selected, dismissed, imagined, invented by the author, and much has to be imagined by the reader as well (similarly, the reader of al-Takarlī's *al-Masarrāt* is asked to imagine and produce meaning: 'you have to read what's not written as well', see the passage quoted earlier). Arguably, this is what happens every time a novelist starts writing – the difference between a novel like *Bāb* and a more traditional one is that in the former the reader is constantly reminded about such operations and invited to reflect on them.

In another typically explanatory passage Khalīl asserts that 'the issue isn't what happened but how we report and remember it' (Khūrī 1998: 281/*266*). The readers of *al-Masarrāt* and *Yālū* are, however, stimulated in a more sophisticated and effective way than they are in *Bāb*, because in the former novels the dramatization of their authors' ideas is usually supplemented by a more credible characterization combined with more convincingly fictionalized situations.

A further comparison is possible between *Bāb* and al-Kharrāṭ's *Yaqīn*, where again there are passages referring to the subject matter of the novel. Mīkhāʾīl reflects as follows: 'Love is never only love. It's always something else, many other things take shape in it, obscure things linked to the meaning of life, of existence. [It is one's] hidden, inner structures, of course, but also mythology and theology.' (Kharrāṭ 1996a: 51). This passage can be regarded either as a spelling out of what the *Rāma* Trilogy is all about (the love story between Rāma and Mīkhāʾīl with its mythological and theological layers of meaning as analysed earlier) or as the author winking playfully at his readers. These references are, however, still different from Khalīl's explanations in *Bāb*. They take place, as almost everything does in the three novels of the *Rāma* Trilogy, in the mind of the protagonist, whose thoughts, we have learned, are far-reaching and all-inclusive. In other words, the very introspective nature of the narration justifies these explanatory passages, which can even be considered playful.

There are also self-referential passages in *Yaqīn*, which explicitly convey the novel's political message. It is possible to draw a parallel between these and *Bāb*'s sometimes didactic spelling out of themes and intentions. In *Yaqīn*, the last novel of the Trilogy, this may be a result of the evident personal distress of the author *vis-à-vis* the increasing number of acts of sectarian violence against the Copts in Upper Egypt during the 1980s and 1990s. As a consequence, Rāma and Mīkhāʾīl are made to comment on these events, continuously reiterating their faith in the national unity of the homeland, stressing that all Egyptians are brothers regardless of their religious faith. In *Yaqīn*, Rāma reads out a list of damage done to Coptic properties and the personal injuries sustained by Copts to Mīkhāʾīl, then interrupts herself, saying: 'Are you interested in hearing the whole list? It will take some time.' Al-Kharrāṭ adds an overt metafictional aside here, the only one of its kind in the whole of the Trilogy: 'It will take three whole pages of this novel' (Kharrāṭ 1996a: 211). As noted in the introduction to this study, it is hard to decide whether the author of fiction is justified in including (or indeed compelled by certain external, political crises to include) lengthy documents in his or her fiction, followed by his or her comments voiced by characters, or whether this procedure remains redundant in a work of fiction and would be more suitable to a newspaper article.[35]

To go back to *Bāb*, it is possible to discern two contrasting intentions in it: on the one hand, the narrative has this metafictional flavour: it makes the reader reflect on how a people's memory can be selective. In making Khalīl question some of the stories which he narrates, Khūrī infers an obvious discourse about history and the way it is constructed, adjusted, and so on. This preoccupation is evident in Khūrī's works. Imposing order on the past, constructing various versions of it, is what people, governments, conquerors and victims alike normally do. Khūrī, as a writer of fiction, tries to subvert this process. At the same time, the reader clearly feels that all these stories are meant to be preserved: their political importance is very much in the foreground (imposing order on the past, to paraphrase our earlier Hutcheon quote, does not mean that the real past does not exist).[36] However, Khūrī writes in this metafictional fashion in order to point to the inevitable flaws of memory and the dubious selections of historiography (and fiction). Khūrī suggests that victims too can take advantage of situations to serve their own discourse. It happens unconsciously to a little survivor of the Shatila massacre, Dunyā, who ends up saying what the international media and the Palestinian fund-raising organizations want her to say, namely that she had been raped (a fact Khalīl doubts, Khūrī 1998: 254–7/*241–4*).

This asserting as true (of the stories of the *nakba*, for instance) and questioning (whether their narrators are unreliable, or when we are offered more than one version) is in line with the ambivalent nature of most postmodern fiction: Hutcheon states that 'postmodern de-naturalizing' is 'the simultaneous inscribing and subverting of the conventions of narrative' and that this paradox governs 'the metafictive reflexivity' of such fiction (Hutcheon 1989: 49). Her claim is that postmodern fiction is not a rejection of representation (a definition which might partly apply to modernism) but a problematization of it. It is possible to draw a parallel between these observations and what Khūrī himself states about his writing, which is so focused on the concepts of memory and forgetfulness as to promote a debate on literary writing itself:

> Literary writing is not an ordered version of reality; the story is not actually the event. It is the event in remembrance and recreation. When the event turns into a story, it takes for itself its own history, considering it as

> awareness of the lived moment, at once separation from it and designation of it. This separation and designation, which we call the literary lie, is the truth. The writer does not look for the truth outside himself. The truth is not ready-made. It is made and told. Telling it is one of the forms of making it.
>
> (Khūrī quoted in Ghandour 2000: 196)[37]

The centrality of memory-forgetfulness in Khūrī's writing is underlined by the novelist himself when he uses the well-known anecdote of Khalaf al-Aḥmar and Abū Nuwās to illustrate an important aspect of Arabic creative writing: Khalaf teaches Abū Nuwās how to be a poet by first making him memorize a thousand poems and then making him forget them (Khūrī, referred to in Ghandour 2000: 195). Khūrī associates literary writing with memory, recollecting, remembering. This appears clearly in a formal aspect of *Riḥlat*. As noted earlier, a brief section is repeated at the beginning of most chapters (from the second to the sixth). The passage mainly deals with two aspects of the whole novel: first of all it depicts the death of Little Ghāndī (through the words of Alice); second the passage conveys the narrator's attempt to imagine what happened when Ghāndī died and to narrate it (despite his own admission that he is not able to narrate anymore).[38] The author points at a connection between narrating and death, and this is also confirmed elsewhere in the novel (when the narrator says that, had not all these people died or disappeared from his life, he would not have begun narrating). This concept can be found in other works by Khūrī: Maḥmūd Sa^{c}īd underlines how three of the four main characters of *Bāb* are dead at the moment of Khalīl's narration (Yūnis, who is clinically dead, Umm Ḥasan and Shams; Sa^{c}īd 1999: 102). In other words, the importance of remembering, telling the stories of the people who have died or disappeared (like Alice) is here emphasized and at the same time questioned.[39]

Of course, this central passage also expresses the gloomy perception of the destructiveness of war, its violent capacity to wipe out lives, cities and maybe even memory.[40] We read in *Mamlakat*: 'We find stories tossed in the streets of our memory and the alleys of our imagination. How can we bring them together, to impose order on a land in which all order has been smashed to pieces?' (Khūrī 1993: 103/*84*). Khūrī's narrators are those who have survived; the heroes of their stories are those who did not survive. In *Mamlakat* the narrator, finding himself telling stories about bloodshed, massacres and wars, underlines the fact that he belongs to those who have survived these devastating events and expresses his sense of guilt for having survived a war which has killed many of his friends.[41]

If writing is central to Khūrī's novels it is also true that the character of the writer is rarely spared criticism. Only to mention a couple of the many possible examples, *Riḥlat*'s Alice is both suspicious and dismissively sarcastic about the narrator's job:

'What do you do for a living?'
'I write. I work as a writer.'
'What the hell is writing for, for God's sake?'
'To compose books and create heroes, so people can read them and enjoy them.'

'Why don't they just watch TV? Wouldn't that be better? [. . .] But what do you want with me?'
'I want to write about you.'
'You're a liar [. . .] Nothing you say is true, you're full of lies. Honestly, what do you want with me? What can I help you with?'
'I want you to tell me stories.'
'Why should I?'
'So I can write.'
'Okay. Instead of telling you, why don't I just write them?'

(Khūrī 1989: 138–9/*130–1*)

Mamlakat's Maryam harshly points out that the narrator and those like him claim that they are in search of the truth (as a general concept), but what they actually do is to search for the truth with the sole aim of writing it down (Khūrī 1993: 64/*51*). Once they have recorded it, they turn it into fiction and betray it. This is also related to another of Maryam's critical attacks, this time more personal. Writers such as the narrator (and another of Maryam's writer lovers, Marwān al-ᶜĀṣī) are unable to love, they are 'lovers on paper' (Khūrī 1993: 65/*52*). They are would-be lovers whose love is an illusion. Here there is a reference to the danger that a writer can spend his or her life in a fictitious world of paper, alienated from the real world. Not only is the category of writers dismissed or misunderstood by characters like Maryam (*Mamlakat*), Alice (*Riḥlat*) and Umm Ḥasan (*Bāb*), but other characters challenge the documentary elements or stylistic features taken from oral narratives, as opposed to a highly literary and more traditional style. Obviously, these self-referring comments are (partly) ironic. In *Bāb*, Khalīl says that he is reading Jabrā's novel *al-Baḥth ᶜan Walīd Masᶜūd*, then he adds:

> I love Jabra because he writes like an aristocrat – his sentences are élitist and beautiful [. . .] he wrote like real writers, meaning he formed expressive, literary sentences. You have to read them the way you read literature, not the way I'm talking to you now.
>
> (Khūrī 1989: 99/*91*)

The way in which Khalīl is talking to Yūnis is obviously a reference to Khūrī's style, which is more colloquial and not as elegant and well-crafted as Jabrā's (let us remember that *Bāb*'s narrator is not the authorial persona, method 1). The irony of this passage is paired with another observation regarding the way writers are perceived socially. In the following passage, from *Mamlakat* this time, Jibrān Khalīl Jibrān is the champion of proper, serious literature, the writer admired by the people, as compared to the authorial persona (the character of the narrator, method 2), who is rejected by his own father:

> [My] father, despite his respect for literature, believed an author should be like Kahlil [sic] Gibran and compose poetry and stories from his

> imagination, not go from place to place looking for them the way I do. 'A writer is not a travelling salesman,' my father said. 'He is the one who writes the things for people to say. He doesn't steal people's ideas and say it's literature.'
>
> (Khūrī 1993: 99–100/*81*)

Here, Khūrī seems to infer that his experimental way of writing will not be appreciated as readily as a more traditional mode would be. Is he anticipating what some literary critics might say about his novels, or is he preoccupied with the average reader's (the narrator's father's) response?[42]

Bāb and other novels by Khūrī lay bare the mechanics governing the writing of fiction (or history). They are comparable to texts which some critics (e.g. Hutcheon) define as postmodernist. In contemporary Arabic fiction there are, however, much more experimental, extreme examples of metafiction. One of these is *Lu^c^bat al-nisyān* by Barrāda. Like Khūrī, Barrāda deals with the problems of memory/forgetfulness, but his writing is even more explicitly metafictional. From the beginning of the novel (which is subtitled *naṣṣ riwāʾī* 'a narrative text' *à la* al-Kharrāṭ), it is clear that this is not a traditional novel: there are two sorts of false starts, two short passages defined as 'plans for a beginning', about the mother of the novel's main narrator. After these two plans the novel finally takes off, but this is hardly the only metafictional passage where the author's intentions, notes and plans are included in the text. The difference between *Bāb* and *Lu^c^bat* is that *Lu^c^bat* is more overtly about the writing of *Lu^c^bat*, while in *Bāb* comments tend to be more general and veiled. Another important difference is a technical one: the presentation of a metafictional discourse. In *Bāb*, this is achieved through Khalīl's continuous hints at what he is doing and the general implications of what is narrated. Barrāda, on the other hand, systematically uses a number of voices including one, 'the narrators' narrator', which is overtly metafictional. This operation has an ironic effect: 'the narrators' narrator', for instance, addresses the reader directly, complaining about the author of the novel and arguing against his ideas (e.g. he says that the variety of voices and narrators is pointless since it makes the reader lose sight of the plot; he suggests the writer should stay away from describing the present time in order not to sadden the reader or anger the censor, Barrāda 1987: 53/*56*, 133/*128–9*). These interventions also have the more serious metafictional effect of making the reader reflect on how a text might be created, how different interests clash in the author's head ('the narrators' narrator' obviously represents one of the many attitudes of the implied author, method 2).

Ultimately, if *Bāb*'s Khalīl is at times unconvincing and didactic in his metafictional stances, Barrāda's experiment systematically breaks up the narration in such a way that it gradually loses its ironic potential and becomes nothing more than a self-conscious game: the 'narrators' narrator's role is not integrated into the text and fails to endow it with any structural or deconstructive sophistication that might serve to justify its existence' (Musawi 2003: 361). Another more subtle intervention from the author is the division of the narrative into sections. Some of these are alternatively entitled 'Illumination' (passages usually narrated by a witness to the events narrated, a secondary character – usually a woman of the houses inhabited by the main characters) and 'Obscuration' (passages narrated by the central character al-Hādī about his childhood). The author gives his narrative different perspectives and moods (only for the 'narrators' narrator' to pop up and question his procedure). From a metafictional point of view, what is most significant here is his entitling of these passages. It is curious that the 'illuminating' sections (*Iḍā'a*) are those narrated by characters who are not talking about their own life but about somebody else's. At the same time al-Hādī, in remembering his own life, seems to carry out a dissembling operation, an obscuration (*Ta^ctīm*). This might at first appear as a contradiction, but the author's editorial choice is in line with his characters' dilemmas about what to remember and what to forget of their lives: is the game of forgetting (what makes us suffer) possible? Is al-Hādī able or willing to play it? More practically, the Illuminations provide the readers with more information about the time, setting and characters of al-Hādī's story, whereas his Obscuration sections are inevitably more introspective.[43]

Barrāda is obviously playing with his narrative, and is probably trying to provide some self-directed irony and lightness to a book which reflects on themes and topics dear to many Arab writers: a sense of nostalgia for childhood mixed with feelings of bitterness and frustration about the hopes for social and political change (usually from a leftist, militant perspective), denied by the totalitarian nature of Arab postcolonial regimes.[44] Boullata writes convincingly about Barrāda's metafictional devices such as the 'narrators' narrator':

> These are conscious attempts by Berrada to highlight the distance of actual reality from the artificial construction of fiction, which some Arab writers take too seriously as fully representable [sic] with little recognition of its ludic, even playful nature as mere art.
>
> (Boullata 1996: 10)

Nonetheless, the same writer's use of less overt metafictional features can achieve similar effects without breaking up the narrative in a way which is at times burdensome and gratuitous.[45]

Barrāda's second novel, *al-Ḍaw' al-hārib* (1993; *Fugitive Light*, 2002), is an example of how a novelist can promote a reflection on the act of writing through an ingenious device which does not break up the narrative in a gratuitous way. This novel's metafictional device is much closer to method 1, which we have admired in al-Takarlī's *al-Masarrāt* and Khūrī's *Yālū*. Like the latter, *al-Ḍaw'* too is divided into chapters, each narrated by means of a different narrative technique.

The novel, set in Tangiers, opens with the protagonist, the ageing painter al-ᶜAyshūnī, receiving a surprise visit from a young woman called Fāṭima. She will soon reveal herself as the daughter of Ghaylāna, al-ᶜAyshūnī's old companion and lover. The two have a short-lived relationship which ends when the young woman leaves the country. In the second chapter, the painter, urged by Fāṭima's questions about his relationship with her mother, recalls his life's crucial moments: his adoption by a rich Spanish man, his life as a painter, his love story with Ghaylāna ended by his refusal to commit to marrying her. The third chapter, taking place one year after Fāṭima's departure, is about al-ᶜAyshūnī's receiving another unexpected visit, in this case from Ghaylāna. The ensuing conversation between the two deals with a series of topics, such as ageing, sex, love and art, and sheds more light on the difficult relationship between mother and daughter, and on the different characters of Ghaylāna and al-ᶜAyshūnī. The fourth and final chapter is made up of two sections, the first includes Fāṭima's letter to al-ᶜAyshūnī (written more than one and a half years after she left him), in which she tells him about her life, including her relationship with her parents and her adventures in France (where she now lives). The second part of the fourth chapter includes extracts from the painter's notebooks.

It is only at the very end of the novel that its metafictional discourse becomes clear. At this point, al-ᶜAyshūnī writes in his diary that he gave his notes to a novelist friend and suggested that he should use them as the basis for a novel. This surprising confession, apart from being an ingenious way to end the novel and reveal its true nature, promotes the usual metafictional discourse in the text on the reasons why a writer writes, on the nature of fiction and the dividing line between reality and fiction. At the end of his notes, al-ᶜAyshūnī writes that if his friend ever chooses to write the novel he suggests he will be free to use the notes. The readers now know that this is exactly what his friend has done with the novel they have in their hands.

While Boullata's comments about the 'ludic' element in Barrāda's fiction are also pertinent to *al-Ḍawᵓ*, it is clear that Barrāda's text implies a serious invitation to his readers to go back and reconsider what they have just read in the light of al-ᶜAyshūnī's confession. At a superficial level, they now understand how some passages they have read in the last section of the novel sound so familiar to them: the editor/writer, following al-ᶜAyshūnī's advice, has already used them in the main body of the novel.[46]

From a metafictional point of view, the most significant of these double uses of the same passage is the one which appears in al-ᶜAyshūnī's diary on p. 180. This depicts a dream where al-ᶜAyshūnī finds himself in the middle of a group of people wearing evening dress. Waiters give them plates to smash against a wall. He hesitates and then gives in. The dream has previously been used by the author to describe an episode included in Fāṭima's letter to the painter in which she narrates her life in France (Barrāda 1993: 141).[47] These two uses of the same episode are significant because more than the others, they invite the reader to consider the role of the editor/writer in narrating a life story, to explore the interaction between fiction and reality (for one thing, apart from the central act of smashing plates which does not change, a lot of details are very different in the painter's dream from how they are in the young woman's experience). It is an original way of making us focus on the fact that we are dealing with fiction, which might be inspired by real life but has its own rules and requirements: the author of fiction edits, decides to include or exclude according to his or her choices as an artist. The illusion of reality persistent in the whole of the novel is therefore broken at the end of it through this metafictional *coup-de-théâtre* which lays bare some of the methods a novelist uses to write.

Another self-referring function of these final excerpts from al-ᶜAyshūnī's notebooks is to promote a reflection on the reasons behind writing. This is one of the cases in which the metafictional methods we loosely labelled 1 (use of fictional situations about reading/writing) and 2 (use of authorial persona) might overlap. The painter is not drawn as precisely as the authorial persona in most of Khūrī's novels, but he voices some of the author's concerns about writing and raises some general issues about the craft of writing, which must be central for Barrāda himself as a writer of fiction. In the introduction to the novel's second edition, Barrāda writes that at the moment of writing the novel he was going through a very difficult period of his life (Barrāda 1993: 7).[48] He began writing with the hope that chasing 'the elusive light' might rescue him. The same happens to his hero at the moment he begins writing his diary: he finds himself pushed to write when he is depressed, and his feelings of loss and uselessness dominate his mind. He too hopes that writing will be a healing process. But there is more than that in the character's reflections on writing. As al-Takarlī's Tawfīq writes to gain awareness of himself (and self-awareness is what Yālū obtains from his writing, albeit incidentally), al-ᶜAyshūnī writes to try to make sense of what has happened to him.[49] For once, he submits himself to a rational examination (i.e. writing), whereas in the past he has always responded to his instincts. At the beginning, writing seems to him a more effective medium than painting to reach what surrounds him and what lies in his memory. Al-ᶜAyshūnī is an individualistic, isolated character, who only starts writing with the intention of reviving the features of places ('spaces') he had known (the first entries are dedicated to his beloved, pre-independence Tangiers). He admits to having succumbed to the desire to appropriate this space for himself through words, to make it a dream-like space and an expansion of his identity, giving him more than one face and one way of living. He concludes that he began writing to make sense of the world and to understand his life but ended up being drawn to the pleasure of creating a world enveloped in dreams, illusions and hallucinations (Barrāda 1993: 194).

In other observations on writing (like the one quoted in Chapter 2), al-ᶜAyshūnī expresses his doubts about writing in general and the effectiveness of words in expressing what a writer wants to express. For example, is it really possible for a writer who portrays his past experiences to use the same language which he actually spoke at the time he was living through such experiences?[50] Is the order which words impose on these experiences something which has to be dispensed with in order to give voice to the illogical, irrational element in real life? On the other hand, even al-ᶜAyshūnī's observations on his painting are relevant to writing in as much as they are both artistic, creative activities. The painter reflects that the more aware he is of the history of painting, the more this impressive heritage seems to frustrate, instead of inspiring, his creative ability. Does this fear not remind us of the 'anxiety of influence' felt by a writer (indirectly voiced by Mīkhāʾīl in al-Kharrāṭ's Trilogy and quoted at the beginning of Chapter 4)?

At the end of *al-Ḍawʾ*, al-ᶜAyshūnī seems to dismiss his writing experience (which nevertheless had given him pleasure and purpose) as 'the barren operation of searching for words which ought to revive something of what our feelings have stored' (Barrāda 1993: 198). The final lines of his diary (and of the novel) are:

> Which of us is not escaping from something? I return to my lines and colours, escaping from the words of these memoirs, abandoning the illusion of recording and characterising what I have experienced, content to repeat: what has passed, is gone. What is left to me is light and colour, and the space which I can dream of through light and colour... all the rest is chitchat and preaching, scattered like dust in the wind.
>
> (Barrāda 1993: 198)

At the end of al-Takarlī's *al-Rajᶜ*, the reader finds the following paragraph:

> This mass of pages does not contain what people believe it does. No sighs, no talk, no groans or smiles. No sublimity, suffering, fear, or desire. No eyes, lips, blood, or tears. If they are thrown away they will not protest. They are dumb pages which are neither harmful nor beneficial, and it is better for them and for everyone if they are left in peace and forgotten.
>
> (Takarlī 1980: 491/*379*)

Unlike al-ᶜAyshūnī's final observations, these self-referred comments are placed by al-Takarlī outside the fictionalized space of the novel. In other words, they clearly come from the author himself. The reasons behind these extraordinary comments might be numerous: they might be read as a sort of ironic disclaimer by the author of his own work. They might also point to the author's fear of being misunderstood by readers or critics. It is possible to draw a parallel between this and Khūrī's ambivalent attitude: the author's noble intentions clash with his narrator's doubts and cynicism about himself and his own craft, not to mention the way other characters view it (the very characters he sets out to represent!). At the same time, the writer/intellectual's fear of his inability to communicate with people (as we have seen earlier, *Riḥlat*'s Alice does not entirely trust the narrator) reminds us of al-Kharrāṭ's similar concerns. The discourse on the role of intellectuals within Egyptian society and their alienation (both from its workings and from the people), is another of those topics further developed within al-Kharrāṭ's metaphorical framework. In both *Rāma* and *al-Zaman*, the writer expands this subject, exploiting the association heroine-nation.[51]

This chapter has shown how Barrāda, al-Kharrāṭ, Khūrī and al-Takarlī are each aware of, and preoccupied with, the implications of their activity as writers and each (more or less consciously) voice such preoccupations in their novels (albeit in very different ways).

In general, the whole of Khūrī's fiction is informed by two main driving forces: one, already exposed earlier, is ideologically motivated: the focus of this writing has to be on the marginalized of history, the victims of war, those who have no voice.[52] The other focus in Khūrī's fiction is on the way we tell stories, create history, write fiction. To create a novel where these two forces are well balanced is difficult since the natural outcome of the former attitude is to impose a discourse, whereas the latter approach tends to question and problematize discourses. A novel like *Riḥlat* shows that an ideal balance between these two trends is possible and successful. In a much longer experiment such as *Bāb*, the metafictional comments dropped by the main narrator, Khalīl, do not seem to enrich the narrative significantly, being at times didactic and/or unconvincing.

There are various reasons why in some passages these comments are successful and in others they are not. In novels like *Riḥlat* and *Mamlakat*, when the narrator is the authorial persona, or at least somebody who writes, he is credible in his mental wanderings: he spells out his aims, interests, what he thinks about magical realism and what he said to Rushdie! A more important reason would, however, seem to be the way Khūrī draws his readers' attention to the craft of the writer/storyteller/historian. As we have seen in this chapter and to the chapter on polyphony, there are some successfully metafictional passages in *Bāb*, and they are the ones which present a series of stories (like that of the piece of cotton, *ḥikāyat al-quṭna*, or that of ᶜAzīz Ayyūb) manipulated by Khalīl-the-narrator: they are told and retold, have different, contrasting sources and portray different heroes. This manipulation is made evident by Khalīl himself, but naturally it alludes to other less visible modifications (metafiction then becomes something more than a method of drawing the reader's attention to the nature of fiction: it also explores the relation between fiction, or art, and non-fiction, or reality). In *Yālū*, a use of the metafictional trope of the writing situation (method 1) is crucial: it is worth considering how the theme of writing as a means of becoming aware is not formulated *ex cathedra* from an authorial persona but depicted fictionally via Yālū's story and experience in prison when he is forced to put pen to paper. This method is more successful than either a mere statement from a character or a declaration of literary intent from an overtly metafictional character (like Barrāda's narrator-in-chief). This is all the more evident when we compare Barrāda's two novels. Even if the questions about writing in *al-Ḍawʾ* are similar to those asked in *Luᶜbat*, in the former they are more effective because they are concerns voiced by somebody who embarks on the adventure of writing. Characterization (however much despised by some of these innovative authors)[53] is an important factor in the attention the reader pays to what he or she is reading: are we not more likely to listen to a voice from a character we know (like al-ᶜAyshūnī in *al-Ḍawʾ*) than to an artificial voice which is not associated with any character (like that of the 'narrators' narrator' in *Lu^c^bat*)?

Moreover, a more traditional narrative (mostly mimetic, after all) can have the same effect as the most daringly metafictional practice. Al-Takarlī's method in *al-Masarrāt* (with its ironic self-referential asides, its reader/writer trope and imaginative fictional conclusion, method 1) is completely different from Khūrī's experiments with the authorial persona in *Riḥlat* and *Mamlakat* (method 2), but through these two completely different methods a similar result is achieved. As has been already considered, especially in Chapter 3, the adoption of one specific technique does not necessarily lead to a specific result. Similarly, the exclusion of one specific style or technique does not necessarily preclude the writer from obtaining a specific effect. We could, however, conclude by saying that these two methods (in *Riḥlat*, *Mamlakat*, *al-Masarrāt*, *Yālū* and *al-Ḍaw*ᵓ) are more effective than both Barrāda's in *Lu^c^bat* and Khūrī's less successful metafictional episodes in *Bāb*. It is not because of the alleged superiority (cf. Henry James) of the mimetic approach over the diegetic; it is more a question of how well one or other approach is executed, and the quality of either approach has to be evaluated on its aesthetic, literary merits: when a metafictional technique fails, it is because it introduces obtrusive, ephemeral features in a pretentious way and seems to involve some lack of focus or effort on the part of the writer.

In conclusion, *Lu^c^bat*'s shortcomings might be partly explained by the fact that it is the first novel by a well established literary critic who probably tried his hand at the novel form with his head full of theoretically abstract concepts.[54] On the other hand, Barrāda's second novel is a more disciplined work, which still works effectively as a metafictional text. We would like to think that he is talking about himself too when he writes about al-^c^Ayshūnī's contemplating the possibility of giving his notebooks to his novelist friend. The painter writes in his diary that he really would like the writer to express an idea which he finds important. Then, he foresees his friend telling him what Mallarmé allegedly told Degas when the latter wrote a poem in which he expressed many of his ideas: 'Ce n'est pas avec des idées qu'on fait des vers, c'est avec des mots' (mentioned in Barrāda 1993: 197).

6

CONCLUSION

On literary innovation (part 2)

Inspired by the idiosyncratic arrangement of the final chapters of al-Takarlī's *al-Raj*^{c}, we have chosen to split an essay on literary innovation in the Arabic novel into two parts: the first is the introduction to this work and the second is this final chapter, which will summarize the findings of our research and place our authors into the wider context of contemporary Arabic literature.

As stated in the introductory chapter, the most significant aspect of the novels by Barrāda, al-Kharrāṭ, Khūrī and al-Takarlī is that they represent different kinds of novelistic writing which depart from Mahfouz's early realism. In fact, our selection of novelists is significant, since the four writers can be seen to represent the different paths along which Arabic fiction is developing today and will possibly develop in the future.

The French scholar Jacquemond and al-Kharrāṭ himself provide us with panoramic views of the different directions taken by Arab writers after the crisis of realistic writing culminated in the late 1960s. Before we summarize their observations, we should stress that they deal mainly with Egyptian writers. Moreover, they are well aware of the fact that their observations are overly schematic (for instance, they stress that some, if not all, of the innovative features they mention might well be found in one single work). First of all, Jacquemond underlines how in Egypt most literary critics were not willing to attack the realist paradigm in itself but rather those mimetic texts which failed to denounce the negative aspects of Egyptian society and prophesy the defeat of 1967. Accordingly, novels like Mahfouz's *Tharthara fawqa al-Nīl* (1966; *Adrift on the Nile*, 1993) and *Mīrāmār* were praised as examples of a healthy 'critical realism'. On the other hand, some critics and writers started to question the very tenets of literary realism. In the introduction we proposed a modified version of the well-known metaphor of art as a mirror held up to the world, in order to stress that the texts analysed in this study are related to the surrounding world, the external reality (despite being quite different from their traditionally realistic counterparts). Jacquemond seems to make a similar point when he writes that the reaction to realism in Egypt is a complex and controlled process which rarely culminates in a total negation of it. What we are dealing with here is a variety of neo-realistic writing: there is a rupture with the conventions of mimetic realism as epitomized by Mahfouz's Trilogy, not with the idea that literature still enjoys a privileged relationship with reality ('le réel, le social, le collectif'; Jacquemond 2003: 120).[1]

Some critics might refer to this development as postmodernist (as we have seen earlier, Hutcheon talks about postmodernist fiction as promoting a problematization of realism, not a total refusal of it), some as modernist (Brenkman relies on Kundera who refers to this constructive attack on realism as the most notable feature of the most successful European modernist writers). As we have seen, it is difficult to disentangle the concept of novelty from the schematic division of literary styles into general categories. The definition of a literary text as modernist or postmodernist can be open to debate even from a purely Western perspective, and even more so from a global perspective (this is why Meyer is led to talk about a variety of postcolonial modernisms, rather than relying on the axis modernism/postmodernism; cf. Meyer 2001: 255–79). Brenkman, relying heavily on Kundera's ideas, questions the schematic depiction of Western literary development from realism to modernism to postmodernism (Brenkman 2006: 809–11). Kundera affirms that the decision of modern novelists to write essayistic passages without inhibition, to digress at leisure, to dispose with the need to create an 'illusion of reality' effect *et similia* (see contemporary writers such as Rushdie and Khūrī) betrays their willingness to reconsider pre-nineteenth century Western pioneering novelists such as Diderot and Sterne. At the same time, Kundera goes on, the most innovative of these novelists have been able to remember the lessons of the nineteenth century 'realistic' tradition and use them in new ways (Kundera 1993: 74–5). As we have already pointed out in passing in the introduction, this phenomenon is present even in the texts analysed in this work: the best examples of this innovative fiction question the preceding fictional production without destroying it, subvert it without deleting it, and go beyond it without ignoring it.

The scheme proposed by Jacquemond is probably influenced by that sketched by al-Kharrāṭ in his monograph *al-Ḥasāsiyya al-jadīda* (1993). According to the Egyptian writer, the trends of the new literary sensibility, inaugurated through the literary journal *Jalīrī 68* (of which he was one of the editors), are: (1) the *objectifying* current (*tayyār al-tashyī*ᵓ) of writers who promote a distancing, neutral kind of writing. These writers depict objects and people in a cold, dispassionate light. Their extremely dispassionate perspective is supposed to make the readers react against the coldness and harshness of what they are reading. This provocative strategy suggests that a world different from the one portrayed is possible and, indeed, necessary.[2] (2) The interior current (*al-tayyār al-dākhilī*) of writers who focus on the inner life of characters, painting a picture which is often obscure, and in which dream, imagination and external reality merge.[3] (3) The revival of the literary heritage (*istīḥā*ᵓ *al-turāth*), both classical (al-Ghīṭānī) and popular (the Egyptian Yaḥyā al-Ṭāhir ᶜAbdallāh, 1938–1981), of which we have spoken earlier (Kharrāṭ 1993: 18–19). (4) Magical realism.[4] (5) The new realism, which is simply defined as a kind of mimetic writing which appears to rely on traditional formal features, but at the same time subverts the prevalent, dominant values (Kharrāṭ 1993: 19–20). This last category, as formulated by al-Kharrāṭ, seems similar to the critical realism we have mentioned earlier. Moreover, Jacquemond comments further on the last trend, relating it to the whole of the development of the post-Mahfouzian Egyptian novel as a sort of neo-realism. He significantly excludes from this trend the anti-realism promoted by al-Kharrāṭ, whom he depicts as the writer who most consistently refuses to compromise with mimetic styles.[5]

Obviously, these schemes, as their authors admit, are only possible through extreme generalizations and oversimplifications. A close textual analysis of the texts shows how such general schemes are only useful to show broad literary trends. For example, if we go back to Meyer's scheme (mentioned earlier), which divides Arab writers into different generations, we realize how difficult it is to group al-Kharrāṭ with other novelists such as Munīf, al-Ghīṭānī and Ḥabībī with whom he shares an interest in reworking themes and forms taken from the *turāth*. At the same time, an author like Khūrī, placed by Meyer in the following generation of writers who supposedly are not interested in the *turāth*, may show in his awareness and use of it a much more ambivalent attitude (as we will see later). Despite the oversimplification and arbitrariness of such schemes and lists, we can see through them as to how the present research may enrich a panoramic view aimed at outlining the development of the post-Mahfouz novel.

If we now try to schematize and put into a wider context our analysis, we can talk about al-Kharrāṭ's as a kind of writing which focuses on the inner vision of characters, on their dreams, thoughts and feelings. It is true that this depiction of his writing can correspond to the second current (*al-tayyār al-dākhilī*) of the new literary sensibility of which he is the main theoretical proponent. It can, however, also be related to a modernist project aiming to create a heterogeneous, rich language derived from different literary traditions (in *al-Ḥasāsiyya al-jadīda*, al-Kharrāṭ refers to the modernity of the *ṣūfī* writers of the past, who, as we have seen earlier, are a source of inspiration to him; Kharrāṭ 1993: 21–2).

With Khūrī and Barrāda we have highly metafictional discourses on writing which rely respectively on an impressive collection of stories told in an oral-like and extremely simple style, and on the (more or less sophisticated) manipulation of traditional novelistic structures. Each of Khūrī, Barrāda and especially al-Kharrāṭ's fiction is not noticeable for one particular innovative technique, but rather for its unusual mixture of a high number of different techniques in a single novel. As Meyer has pointed out, what we find in Khurī's novels is not a depiction of the same event from different points of view, but rather an attempt to 'get away from any central event altogether' (Meyer 2001: 270). Khūrī's innovation appears to be in 'his wholesale investment in so many of these narrative techniques in a single text' (*Ibid.* 271).[6] We can make a general observation here to the effect that writers like Khūrī and al-Kharrāṭ rely on a mixture of a wide variety of different techniques which are juxtaposed and merged into one another. Al-Takarlī and Barrāda, on the other hand, while using various techniques, tend to employ them in a more orderly fashion.

Another trend listed in the scheme summarized earlier, which can be found in some of the texts analysed in this study, is the employment of the *turāth*. Even in the novels of Khūrī, who is not as consistent as al-Kharrāṭ in his reliance on themes and forms inspired by the Arabic literary heritage, we can see a sort of acknowledgement of, an awareness of belonging to, that literary tradition, in which the writers of the previous generations were hardly interested. Meyer, however, claims that Khūrī is not interested in the *turāth*. More than that, he draws a parallel between what Gerald Martin writes about Jorge Luis Borges, and contemporary Arabic literature. Martin sees the Latin America depicted in the works of Borges as

> nowhere, a place cursed to be empty of history, culture, and even people, mere shadows or echoes of other places and other times; or if there is a Latin America, it is just a hybrid chaos of imperfect copies, incoherent fragments, second-rate gestures.
>
> (Martin quoted in Meyer 2001: 272)

Meyer goes even further by stating that 'the impression which Khūrī's work makes on many Western readers'[7] is well described by Martin when he depicts Borges as 'a middle-class member of a Third-World community who is ashamed of his background' (*Ibid.*). All this is contradicted by what we have shown throughout this book: the fact that Khūrī is aware of, or indeed inspired by, contemporary non-Arabic literary trends (or, to use Meyer's words, 'writes under the conscious influence of Western postmodern literature and criticism'; Meyer 2001: 273), does not mean that he is ashamed of his cultural background. As we have seen, even for the other writers analysed earlier, adopting styles and techniques previously adopted by Western writers does not preclude them from appreciating their literary background; on the contrary, it seems to enhance their reworking of it. Al-Kharrāṭ, for example, can be seen to use a Joycean way of writing, but he does so also in order to include narrative forms and structures typical of classical Arabic literature, not to mention his reworking of Islamic mystical concepts. This procedure is echoed by a writer like al-Takarlī who likes to describe his novel *al-Raj*ᶜ as the treatment of traditional themes in an innovative form. Admittedly, the *turāth* does not exercise the same influence on al-Takarlī as it exercises on many Arab writers today (however, even if the Iraqi writer considers the Western novel to be more developed than the Arabic novel, it would be difficult to conclude that he is ashamed of his background).

Al-Takarlī differs from other writers discussed here in other respects too. The most important one is that his writing seems deceptively to rely on mimetic representation, when in fact it transcends it through technical sophistication. The case for al-Takarlī, as we noted in passing in the introduction, is one which needs to be made. The Iraqi is rarely considered as an innovative novelist by Arab critics[8] and writers,[9] while he is more or less ignored by Western critics.[10] The detailed analysis of his two major novels earlier should help make clear why this underestimation of the novelist occurs and why it is inappropriate. If we compare al-Takarlī's innovative writing with that of any other of the authors studied earlier (and we have contrasted his style especially with Khūrī's), it is clear that his writing at first reading is much more recognizable as mimetic: it lacks the total focus on a character's mind which we find in al-Kharrāṭ's novels, it is devoid of Barrāda's overtly metafictional characters (in *Lu^{c}bat*), it does not emulate the storytelling frenzy of Khūrī's multiple narrators. However, like Barrāda, al-Takarlī ventures into metafiction; like Khūrī, he engages with multiple narration; and we have seen how successful he is in both cases. As Cobham observes in relation to the metafictional features of *al-Masarrāt*:

> It is these features of al-Takarlī's writing – the recurrent questioning of the processes of fiction, and the dramatisation in many different ways of the reader's contribution to making the text – which link him to post-Mahfouzian writers whose style is more obviously experimental than his. However, the subversive and iconoclastic attitudes underlying al-Takarlī's metafiction are distinctive and make him stand out from his peers.
>
> (Cobham 2004: 43)

What sets al-Takarlī apart from other writers who employ more overtly innovative strategies is his sober and disciplined style, which allows him to introduce innovative features in an efficient but controlled fashion (we find the same feature in Barrāda's second novel). This self-imposed discipline does not allow al-Takarlī to compromise with features which, according to some other innovators, are obsolete: convincing characterization, solid spatio-temporal settings. In the light of the observations made about the constructive questioning of old techniques found in truly innovative texts, al-Takarlī's fiction, if given the careful critical evaluation it deserves, should make an important long-term contribution to innovation in the Arabic novel. We hope to have shown earlier what we mean by a proper analysis of al-Takarlī's works. The formal and critical analysis we have tried to promote is the same critical approach adopted by Cobham (in both of her articles on al-Takarlī's major novels, Cobham 2002, 2004): it is clear from these articles that even if a critic of fiction focuses mainly on its themes and content, he or she cannot do so efficiently without discussing its form in some detail. We argue that a lack of consideration of such formal features has so far prevented critics from appreciating the innovative value of al-Takarlī's work.

Al-Takarlī, when compared to al-Kharrāṭ, Khūrī and Barrāda, is the writer whose position within the text is the most discreet: whereas it is impossible, and ultimately pointless, to establish to what extent al-Kharrāṭ's Mīkhā$^{\supset}$īl, Khūrī's narrators and Barrāda's intellectual protagonists contain autobiographical elements, it is undeniable that all of these characters more or less directly voice their creators' concerns. Mīkhā$^{\supset}$īl obviously conveys some of al-Kharrāṭ's beliefs (both religious and political); the writers/narrators in *Riḥlat* and *Mamlakat* can be identified with Khūrī, at least in the way he carries out his research/writing; the heroes in Barrāda's novels voice some of the author's political and intellectual concerns.

Whereas all of these strategies are obviously legitimate, we have to appreciate al-Takarlī's intellectual effort in portraying convincingly characters whose visions and concerns are completely different from his own. The same effort is made by Khūrī in trying to enter Yālū's consciousness.

Characterization, especially that of another's consciousness, is a complex technical and imaginative exercise (and we could be cynical and observe that it is no wonder some authors declare that they do not have time for it). Obviously, there can be valid reasons for abandoning a traditional form of characterization: al-Kharrāṭ, for instance, abandons it, or rather revolutionizes it, in order to shift the focus of writing on to the inner life of his character: this subjective perspective is his priority. In al-Kharrāṭ's case, a traditional sort of characterization would not have fitted his strategy.[11] At the same time, we have to ask ourselves whether traditional characterization should always be dismissed in order to promote innovative forms. As we have seen earlier, in considering the female characters of *Bāb* and *al-Raj^{c}*, we are left to wonder whether a character like Munīra (with all her strengths and weaknesses) would not have served Khūrī more effectively than the over-idealized Nahīla.[12] An even clearer example of how traditional characterization can be accommodated within a genuinely innovative piece of fiction is given by contrasting two different novels by the same author: Barrāda's *Lu^{c}bat* and *al-Ḍaw$^{\supset}$*. Al-^{c}Ayshūnī in *al-Ḍaw$^{\supset}$* is much more fully drawn than 'the narrators' narrator' of *Lu^{c}bat* and, even if it is true that seeking the reader's sympathy and empathy can seem to be a vestige of Mahfouz's early novels (or the European nineteenth century realistic novel which inspired him), it is also true that a reflection on writing remains better portrayed by a convincingly drawn fictional character (like al-^{c}Ayshūnī and *al-Masarrāt*'s Tawfīq) than by an overtly artificial voice ('the narrators' narrator'). Patricia Waugh, in the very article in which she sets out to defend a certain metafictional writing, argues that if such writing has no proper balance between its most experimentally adventurous elements and a more traditional redundancy, it runs the risk of being as ephemeral as the phenomena it strives to portray: 'some degree of redundancy is essential for any message to be committed to memory' (Waugh 1984: 48).[13]

Our appreciation of al-Takarlī's efforts does not have to be read as a dismissal of other more explicit experiments. As we have repeated throughout this study, the aesthetic success of a novel has more to do with the skill with which a writer executes a certain technique than with the technique in itself.

If al-Takarlī's work has not attracted the critical attention it merits, al-Kharrāṭ's innovative shift towards depiction of the inner self, and the way he executes this, has not always been praised by critics. The Palestinian critic Darrāj attacks both the language and the content of al-Kharrāṭ's Trilogy. Darrāj points to the fact that the search for the absolute in man and for a language which can suitably convey it is typical of a neo-classical author rather than a modernist and innovator: according to Darrāj, al-Kharrāṭ is not a novelist but a mere *ṣāni^{c} lughawī*, 'a producer of language'[14] and *Rāma* is not a novel but a 'linguistic experiment' (Darrāj 1999: 260, 264). Al-Kharrāṭ's fiction is dismissed as elitist and Darrāj claims that the Kharrāṭian man is a sort of demigod (inferior to immortal gods but superior to mortal men) who 'walks with his feet on the ground and his head in the clouds' (Darrāj 1999: 269). Darrāj goes on to define the present in al-Kharrāṭ's first novels as an 'absolute present', relying on Bakhtin's observations on the absolute past of the epic:

> The epic past is called the 'absolute past' for good reason: it is both monochromic and valorized (hierarchical); it lacks any relativity, that is, any gradual, purely temporal progressions that might connect it with the present. [...] By its very nature the epic world of the absolute past is inaccessible to personal experience and does not permit an individual, personal point of view or evaluation.
>
> (Bakhtin 1975: 15–16)

We find similar observations in Auerbach's article 'Odysseus' Scar', in which Homer's style is contrasted with that of the Old Testament (Auerbach 1946: 3–23). Auerbach underlines the differences between the two texts by contrasting the *Odyssey*'s scene of Odysseus's return home (book 19) with that of the sacrifice of Isaac (Genesis 22). In the classical text, all phenomena (including the characters' thoughts) are clearly present before our eyes, 'this procession of phenomena takes place in the foreground – that is, in a local and temporal present which is absolute' (Auerbach 1946: 7). In the Old Testament, on the contrary, much is concealed from the readers, who are expected to investigate and interpret – the context is historical rather than legendary, and this makes characters change and evolve (another crucial difference is that, in the Bible, the focus is also on characters with humble origins, who are significantly portrayed as owners of a complex consciousness). With al-Kharrāṭ's depiction of his hero, we seem to have the whole of Mīkhāᵓīl's consciousness, given in one moment, always present in front of us: everything he has to say is said (another reference to the use of the verb *qāla* in classical Arabic literature?),[15] and because he is depicted in a moment of crisis, fraught with doubts, he sometimes seems to say everything and its opposite. Even if Mīkhāᵓīl's background is humble, his and Rāma's sophisticated and refined way of living, which is stressed throughout the Trilogy,[16] perforce places the couple on a culturally superior level to the rest of the characters (and the average reader). Some of these secondary characters are clearly from the lower strata of society and, while they are portrayed favourably,[17] as Darrāj points out, they are just not portrayed enough: they work as extras in a film which always focuses on the heroes. This is not to say that al-Kharrāṭ should be forced to focus on characters from the lower strata of society, but since such characters are present in his novels, a critic like Darrāj can mention their characterization to reinforce his depiction of the protagonists of the novels as demi gods. We have, however, observed earlier how al-Kharrāṭ's primary goal is to focus on the inner self of Mīkhāᵓīl only. Moreover, if it is possible to define the atemporality of al-Kharrāṭ's narrative act as an absolute present, it is also true that the presence of the present (which is crucial for Bakhtin to distinguish the novel from the epic, cf. Bakhtin 1975: 11) is clearly felt in al-Kharrāṭ's novels. Darrāj's reading of al-Kharrāṭ's Trilogy crucially overlooks one of the most significant features of the contemporary Arabic novel: the socio-political element. In the introduction, we have stated that this element is probably one of the most striking differences between Western literary modernism and what might be defined as Arab literary modernism. In dealing with the Trilogy, we have an example of the different ways in which a political discourse can be introduced into fiction.

The *Rāma* Trilogy does indeed focus on Mīkhāᵓīl's striving to reach Rāma (his other self), but the problem of how to reach perfect unity is never solved: the Kharrāṭian hero might have divine aspirations to eternal glory, he might strive to achieve the absolute within himself, but he fundamentally fails.[18] The *Rāma* novels depict human life as a continuous struggle to reach a goal, a perpetual search (hence the works' repetitive, open-ended nature). The author regards this as an important element of human experience: whether this is an admission of the way man is, or a praise of the superhuman in man (as Darrāj has it), is left to the reader to decide. The distanced, positive, *epic* image of Rāma as Egyptianness (pure, immortal, and so on.) is contextualized on many different levels: we have, for instance, a historical context which is unmistakably a contemporary one and, accordingly, is questioned. The would-be distanced, closed image is now dramatically put very close to Mīkhāᵓīl, who has to deal with it in his own present. His praise of Rāma/Egypt contrasts, on an immediate level, with his inability to be Rāma's only lover and, more importantly, with his alienated position as an intellectual in contemporary Egyptian society.

What al-Kharrāṭ does, especially in *Rāma*, is to allow cultural and political statements to undergo a process of 'fictionalization'. In other words, in a truly artistic novel, such statements will be fictionally contextualized (they will be conveyed by a particular character, in a particular situation, at a particular moment). By virtue of this contextualization (which, it has to be said, reproduces what happens in the life of real people), these statements will not be made in an abstract vacuum – they will probably be confronted by other statements, they will be questioned, they will be problematized, they will be expanded, they will work on many levels, and so on. Kundera reflects on the nature of novels as follows:

> the moment it becomes part of a novel, reflection changes its essence. Outside the novel, we're in the realm of affirmation: everyone is sure of his statement [. . .] Within the universe of the novel, however, no one affirms: it is the realm of play and of hypotheses. In the novel, then, reflection is essentially inquiring, hypothetical.
>
> (Kundera 1986: 78)

Kundera offers a good example of this shift from a non-fictional to a fictional environment (hinted at earlier in this study): in discussing how Dostoevsky's ideas can be voiced by some of his characters, Kundera says that these ideas, upon entering Dostoevsky's novels, immediately become relative: 'a dogmatic thought turns hypothetical' (Kundera 1986: 78–9).[19] Similarly, it is likely that al-Kharrāṭ's ideas are given to Mīkhāʾīl, but they become relative and problematic, first by clashing with Rāma's and then, especially, through the fictional framework in which they appear. For example, it is possible to relate Mīkhāʾīl's ideas to a sort of Egyptianism with a strong Coptic element.[20] At the same time, Mīkhāʾīl's seemingly uncompromising beliefs about his national identity are contextualized (in a period of socio-political and personal crisis), questioned (by other voices), and problematized (in the dramatization of the couple's relationship). In other words, al-Kharrāṭ goes far beyond the undoubtedly beautiful and poetic idealization of an image of Egypt as Rāma–Isis and all the lofty concepts he attaches to it.[21] It is therefore evident that whereas Arab novelists sometimes choose to, or are called upon to, contribute to historiography, the literary form of the novel encourages skilful writers to go beyond mere historiography and promote a reflection which, from an intellectual point of view, is more sophisticated because it involves questioning their own and other people's beliefs.[22]

We have seen earlier that there are some political beliefs which al-Kharrāṭ is not ready to question and wants to voice forcefully: in *al-Zaman* and especially in *Yaqīn*, the two protagonists voice their author's condemnation of the sectarian violence of Islamist groups and his support of national unity and tolerance.[23] Whether the intrusion of such overtly political arguments into a work of fiction is obtrusive or, considering the circumstances underlined in the introduction, inevitable perhaps even praiseworthy is difficult to decide.[24] A political statement can be introduced into fiction successfully if it does not emerge as an alien body which does not fit with the rest of the work: in the Trilogy, it seems natural that Mīkhāʾīl and Rāma talk to one another about problems which, like those related to sectarian differences, directly interest them.

If al-Kharrāṭ's concern about the socio-political crisis of Egypt is increasingly mirrored in his Trilogy, it is not as central as the position occupied by the themes of war and conflict in the novels of Khūrī. If the fiction of al-Takarlī and al-Kharrāṭ points at two ways in which the Arabic novel can evolve and develop from a more traditionally mimetic writing, the fiction of Khūrī represents yet another innovative direction. As we have seen earlier, Khūrī is innovative in many ways: the most prominent feature of his writing to set him apart from the other novelists studied here is his language. His style represents a significant shift towards the more agile syntactical structure of the vernacular language, while fundamentally remaining a standard variety of written Arabic, understandable to all literate Arabs. The sophisticated language of al-Kharrāṭ, with its wordplay and lyrical passages, contrasts with an extremely economic style made up of brief and simple sentences in Khūrī's novels. The style is, however, not an aesthetic exercise *per se*: it is a suitable vehicle for an oral-like narration, in a style much influenced by the oral tradition, of a large number of stories which reflect on various matters, including war and violence and their impact on the victims and marginalized individuals from the lower strata of society. In developing such a style, Khūrī draws on the folk tradition of storytelling, with its repetition of situations and sentences and lack of unnecessary detail. The language and the highly fragmented narrative (by numerous narrators with contrasting versions of what happened) are innovative features, to which Khūrī adds a self-reflective dimension, where he questions storytelling and writing (and by extension, historiography). The latter innovative feature is introduced sometimes overtly and sometimes discreetly by Barrāda and al-Takarlī too. This phenomenon, analysed in the chapter devoted to metafiction, connects these authors to other non-Arab contemporary novelists, who are often defined as postmodernists. We have seen earlier how a metafictional discourse can be promoted in different ways, and how the most daring techniques do not necessarily draw the reader in more than the more traditional ones (Barrāda's limited novelistic production is a case in point).[25] What we want to underline here, however, is that no matter what metafictional form is privileged, this kind of fiction introduces an innovative feature into the Arabic novel, in so far as the centre of the reader's attention shifts onto the mechanics of fiction itself. Literature is not a mere representation of the real world, as is the case with the traditionally mimetic novel.

At the end of the introduction to this study, we dismissed Meyer's point about the lack of ironic distance in Arab culture. Nonetheless, it is true that most of the texts under scrutiny in this study, though not devoid of humour, ironic asides and comic sketches, have a non-ironic purpose. For example, Joyce's use of alliteration and different styles of English is ironic and playful, while al-Kharrāṭ's similar displays of virtuosity are usually meant to be a serious display of his linguistic skill. In broader terms, the very approach to the myths of the past is different. Joyce's use of Homer's *Odyssey* is ironic whereas al-Kharrāṭ's use of the myth of Isis, for instance, is part of a self-conscious enquiry into identity. Declan Kiberd writes in his introduction to *Ulysses*: 'Joyce's and Eliot's use of myth may be called ironic and even playful. Such treatment contrasts with that in Robert Musil's *The Man Without Qualities*, whose central characters try knowingly and deliberately to relive the myth of Isis and Osiris' (Kiberd 1992: xxx–xxxi). Like Musil's characters, al-Kharrāṭ's Mīkhāᵓīl is all too conscious of the Isis myth and deliberately relates it to himself and Rāma, while Leopold Bloom is unaware of his modern mythmaking.

We often find the same serious approach to socio-political criticism and discourses on historiography, which in contemporary writers like Rushdie are mainly conveyed through irony and humour. Other contemporary Arab writers, like Ṣunᶜallāh Ibrāhīm for example, use irony to convey their political criticism and Ḥanān al-Shaykh (b. 1945) is one of the few Arab writers who portrays serious themes (such as the life of Arab exiles in London in *Inna-hā Lundun yā ᶜazīzī*, 2001; *Only in London*, 2001) in an often lighthearted and humorous style.

One of the reasons behind the relative lack of irony in the texts we have discussed might be the fact that all of their authors, unlike Rushdie and al-Shaykh, are living in the Arab world and might feel more directly the pressure deriving from their status as 'underground historians', or spokesmen for the voiceless. Obviously, the same social and intellectual status does not preclude other writers, such as Ibrāhīm, from taking another direction, but we can claim that most of the novels by Arab authors living in the Arab world reflect a sense of pessimism about external events and when their authors want to make a political point they usually want to be taken extremely seriously.

In his critical works, Kundera addresses problems related to the novel in the West. One of his observations is relevant to our study on the innovative Arabic novel: it deals with the nature of the novel in general, and indirectly touches upon problems related to the literary criticism which is supposed to analyse and evaluate this form. In lamenting how mainstream criticism of Kafka's work has rarely been as rigorous as he would like, he indirectly gives his definition of the criticism of fiction. The questions the serious literary critic should ask about a novel are: does it make us aware of something we did not know before? In other words, does it change our understanding of human life? Does it have aesthetic ambitions or does it change our understanding of novelistic form? In other words, is it formally innovative? Does it exercise an influence on posterity? (Kundera 1993: 18 and Kundera 1986: 5–6). In order to answer these questions, a critic studying a novel should always consider the place it occupies within a novelistic tradition, within the history of the novel itself.[26]

By adopting the literary approach we have described in the introduction, we hope to have achieved this goal and we will now try to summarize the answers we have found to the questions Kundera proposes.

1 Al-Kharrāṭ introduces into the Arabic novel his particular philosophical vision. Boutros Hallaq reflects on the fact that al-Kharrāṭ's fiction (defined as *transgeneric*) shows how the goal of literature is neither to represent the real world nor to change it. According to Hallaq, the great socio-political and economic crises of Arab society, not to mention the stagnation of Arab culture, require Arabic literature to fulfil the role once assigned to philosophy, religion and science, and to be the privileged instrument for reform.[27] In this context, the writer/poet is seen as a prophet whose main goal is to reveal man to himself (Hallaq 2001: 163). In more practical terms, al-Kharrāṭ's *oeuvre*, for the first time in such a consistent way, strives to articulate a philosophical conception of man which is significantly syncretic in its attempt to marry the Arab–Islamic, *ṣūfī* understanding of human existence with Christian and Pharaonic beliefs. This is, according to him, the essence of Egyptian identity. If, on the one hand, this idea has clear political implications, from a cultural perspective it points towards an Arabic literature able to investigate its past and at the same time open to other cultures.[28]

2 Al-Takarlī convincingly portrays the struggle of individuals to gain self-knowledge. This often painful striving can reveal even to the most independent and strong-minded characters how their identity is shaped by the weight of the society in which they live (with its ancestral rules and laws). The connections between inner and external worlds are often depicted in his works through the

violent impact of history on the lives of characters who are modelled on common people. These human beings, often victims of history or, more simply, of backward social conventions and traditional, middle-class moral values, often egotistic and self-centred, sometimes exploitative and cruel, show all their humanity in their attempts to become aware of themselves, even if this awareness will not lead them to improve their lives and solve their problems.

3 Khūrī treats the violence of war in a way which gives dignity to its victims, and at the same raises questions relevant to writing, storytelling and historiography. In so doing he underlines the importance of his craft as a writer, though he is ready to be self-critical and sceptical: like al-Takarlī's Tawfīq, Khūrī's writer/character finds himself compelled to write even if such an enterprise might not bring about any immediate change. As underlined earlier, Khūrī's writing seems to reject focusing exclusively on one main story and one main theme. Another aspect of violence investigated by Khūrī is the way it affects the memory of its victims. Typically, even this phenomenon is ambivalent and controversial: the characters are depicted as they alternatively attempt to recall what they have suffered (to make sense of their lives and learn from their mistakes), try to *edit* some of the events they have lived to make political use of their narratives (at times, unconsciously), and finally decide to forget in order to go on with their lives.

4 The theme of memory and forgetfulness is similarly explored by Barrāda: in his case a more individual and personal portrayal is given. Another unusual feature of Barrāda's novels is that their characters are either individualistic and apolitical or disillusioned with politics. The post-independence Arab characters he portrays are far removed from the initial optimism generated by political independence from the colonial powers. In some cases even a nostalgic view of the pre-independence, cosmopolitan period is expressed.[29] Even Barrāda, like Khūrī and al-Takarlī, promotes a self-referential discourse on writing and gives us sketches of characters who, although not professional writers, embark on the writing experience and voice some of his reflections on his own craft as a writer.

Throughout this chapter we have tried to summarize the formal innovations introduced in the texts of these authors. It is too early to asses the impact of these novels on subsequent fiction. Nevertheless, it seems clear that, however marginal to the mainstream literary production these currents may be, however different from one another these styles are, they all contribute to shaping a sort of fiction which is richer, more complex and probably more artistically ambitious than the preceding tradition. Jacquemond insists that, at least in Egypt, realism has returned triumphantly to the mainstream after the early experimentations inaugurated in the late 1960s (Jacquemond 2003: 123–5). It is significant that al-Kharrāṭ's work, defined by Jacquemond as unique, has already exercised some influence over writers such as Maḥmūd al-Wardānī,[30] Badr al-Dīb, and possibly Bahā᾿ Ṭāhir and Barrāda himself. In Lebanon, a kind of writing similar to Khūrī's has been adopted by Rashīd al-Ḍaᶜīf, and the same sort of technical sophistication and discipline admired in the works of al-Takarlī is found in the best works of the late Iraqi Mahdī ᶜĪsā al-Ṣaqar (1927–2006). This last, least obvious of literary currents, seems to suggest how literary skill and discipline can subvert the old assumption that everything has already been written: maybe this is true, but as al-Takarlī implicitly states in his novels, you can always find a way to treat a traditional theme in an innovative way and, we would add, in so doing you inevitably say something new or at least render a certain situation or concept in a deep and far-reaching way.

In conclusion, one of the most important observations one can make about these texts is that, while dealing with the specific problems of Arab societies and identities, they all propose concepts, ideas and questions which are universally valid. The journey of self-discovery described in al-Kharrāṭ's works, the need for a constant striving to be and remain aware in al-Takarlī's, the personal reflection on the past depicted in Barrāda's; the importance of memory and forgetting from a communal and collective perspective; the importance of storytelling even, or especially, in extreme circumstances in Khūrī's; all of these can be easily related to different people and communities throughout the world.

Similarly, the tendency of Barrāda, al-Kharrāṭ, Khūrī and al-Takarlī to seek inspiration from intertextual references to Arabic and non-Arabic literary traditions, and their recurrent, if varied, reflections on fiction itself show that they are increasingly preoccupied with their craft as writers of fiction. This preoccupation connects them with their non-Arab peers and shows that they not only occupy a well-defined position within the history of their societies but also belong to the international history of their art.

NOTES

1 INTRODUCTION: ON LITERARY INNOVATION (PART 1)

1 For an overview of the history of the magazine and its importance as far as literary matters in the Arab world are concerned, see Ruocco 1999.
2 So impressive that the magazine actually dedicated two issues to the Arabic novel: the one mentioned earlier and the following. Idrīs's main reaction to such a positive response confirms the impression of most critics of contemporary Arabic literature: in the last few decades the novel has acquired such a status that it is considered the privileged literary genre.
3 Our starting point is the year in which Idwār al-Kharrāṭ's groundbreaking novel *Rāma wa-'l-tinnīn* appeared (the author himself financed the first publication and the novel was published one year later in Beirut by *al-Mu$^{\supset}$assasa al-^{c}arabiyya li-'l-dirāsāt wa-'l-nashr*). The novel has been translated into English as *Rama and the Dragon* by Ferial Ghazoul and John Verlenden (2002). Hereafter, when first referred to, the Arabic title of a novel will be followed by the year of its first publication, and the title and date of its published English translation (when available). Subsequent citations will include only the Arabic title, or the first part of it if the novel is frequently mentioned: *Rāma wa-'l-tinnīn* (1979; *Rāma and the Dragon*, 2002), subsequently *Rāma*. When quoting entire passages from these novels, a plain number referring to the page/s of the Arabic edition used will be given, followed by a number in italics referring to the English translation. For those novels for which no published English translation is available, the Arabic title will be followed by our translation of it, for example, *Yālū* 'Yalu' (2002). This novel by Ilyās Khūrī is the most recent of those studied.
4 While the literary quality of the works analysed here and the critical consensus are the most important criteria of selection, we have also deliberately chosen writers who can loosely be said to represent every major region within the Arab world (the East or Iraq, the Eastern Mediterranean, Egypt and North Africa).
5 Cf. Allen 1995: ix.
6 Khūrī confesses: 'My basic fear has always been that my works would be translated as social documents, as is the case for most examples of Arabic literature in translation, including those of Naguib Mahfouz. I am not interested in presenting a social document, because literature is only partially a social document' (Khūrī quoted in Haydar 1996: viii).
7 Hence to conclude our reference to Bakhtin and the concept of polyphony, we can say that the Russian critic provides us with a suitable tool with which to analyse the narrative structure of one of al-Takarlī's novels. As will be clear in Chapter 3, our discussion of the novel begins with Bakhtin but later parts company from him, reaching different conclusions.

8 Cf. Anna Xiao Dong Sun's review of a Chinese novel (Sun 2004) to see how this problem can afflict any author with a strong political agenda.

9 See the introduction to Mehrez 1994 (1–16) for a justification of, and a call for, an interdisciplinary (historical and literary) study of contemporary Egyptian fiction. Waïl Hassan too calls for a more interdisciplinary approach and argues that Arabic literary scholarship will benefit greatly from postcolonial theory (Hassan 2002: 59). This is how Richard Jacquemond comments on the character of the public writer in Mahfouz's *Awlād Ḥārati-nā* (1959; *Children of Gebelawi*, 1981), a character he defines as Mahfouz's *alter ego*: 'l'écrivain selon Mahfûz serait le titulaire d'une compétence socialement rare (la maîtrise de l'écrit), qui lui donne le pouvoir de rassembler le savoir fragmentaire, déformé par les "intérêts et les passions", produit par les autres intellectuels, et de donner le vrai récit de l'Histoire, celui qui fera autorité' (Jacquemond 2003: 18). The Egyptian novelist Jamāl al-Ghīṭānī (b. 1945) seems to echo Mehrez's observations on the 'underground historian', when he writes: 'In my view [the artist] is a very particular kind of historian, since his task is to preserve the essence of a particular temporal period from oblivion' (al-Ghīṭānī quoted in Allen 1995: 196).

10 We could not find such a statement in the source quoted by Meyer (Cachia 1990: 18–19). As we will see later, Cachia's argument is more subtle than Meyer's version of it. Cf. Jacquemond 2003: 113, for similar statements on the role of the Arab intellectual.

11 Cachia himself depicts the emergence in the early 1950s of a new generation of Egyptian writers (like ᶜAbd al-Raḥmān al-Sharqāwī) with leftist leanings and little time for the paternalism of the Tawfīq al-Ḥakīms and the Muḥammad Ḥusayn Haykals (Cachia 1990: 20).

12 Al-Kharrāṭ admits that Arab writers can aspire to influence only the so-called elite (Kharrāṭ 2001). Similarly, the late Egyptian writer ᶜAbd al-Ḥakīm Qāsim observes: 'with regard to the question of literacy, I think the problem is that we're writing for the public at large, but that particular public is not one that reads' (Qāsim quoted in Allen 1995: 129).

13 See Jacquemond 2003: 95–6 for the marginality of literature in the Egyptian book market.

14 See Jacquemond 2003: 107–12 for some observations on the connection between literature and audiovisual media in Egypt.

15 Tawfīqᶜ Abd al-Raḥmān's *Qabl wa-baᶜd* 'Before and After', Yāsir Shaᶜbān's *Abnāʾ al-khaṭaʾ al-rūmānsī* 'Sons of the Romantic Mistake' and Maḥmūd Ḥāmid's *Aḥlām muḥarrama* 'Forbidden Dreams'. See Hafez 2000 for a detailed discussion of the *Walīma* affair and Jacquemond 2003: 15–19 for a comment on the assault on Mahfouz and on his novel *Awlād ḥārati-nā*. Cf. Allen 1995: 128–31 for general views on the readership of the Arabic novel.

16 It is also evident that, in certain cases, as a result of opportunistic political calculations, the regime withdraws such patronage and gives in to the most reactionary forces (Jacquemond 2003: 45–6).

17 See Allen 1995: 136–7 for a sketch of the way pressure is exerted by the political power on the intelligentsia; cf. Stagh 1993 (especially chapters IV and V) and Jacquemond 2003 (especially chapters I to III) for a more detailed analysis of the Egyptian situation.

18 Public lecture delivered in May 1997, in Modena (Italy).

19 Throughout the present work we will only tackle the problem of language in passing, as we feel that this subject deserves an altogether independent study.

20 Cf. Allen 1995: 120–3 on the emergence of Arabic metafictional writing.

21 '[T]he air of reality (solidity of specification) seems to me to be the supreme virtue of a novel – the merit on which all its other merits [...] helplessly and submissively depend. If it be not there, they are all as nothing, and if these be there, they owe their effect to the success with which the author has produced the illusion of life. The cultivation of this success, the study of this exquisite process, form, to my taste, the beginning and the end of the art of the novelist' (James 1884: 195).

22 Al-Kharrāṭ, who is arguably the Arab writer most consistent in his rejection of a traditional, realistic representation in literature, rejects the notion that art is an attempt to represent reality. At the same time, he feels the need to defend himself (and he does it forcefully and efficiently) from those critics who question his commitment to dealing with real socio-political issues. For example, he stresses that he, like the majority of the writers from what he calls 'the third world', is highly concerned about issues such as human dignity, justice, democracy, rationality and freedom. Consequently, al-Kharrāṭ finds for himself a position of balance between art's higher goals (intrinsic in the work of any good fiction writer) and the more practical socio-political concerns (which, he stresses, the Arab public expects him to treat): art can very well deal with the latter, but it always transcends them through the former (Kharrāṭ 2001).

23 In the final chapter of this work we will summarize the results of our analysis and give a more detailed survey of how the works of these novelists exhibit the different innovative trends.

24 'In the old period [up to 1959] Mahfouz [. . .] used to write a number of novels in one form before moving on to another in which he wrote several more before a further change. Each time many followed in his footsteps and this perpetuated the static sense of form' (Hafez 1994: 105). On Mahfouz's intimidating stature as the father of the Arabic novel see also Musawi 2003: 22.

25 Similarly to Mahfouz, another influential Egyptian writer, Yūsuf Idrīs (1927–1991), first employed a realistic style and then played an important role in innovating and experimenting beyond the boundaries of the realistic short story.

26 Such changes involved both the form and the content of fiction. As far as the latter is concerned, some intellectuals in Egypt, for instance, had produced works critical of their society and of the Nasserite leadership before 1967. Cf. Allen 1995: 120 and Jacquemond 2003: 117–25. See also Kharrāṭ 1993: 11 for the writer's reflections on 1967 as a turning point for literary change. According to Boutros Hallaq, it is in the period we are analysing that realistic fiction, still dominant in the 1970s, becomes problematic (Hallaq 2001: 165). Analogously, Kamal Abu-Deeb had predicted that the process of fragmentation and increasing multiplicity of voices in Arabic fiction would intensify in the decade 1985–1995 (Abu-Deeb 2000: 339).

27 See the following footnote and footnote n. 21 in Chapter 4 on how much critical attention al-Ghīṭānī's novel *al-Zaynī Barakāt* (1971; *Zayni Barakat*, 1988) has attracted.

28 As we have seen earlier, Roger Allen does not include a discussion on experimental works in his monograph on the Arabic novel. Consequently, a novel like *Rāma* is only mentioned in passing. It is indicative of the difficulty encountered by innovative writers like al-Kharrāṭ in having their works published and properly distributed (at least at the beginning of their careers) that Allen had to rely on secondary sources (namely, Fontaine 1986). In her article about the Egyptian novel, Hilary Kilpatrick dedicates a page to *Rāma* which contains a very limited descriptive commentary (Kilpatrick 1992: 268). Fontaine, on whom Allen relies, includes in his article on the Egyptian new novel some brief observations on al-Kharrāṭ's early novels, but focuses more on *al-Zaman al-ākhar* 'The Other Time' (1985) (Fontaine 1986: 25–6, 37–8, 45–8). Both Musawi and Meyer discuss al-Kharrāṭ's fiction, especially from the perspective of male–female discourses, but neither analyses satisfactorily the other aspects of his writing (and Meyer does not deal with al-Kharrāṭ's early novelistic production) (Musawi 2003: 250–4; Meyer 2001: 210–13). Sinan Antoon draws our attention to Hamdi Sakkut's dismissal of the post-Mahfouz novel in the latter's critical introduction to his bibliographical research on the Arabic novel (Sakkut 2000): 'The author is mostly dismissive of the post-Mahfouz world of the Arabic novel. There is a very telling addition in the Arabic version of the preface (which does not appear in the English version): 'What is even more astonishing is [sic] the claims on the part of some that Mahfouz has been actually 'transcended' by some of the writers of the 1960s

[generation]. To these we say … if some novelists write experimental novels or use modernists or formalistic tools never used by Mahfouz, that does not mean that they have transcended him!' Then he finishes off by asserting that the 'modest works of Alain Robbe-Grillet, for example can never transcend the works of Shakespeare and others!' (vol. 1, p. 19)' (Antoon 2003: 299). All in all, the best description (in English) of al-Kharrāṭ's early novels remains M. M. Badawi's (Badawi 1993: 174–6), which is brief and void of any illustrative examples, but touches on more or less all the significant aspects of such texts.

29 Both al-Kharrāṭ and al-Takarlī had been experimenting with short novels or short stories before 1979/1980, the years in which their most significant novels appeared. While al-Kharrāṭ's experience as an innovative short story writer is evident in the structure of *Rāma* (see later), al-Takarlī's short novel *al-Wajh al-ākhar* 'The Other Face' (1960) can partly be seen as a blueprint for his major novel *al-Raj*^{c} *al-ba*^{c}*īd* (1980; *The Long Way Back*, 2001), much as his first novel *Baṣqa fī wajh al-ḥayāt* 'Spitting in the Face of Life' (2000, but written in 1948) already presents some themes expanded in his more mature *al-Masarrāt wa-'l-awjā*^{c} 'Joys and Pains' (1998) (cf. Cobham 2004: 26 *passim*).

30 Hassan laments the fact that scholars in the field of postcolonial studies have paid considerable attention to South Asian, African and Caribbean literatures while disregarding Arabic literature. He sees this phenomenon as a continuation of neo-colonial hegemony which is guilty of privileging the languages (and the canons) of the two major colonial powers, Britain and France, and not paying enough attention to texts written in the languages of the colonies (Hassan 2002: 45–6).

31 The phenomenon of Arabic literature here observed is seen by Jacquemond as a common feature of the literatures of developing countries: 'après une phase d'extraversion qui produit une littérature calquée sur les modèles euro-américains, les nouvelles générations d'écrivains redécouvrent et réexploitent les patrimoines narratifs indigènes' (Jacquemond 2003: 122).

32 'If we wish to bridge the gap between literary perspectives in the Arab world and the West, we need to look at literature in a way that represents the non-Western viewpoint with the least distortion' (Meyer 2001: 276).

33 See for instance al-Takarlī on the Western origins of novelistic art, Ḥalāwī 1995: 29. Maybe Harold Bloom's theory of 'the anxiety of influence' can apply to the Arab authors of today on two levels: they face the influence of both their own heritage and that of Western literature, as most of them are familiar with its forms and themes. While Meyer states that '[e]xperimental Arab writers have [. . .] suffered from two immense strains in their literary practices – the weight of Western influence and literary precedent' (Meyer 2001: 7), we would like to point out that Shakespeare in his sonnets occasionally uses the term 'influence' to mean 'inspiration' (as Bloom notes in the Preface to his book's second edition; Bloom 1997: xii). That is to say that the two 'immense strains' can also be stimulating forces.

34 Here we do not mean to say that all Western literature today is devoid of political discourse, but that, for the reasons set out earlier, the political element is usually more prominent in Arabic literature. Calvino writes about the power of literature as follows: 'it seems that only when [literature] is persecuted does it show its true powers, challenging authority, whereas in our permissive society it feels that it is being used merely to create the occasional pleasing contrast to the general ballooning of verbiage' (Calvino quoted in Mehrez 1994: 80).

35 Bakhtin traces back to this literary form some of the fundamental features of novelistic discourse, such as its dialogic and multi-styled nature, its subverting power of laughter, its spirit of inquiry, its stress on an inclusive present, and so on (Bakhtin 1975: 26–7).

36 Brenkman criticizes Linda Hutcheon for assuming that in what she defines as historiographical fiction, political consciousness and metafictional practices necessarily merge successfully (cf. Hutcheon 1989). He sees this association of literary experimentalism with political radicalism as a heritage of the beginning-of-the-twentieth-century European avant-garde, which is not necessarily applicable today (Brenkman 2006: 818).

37 See previous footnote on the same point made by Brenkman regarding Hutcheon's assumptions.

2 FRAGMENTATION

1 In the introduction, we have seen how Khūrī relates the formless nature of the modern Arabic novel to classical Arabic narratives (Khūrī 1990: 4–5).

2 It is not incidental that the Egyptian critic al-Sayyid Fārūq dedicates his monograph *Jamāliyyāt al-tashaẓẓī* 'The Aesthetics of Fragmentation' (1997) partly to the works of al-Kharrāṭ (and partly to those of another Egyptian writer, Badr al-Dīb – b. 1926).

3 This does not mean that the author does not allow other views to be expressed as we will see in the following chapter. On the other hand, whether the hero's point of view coincides with the author's is a matter for debate. See for instance, the author's statements such as 'I had to point out that though there are quite a few areas of resemblance between the author and his hero or rather, anti-hero, I do not subscribe to many of Mīkhā᾿īl's ideas or attitudes' (al-Kharrāṭ 1998: 11). Cf. also Halim 1994: 18. At the same time, some of al-Kharrāṭ's values are clearly voiced by Mīkhā᾿īl (see for instance his reaction to the sectarian violence suffered by Copts, depicted throughout *Yaqīn*). How much autobiographical material there is in al-Kharrāṭ's work is an unsolved and probably insoluble question.

4 Said in his introduction to Auerbach's *Mimesis* talks about the eighteenth century Neapolitan professor of Latin eloquence and jurisprudence, Gianbattista Vico, as follows: 'Thus the line between actual events and the modifications of one's own reflective mind is blurred in Vico, as it is in the numerous authors who were influenced by him, like James Joyce' (Said 2003: xiii).

5 In this case, we have chosen not to rely on the published English translation of the novel by Ferial Ghazoul and John Verlenden because the translated passage is not complete and turns the original into a first person narrative (cf. Kharrāṭ 1979: 254/*237*).

6 Cf. Genette 1972: 172 ff for a discussion of this style.

7 The following is a rather literal translation. It follows faithfully the sequence of paragraphs of the original text in order to facilitate a formal analysis and show how the different parts of the narrative are juxtaposed. Again, we decided not to use the Ghazoul–Verlenden English translation because, despite being very similar to ours, it omits some repetitions of the original which might be superfluous but help us to illustrate the fragmented nature of the passage (cf. Kharrāṭ 1979: 104–5/*92–3*).

8 See Kharrāṭ 1969: 210–11 for another, earlier example (from the short story *Jurḥ maftūḥ*; *An Open Wound*, 1984) of how al-Kharrāṭ freely switches from a third person to a first person narration in the same paragraph. Such a mixture of techniques and styles is present throughout the Trilogy: see another excellent example in *Yaqīn* (Kharrāṭ 1996a: 92–5), where Rāma's lengthy reportage on the Upper Egypt sectarian violence is followed by Mīkhā᾿īl's interior monologue, an old brief message written by Rāma about her new house, alliteration paragraphs (in which the letter *bā᾿* appears in almost every word), Mīkhā᾿īl's visions equating Rāma to Venus, domestic scene depicting Rāma getting annoyed with Mīkhā᾿īl, dialogue, and so on.

9 This development between *Rāma* and *al-Zaman* is not lost on M. M. Badawi, Badawi 1993: 175–6.

10 One of the many possible examples occurs when Mīkhā$^{\supset}$īl's usual gloomy thoughts, this time about how it is still impossible for him to get rid of his illusions, are followed by a sketch depicting Rāma losing her patience and asking Mīkhā$^{\supset}$īl to hurry up in the bathroom (Kharrāṭ 1996a: 222–3).

11 See for example, *al-Ḥasāsiya al-jadīda* (Kharrāṭ 1993) and *Muhājamat al-mustaḥīl* (Kharrāṭ 1996b) both mentioned by Darrāj. Jacquemond, who defends al-Kharrāṭ's innovative qualities, underlines how only after considerable work done by al-Kharrāṭ the literary critic, did the modernist plan of al-Kharrāṭ the novelist come to be properly valued (Jacquemond 2003: 123).

12 Darrāj blames the Egyptian novelist for disregarding the contributions of other scholars such as Muḥammad Ḥusayn Haykal who, long before him, had studied the renewal of Arabic literature (Darrāj 1999: 255–6). He also attacks al-Kharrāṭ for using over-complex terminology to describe a novelistic style which was present in many novels predating his (Darrāj 1999: 258–9).

13 These novels include the aforementioned *Mā tabaqqā la-kum*, and go as far back as 1946 with the Palestinian Jabrā Ibrāhīm Jabrā's *Ṣurākh fī layl ṭawīl* 'A Cry on a Long Night'; Darrāj 1999: 258–9). Although Darrāj states that the novel was written in 1946, it was published in Baghdad only in 1954 (cf. Musawi 2003: 349, n. 20).

14 Such is the innovative breakthrough represented by al-Kharrāṭ's writing within modern Arabic fiction that it is probably unfairly dismissive on Meyer's part to criticize such experimentalism as a mere tool serving 'the purpose of masculine self-representation' (Meyer 2001: 213).

15 For a more detailed description of the structure of the novel, see Cobham 2004: 28–9. We will see in the next chapter how in al-Takarlī's *al-Raj^{c} al-ba^{c}īd* the chronological succession of events is subverted at the end of the novel.

16 'Although the first section is *ostensibly* historical and dispassionate, it contains elements of myth and parody. [. . .] The family into which Tawfīq is born is made up of archetypal outsiders. They arrive in a border area from an unknown starting-point in the late nineteenth century [. . .], work as woodcutters, speak Arabic with a foreign accent and all resemble monkeys and freakshow characters' (Cobham 2004: 29).

17 Barrāda's *al-Ḍaw$^{\supset}$ al-hārib* (1993; *Fugitive Light*, 2002) presents a structure similar to al-Takarlī's *al-Masarrāt* in that each chapter has its own narrative style. The novel opens with a chapter narrated through a third person omniscient voice (zooming in on Fāṭima's consciousness and more especially on that of the protagonist, the painter al-^{c}Ayshūnī; Barrāda 1993: 11–44); the second chapter is narrated in al-^{c}Ayshūnī's first person narrative (in which he addresses Fāṭima; Barrāda 1993: 45–79); the third chapter returns to the omniscient third person voice (from al-^{c}Ayshūnī's perspective; Barrāda 1993: 81–105); the final chapter includes two sections, the first, Fāṭima's letter to al-^{c}Ayshūnī (Barrāda 1993: 107–70) and the second made up of excerpts from al-^{c}Ayshūnī's diary, his 'notebooks' (Barrāda 1993: 171–98). Even with a much more radical experiment and complex narrative structure such as Barrāda's *Lu^{c}bat al-nisyān* (1987; *The Game of Forgetting*, 1996), we still have a narrative divided into well defined sections (given to different narrators). See the following chapter for a more detailed analysis of the novel's structure.

18 Sabry Hafez has the following to say to al-Kharrāṭ while interviewing him: 'Unfortunately, *Rama wa-l-tannin* [sic] appeared in a period of literary and critical stagnation and vacuity. Thus a great number of people who could have received sympathetically this experiment [sic], and could have tried to mobilize a literary current around its vision and ideas, were unable to tackle it. It is unfortunate that some of them were even unaware of its existence' (Hafez 1982: 235).

19 The short paragraph in which Mīkhā'īl recalls her whispering this sentence to him in the first chapter is completely omitted in the English translation of the novel, cf. Kharrāṭ 2002: 20. The same short sentence is remembered even in *Yaqīn*, Kharrāṭ 1996a: 50.
20 At times these shifts are less clear and logical and occur only through a key word connecting two different episodes, ideas or facts in the mind of the narrator. For example, in the same novel (Khūrī 1993: 18–19/*14–15*) the unnamed narrator is narrating how Maryam goes away with a young Lebanese soldier: '[Maryam] didn't come back for a long time. Time is long. [*shift: linking concept (time is long)*] That's how I felt when I sank in the sea, that time is long.' This passage is then followed by the parenthetic episode of the narrator's attempt to walk on the water, after which the narration again focuses on Maryam and the soldier.
21 Written in 1973 according to Ḥusnī Ḥasan (Ḥasan 1996: 128).
22 The influence of the Arab literary past on al-Kharrāṭ is manifold and it influences both themes and forms, as we will see in Chapter 4. It is, however, apparent even in small details like the way each chapter of *al-Zaman* is called *bāb*, a term traditionally indicating the sections of a work.
23 The recurrence of the same themes in al-Kharrāṭ's first two novels has not been lost on the Egyptian critic Muḥammad Badawī. In an illuminating and precise analysis he writes about the 'cyclical' and 'repetitive' structure of the chapters (Badawī 1993: 112).
24 Other examples are: *Ikhtirāqāt al-hawā wa-'l-tahluka* 'Penetrations of Love and Perdition' (1993) defined as 'narrative outbursts'; *Tabārīḥ al-waqā'i^{c} wa-'l-ḥanūn* 'Torments of Facts and Nostalgia' defined as 'narrative miscellany' (1998). To these we can also add Barrāda's less fanciful 'narrative text' as the subtitle for his *Lu^{c}bat*, see Nowaihi 2000: 383 for a comment on Barrāda's subtitle.
25 Cf. Bakhtin 1975: 3 and *passim* and Allen 1995: 1–10.
26 Bāb al-shams is the name of a geographical area of pre-1948 Palestine.
27 Cf. Meyer 2001: 132.
28 As we will see in Chapter 5, the author, who might well be unaware of this comment, subverts it in a self-referential passage from his novel *Yālū* when the protagonist, who is forced to write the story of his life, is said not to be a *ḥakawātī*: not because of his style of narrating (which is indeed similar to that of a traditional story-teller), but because of the non-heroic subject matters his life provides (Khūrī 2002: 177).
29 In Rushdie's *Midnight's Children* the narrator, trying to explain his technique of storytelling, says that his stories, like people and things, leak into one another (Rushdie 1981: 38). The leaking stories image is equally applicable to Khūrī's main storytelling technique.
30 Cf. Khūrī 1990: 6; Meyer 2001: 117 and Abu-Deeb 2000: 339, and his reference to a paper he had written in 1984 in which he argued 'that a process of *fragmentation* had begun to dominate Arab cultural and political life and to produce marked effects on the *structure* of literary texts'.
31 For a detailed synopsis of the novel, see the following chapter.
32 The temporal sequence is completely subverted, as Muḥammad Badawī has pointed out in his analysis of the initial part of *Rāma* (Badawī 1993: 100–4).
33 Darrāj is right to underline that al-Kharrāṭ's narration takes place in an 'absolute present', but he then criticizes al-Kharrāṭ for creating semi-divine characters who are as static and finalized as the epic heroes are in their 'absolute past' (Darrāj 1999). In general, the atemporality is that of remembrance. At times, this atemporality is also explicitly ascribed to sexual intercourse which is said to take place outside the temporal boundaries: this ideal depiction of sex is present in both al-Kharrāṭ and Barrāda.
34 Jean Fontaine writes about the style of *al-Zaman*: 'De très nombreuses phrases nominales rendent bien l'effect de synchronie et le facteur *kāna* du passé de narration est en

general marqué du signe neuter au point de se confondre avec ce present majoritaire' (Fontaine 1986: 46). Musawi, on the other hand, sees narrating, in *Yaqīn*'s intertextual hints at Rāma/Shahrazād, as the rejection of time, hence of death: this is what makes Mikhāʾīl/Shahriyār tell her: 'You shall live forever' (Musawi 1999: 164; Kharrāṭ 1996a: 287).

35 The novelist stresses that his novels are not about memories, they do not express any nostalgia for the past (Kharrāṭ 1996b: 27).

36 This is the main reason behind the continuous repetitions and reworking typical of al-Kharrāṭ's style, which are not motivated by the desire to give the reader a gradual knowledge of events, as we have mentioned earlier.

37 This is not only evident in his critical work, but obviously, prominently, in his fiction. In some passages from his novels the topic is openly touched upon by Mīkhāʾīl, who asks himself what reality (*al-wāqiᶜ*) is (Kharrāṭ 1985: 250).

38 Kundera notes that the fusion of dream and reality of which Breton speaks had already occurred, thanks to Kafka, in the very literary genre Breton harshly criticizes in his manifesto: the novel (Kundera 1993: 50).

39 For example, if in al-Kharrāt's Trilogy various linguistic varieties and styles are juxtaposed within the narrative whole, in Barrāda's *Luᶜbat* the rich heterogeneity of the Arabic language is disposed in a more orderly fashion, more or less according to the division into chapters and sections and therefore according to who is speaking: as Issa J. Boullata notices in his preface to his English translation of the novel, 'the women of the household are quoted speaking in the Moroccan dialect of Fez [...] In the "Obscuration" sections, Hadi [al-Hādī, the protagonist] speaks in modern standard Arabic, although he also reports quoted speech in the Moroccan dialect' (Boullata 1996: 7). Moreover, Sī Ibrāhīm, the pious husband of al-Hādī's sister, who is of humble origins, speaks in his own dialect of Rabat (Barrāda 1987: 57–64/*60–6*).

40 Al-Nowaihi observes that even al-Hādī in *Luᶜbat* struggles with words: 'Often all that he can recall are vague, legendary images that remain powerful in his memory, and although he thinks there must be words that are suitable for expressing these memories, his search for them is futile' (Nowaihi 2000: 382).

3 POLYPHONY

1 Especially in its discussion of al-Takarlī's *al-Rajᶜ* this chapter includes edited excerpts from a published article by the present writer: 'Polyphony and Narrative Voice in Fuʾād al-Takarlī's *al-Rajᶜ al-baᶜīd*' (Caiani 2004).

2 Jabrā's translation was published in 1963 in Beirut as *al-Ṣakhab wa-'l-ᶜunf* by Dār al-ᶜilm li-'l-malāyīn. The Iraqi critic Fāḍil Thāmir also refers to the American novel in his analysis of Fuʾād al-Takarlī's *al-Rajᶜ al-baᶜīd* (Thāmir 1992: 82).

3 Apart from the novels mentioned in this chapter, this technique is used in novels as diverse as Lawrence Durrell's *The Alexandria Quartet* (1957–1960) and *My Name is Red* (1998) by Turkish novelist Orhan Pamuk. Mahfouz experiments with it again in *Afrāḥ al-qubba* (1981; *Wedding Song*, 1984) and *Yawm qutila al-zaᶜīm* (1985; *The Day the Leader Was Killed*, 1989). Another Egyptian example of the same technique is *al-Rajul alladhī faqada ẓilla-hu* (1961–1962; *The Man Who Lost His Shadow*, 1966) by Fatḥī Ghānim. A more recent Arabic example is *Inna-hā Lundun yā ᶜazīzī* (2000; *Only in London*, 2001) by the Lebanese Ḥanān al-Shaykh.

4 Phrase borrowed from Bakhtin 1963: 56.

5 As we will show later in more detail, a similar dominating voice is also present in Mahfouz's *Mīrāmār* (even if this novel is more sophisticated than Munīf's).

6 Marlé Hammond, in her discussion of the use of various linguistic registers and intertextual references in al-Kharrāṭ's works, uses the term 'overarching polyphony' to

characterize these features (Hammond 2000: 41). This tendency to group different aspects of a novel under the attractive but often ill-defined heading of polyphony is present also in Boutros Hallaq's article (Hallaq 1998) on Maḥmūd Darwīsh's *Dhākira li-'l-nisyān* (1987; *Memory for Forgetfulness*, 1995) and al-Kharrāṭ's *Ḥarīq al-akhyila* 'Fire of Fantasies' (1994). Hallaq fails to explain in enough detail how the presence of different genres and styles grants a true autonomy to each of the voices in Darwīsh's narrative text (Hallaq 1998: 197).

7 'The dominant may be defined as the focusing component of a work of art: it rules, determines, and transforms the remaining components. It is the dominant which guarantees the integrity of the structure.' (Roman Jakobson quoted in Bakhtin 1963: footnote c, p. 13).

8 As we have seen in the introduction, although Meyer analyses al-Kharrāṭ's novel *Yā banāt* (1990) and not the Trilogy, because of the repeating themes and techniques the Egyptian writer adopts, it is sometimes possible to draw a parallel between this later novel and those on which we are focusing.

9 The vividness of this argument cannot be lost on the reader, as it gives the distinct impression that the author must have been involved in this kind of debate during his Trotskyite phase (which provides the background to one of his novels, *Ṭarīq al-nisr* 'The Way of the Eagle', 2002). Moreover, when Aḥmad claims that killing somebody is to kill what he represents at a symbolic level, not the human being he or she is, he is restating one of the clichés of European political terrorism. For another reference to the same problem (symbol/human being) within the Egyptian national struggle for independence against Britain, see Kharrāṭ 1996a: 111.

10 Mīkhāʾīl draws an interesting parallel between Islamic and leftist terrorists, saying to Rāma and Aḥmad: 'The absolute [value] for them [the Islamists] is the past. For you [the Communists] it is the future. Both are unrealizable dreams' (Kharrāṭ 1985: 280).

11 As we have observed elsewhere, 'while the theme of Mīkhāʾīl's Coptic pride and his corresponding anti-pan-Arab discourse is only hinted at in *Rāma* [...], in *al-Zaman* [...] it is fully-fledged. The tumultuous events of the early 1980s – violent clashes between Muslims and Copts in Egypt, Sadat's assassination, the Israeli invasion of Lebanon, the massacre of Palestinians in Sabra and Shatila – certainly had an impact on al-Kharrāṭ. No wonder then that each of these violent episodes is mentioned in the novel. If we add to this gloomy picture the effects of the *infitāḥ* era (depicted in the novel as disastrous, see the insertion into the narrative of letters of distress and desperation addressed to newspapers by their readers), then Mīkhāʾīl's stigmatization of the decadence of contemporary Egypt and a consequent idealization of Egypt's "glorious" past (not only Pharaonic) seems at least easily understandable, if overstated at times. An analogous observation can be made about Mīkhāʾīl's intransigent ideas about the Coptic nature of Egypt (he himself admits to being a "chauvinist of Egyptianness", Kharrāṭ 1985: 99): al-Kharrāṭ could be readier to voice such feelings as a reaction to the ascendancy of an extreme and violent branch of political Islam (and its attacks on Copts), typical of the period in which the novels were composed and set' (Caiani 2005: 41–2).

12 The last part of the fourth chapter of Musawi's monograph (in Arabic) on the post-Mahfouz novel is dedicated to *Yaqīn* (Musawi 1999: 163–74). This section is only partly reproduced in English in the author's monograph on the postcolonial Arabic novel (Musawi 2003: 252–4).

13 This technique is consistently adopted in entire chapters by the Israeli novelist Abraham Yehoshua in his novel *Mar Mani* (1990; *Mr. Mani*, 1992).

14 Rāma's protest against what she perceives as Mīkhāʾīl's male attitudes has already been forcefully voiced in *al-Zaman*. For example, she tells him that however rational and progressive men would like to appear, they (including him) are still the men of *The Arabian Nights* who want their women to wear chastity belts and are persuaded that the trickery of women is superior to that of men; Kharrāṭ 1985: 310.

15 Despite praising *Yaqīn*'s narrative for allowing Rāma's voice to emerge, Musawi observes that it neither totally subverts the male protagonist's dominating position nor always prevents him speaking for the female Other. The Iraqi critic illustrates this claim well by quoting a passage from the novel where Rāma surprises her partner with a racist comment (on black men). Mīkhā᾽īl reacts by saying to himself that she actually meant the opposite of what she said (Musawi 1999: 355; cf. Kharrāṭ 1996a: 144; the passage could also show the author's ironic criticism of Mīkhā᾽īl's idealization of Rāma). Ḥasan makes a similar analysis of the way readers only meet Rāma's character through Mīkhā᾽īl's voice. From this perspective, Ḥasan depicts the text of the Trilogy's first two novels as a prison made of words and images (*sijn lughawī wa-ṣūrī*) built by the author in order to capture Rāma (Ḥasan 1996: 126).

16 See Boullata 1996: 5–11 for a more detailed analysis of the narrative methods of the novel.

17 'Hādī only vaguely realizes that he is driven to this rediscovery of his sister by his own needs, for the death of his mother requires finding a new bond with childhood, which he hopes Najiyya will be able to supply. He is not really uncovering her but creating for her a new role that fits his emerging needs' (Nowaihi 2000: 373).

18 Cf. Nowaihi 2000: 371–3 on the characterization of F. B. and Najiyya.

19 We will see in the chapter on metafiction how Aghacy's reading (backed up by Meyer) labels *Riḥlat* a self indulgent work which does not depict the reality of the war (even in this case, we disagree with Aghacy). For a completely positive evaluation of *Riḥlat*, see Ghandour 2000.

20 Naturally this is in itself an ideological position.

21 As is that of Alice, on whom Aghacy would like to impose an apparently feminist point of view (Aghacy 1996: 170).

22 The same thing happens in the same novel to the character of Widād the Circassian (an outsider in Beirut).

23 If we consider Bakhtin's reflections on the fundamental differences between the epic and the novel, we can see *Bāb* as a typically novelistic attempt to subvert the 'epic' tendencies within Palestinian imagery. Each of the epic's three features proposed by Bakhtin in his essay 'Epic and novel' is depicted but also challenged in *Bāb*: '(1) a national epic past [. . .] as the subject of the epic; (2) national tradition (not personal experience [. . .]) as the source of the epic; (3) an absolute epic distance [separating] the epic world from contemporary reality' (Bakhtin 1975: 13).

24 The overall narrative structure of the novel is that of the frame-story (Khalīl narrating to Yūnis in the Galilee Hospital).

25 At the beginning of the novel, Khalīl speaks of Yūnis using the third person, explaining that there is a man with him in a room, he is in a coma, and so on.

26 As we have seen in Chapter 2, however, in the second part of the novel it becomes clear that Khalīl has not told the whole truth about the reason why he is staying beside his unconscious friend. Shams, Khalīl's former lover, has been killed and, despite the fact that he claims to be innocent, the woman's male relatives are searching for him to take revenge for her murder. Hence, Yūnis's room in the Galilee Hospital is also Khalīl's refuge. However, Khalīl says to Yūnis: 'I'm certain you'll wake up one day and discover that I bathed you in words, and washed your wounds with memories' (Khūrī 1998: 303/*286*).

27 Although Umm Ḥasan, the midwife of the Shatila camp who dies at the very beginning of the novel, tells Khalīl that Yūnis is actually talking and that he should listen to his voice (Khūrī 1998: 12/*5*).

28 Mīkhā᾽īl's consciousness dominates al-Kharrāṭ's novels as much as Khalīl dominates the narration in *Bāb*. The crucial difference is that in the latter's random and imperfect recollection many more voices emerge.

29 The parallel between Nahīla and the Virgin Mary is reinforced when the 'fourth Nahīla' is called Umm al-Nūr by Yūnis (Khūrī 1998: 390/*372*). Apart from the fact that

the couple actually had a daughter called Nūr, the *kunya* is one of the designations applied to the Virgin.

30 It is curious to notice how 'the seventh Nahīla', coming at the end of the chain of alternative depictions of the heroine, can be regarded as both negative and positive. It is true that she has had enough of her life ('The seventh Nahīla was tired of being tired. A lonely and poor woman', Khūrī 1998: 391; our translation), but she also embodies a thoughtful compromise between a woman bravely making a stand and one who understands her husband's difficult situation.

31 When a distraught Yūnis, after having listened to his wife's recriminations, sets out to return to Lebanon, Nahīla prevents him. She takes him to the cave and she makes love to him. The scene's symbolic value is clear: 'This time she was the one who began and he felt her hands possess him, his manhood extinguished' (Khūrī 1998: 403; our translation).

32 The novel begins with Khalīl's recalling how Umm Ḥasan was the only one who cried amid general scorn when the so-called Six-Day War broke out. She was the only one who understood that the war was going to mean for her generation the definitive loss of their homeland (Khūrī 1998: 10/*4*).

33 For some examples, see later, Chapter 5.

34 Abū Ma[c]rūf, a Palestinian man who once fought alongside Khalīl, narrates to him the story of his first marriage when he was 15 and his bride 14. The girl was showed by his mother how to put a piece of cotton between her thighs to remind her where she should put her groom's member. After they finally have intercourse the girl is scared because at first she cannot find the cotton and thinks it might be inside her. Abū Ma[c]rūf's story underlines the backwardness of the tradition of early marriages, which Yūnis disapproves of and Khalīl finds odd.

35 Cf. Accad 1990: 135–6.

36 Self-criticism is quite common in Palestinian fiction, cf. for instance Kanafānī's novels.

37 For instance, Yūnis emerges as a pragmatic leader who dislikes easy rhetoric (the Arab armies are not the only ones to blame for the *nakba*) and terrorist actions (he opposes the attack at the 1972 Olympic Games in Munich).

38 Curiously, if the love story Yūnis is said to represent is over-idealized, so is the novel's depiction of Nahīla (see earlier).

39 Much of Barrāda's fiction is built on the same tension between the human needs of remembering and forgetting.

40 Maḥmūd Sa[c]īd writes a positive review of the novel in which he nevertheless points out how a creative writer can sometimes fall 'into the net of reportorial writing', especially when he is a journalist (Sa[c]īd 1999: 101).

41 Are dramatization and characterization vestiges of novelistic realism (which is rejected in these texts)? Are they only *mimetic* tools (which, as we noticed earlier, are not necessarily superior to *diegetic* ones – such as Khūrī's reportorial style)? We will try to answer these questions in the conclusion.

42 Cf. Khūrī 1999: 14 where he claims that writing means to give a voice to those who do not have one. Incidentally, this is exactly what al-Kharrāṭ too claims to want to achieve (Kharrāṭ 1996b: 14).

43 It is fair to say that the challenge to heroism is already present in earlier modernist works. For example, it is ironically present in Joyce's *Ulysses*, where the Homeric hero is dressed in the clothes of a twentieth century common man.

44 Conversation with the author, Tunis, December 2001.

45 'Ma conception du roman – la structure que je lui ai donnée – est telle qu'elle cherche à impliquer le lecteur' Takarlī 1985: 11.

46 Thāmir relates *al-Raj*[c] to a somewhat similar earlier experiment in multiple narration within Iraqi fiction: Ghā[ɔ]ib Ṭu[c]ma Farmān's *Khamsat aṣwāt* (1967), Thāmir 1992: 79, 82, cf. on the same novel Allen 1995: 82–3.

47 We have observed earlier how Barrāda's *Luᶜbat* presents similar characteristics: a pluralistic narration and a variety of linguistic varieties. As far as the stylization of the characters' speech is concerned, it is curious to contrast Genette's view of 'the stylistic autonomy of the characters' as the height of dialogic mimesis (Genette 1972: 210–11) with Bakhtin's observation that stylistic characterization can lead more easily to an objectification of the characters' discourse by the monological author. Of course, the critics are addressing two different topics. Bakhtin concedes that 'language diversity and speech characterizations remain important in a polyphonic novel' but he argues that its most important aspect is 'the *dialogic angle* at which [. . .] styles and dialects are juxtaposed or counterposed in the work' (Bakhtin 1963: 182). He therefore disregards the fact that all of Dostoevsky's heroes seem to speak the language of their author. In Meyer 2001: 38, Hamarneh is quoted lamenting that in Jabrā's *al-Safīna* the characters all speak with the author's voice.

48 Cf. Cobham 2002: 187.

49 Little Sanāᵓ sees her father Ḥusayn in the street at the beginning of the novel, frustrating her grandmother's attempt to conceal him from her. Later, she will be present both at ᶜAdnān's dramatic confrontation with Munīra, and when Midḥat proposes to Munīra. In both situations she is the unwanted witness. In the two chapters focused on Sanāᵓ (see later) we have approximately the same situation as Genette identifies in Henry James's *What Maisie Knew* (1908): 'we [. . .] never leave the point of view of the little girl, whose 'restriction of field' is particularly dramatic in this story of adults, a story whose significance escapes her' (Genette 1972: 189).

50 Apart from the story which we are about to refer to, see also the story narrated to Midḥat by his father (Takarlī 1980: 153–6/*118–20*). The anecdote is about al-Sayyid Ismāᶜīl, Abū Midḥat's father, and his neglecting his wife to spend entire days with his lover, a singer called Riḥāna.

51 Another important contribution which these background characters make to the novel is the linguistic richness of their dialogue: we will see later how the main characters express their own different perspectives and how their tones change rhetorically too. However, as far as style and linguistic variety are concerned, the heroes (Midḥat, Karīm, Munīra, and also Ḥusayn and Madīḥa) speak roughly the same language. The great range of linguistic varieties comes from the minor characters: the Christians speak their own variation of *ᶜāmmiyya*, the drinkers of Uwānīs's back room offer their own peculiar bar slang, and most notably, the old man who hosts Ḥusayn and Midḥat will end up speaking Turkish! The older generation of the family, especially Abū Midḥat, speak in a more pious language (see the scene where he sends a message consisting of some verses from the Koran to his son via Ḥusayn, the non-delivering messenger, Takarlī 1980: 380–1/*291–2*).

52 Meyer adds that Faulkner's novel is more sophisticated because Mahfouz does not 'deal with the validity of the different types of perception. In Faulkner, on the other hand, the emphasis is as much on the quality and nature of the narrators' awareness as on how each one contributes to building a complete picture of events' (Meyer 2001: 26).

53 We could well add *Crime and Punishment* to Genette's list of such mysterious beginnings.

54 The physical descriptions of Munīra are more numerous in Midḥat's first chapter (5), denoting his interest and attraction; cf. Takarlī 1980: 158/*121*.

55 Which by the way, was easily recognizable in his fiction because of his work as an editor, critic and publicist (cf., e.g. Grossman 1962: 223–9). The same can be said about Khūrī but not about al-Takarlī.

56 When challenged by Ghālī Shukrī about the alleged neutrality of his works, Mahfouz replies: 'My sympathies for a certain character appear one way or the other within the novel. [. . .] Do you not sense that I am for, or against, [a certain character]?', quoted

in Mehrez 1994: 36. In the context of Shukrī's interview, being partisan is a positive value: it means that the writer is brave enough to make a stand. Mahfouz was famously criticized for his alleged unwillingness to speak out. Of course, the attitude of the critics and writers mentioned earlier (who see in the author's neutrality and objectivity that elusive mark of artistic sublimity which is almost impossible to attain) is very much the opposite of the attitude of those critics who want the writer to lead by example, taking up arms against injustice and taking a clear political, ideological stand.

57 It is true that the epilogue to the novel (celebrating Raskolnikov's new life regenerated through Sonya's Christian values) looks like an alien body which, Bakhtin insists, does not destroy the polyphonic value of the novel, Bakhtin 1963: 92.

58 Genette uses the term 'narrating instance' to mean a sort of general narrating context, that is: 'the narrating situation, the narrative matrix – the entire set of conditions (human, temporal, spatial) out of which a narrative statement is produced' (Genette 1972: n. 10, p. 31). We could include *al-Raj*[c] in Genette's comments on Joyce's *Ulysses* and Faulkner's *The Sound*: 'In the case of an isolated monologue, one not taking up the whole of the narrative, as in Joyce or Faulkner, the narrating instance is maintained (but in the background) by the context: all the chapters before the last one in *Ulysses*, the fourth section in *The Sound and the Fury*' (Genette 1972: 174–5). Similar enigmatic endings are present in these two novels.

59 Cf. Batatu 1978: 282–3.

60 *Al-Raj*[c]'s open-endedness can be compared, despite the many differences, to the open-endedness admired by Meyer in Kanafānī's *Rijāl fī-'l-shams* (Meyer 2001: 28).

61 '[W]e should regard the ideas of Dostoevsky the thinker as the *idea-prototypes* for certain ideas in his novels (the idea-images of Sonya [. . .])' Bakhtin 1963: 92.

62 In a way this is exactly what happens in *Crime and Punishment* as well: as we know from secondary sources analysing the ideas of 'Dostoevsky the thinker', we can find in Porfiry Petrovich the author's ideal for a new method of police investigation; in the *déclassé* aristocratic young man Razumichin we have his hope for a national revival (from a Slavonic nationalistic point of view); in Sonya we have already seen the Christian ideal. In this respect, Dostoevsky's point of view is recognizable but it is not that of a single character.

63 The portrayal of [c]Āmir is extremely positive: he appears as a member of an heroic generation of Egyptian history which has been too easily dismissed by Nasser's regime: he always provides a wise comment on the episodes involving the people living at the pension *Mīrāmār*, and he is clearly the character closest to Mahfouz.

64 As for *Crime and Punishment*, its characters can be easily associated with social and ideological types typical of 1865 Russia. Cf. Grossman 1965: 345–70.

65 Cf. for example Musallam 1983: 40–1 and Cobham's discussion on the dubious usefulness of these symbolic readings, Cobham 2002: 191–2.

66 As we have seen earlier, *Bāb*'s idealized Nahīla lacks the three-dimensional characterization of Munīra.

67 Obviously we could ask the same question about Khūrī's and Barrāda's novels and the answer would be negative.

68 Raskolnikov does not collapse merely because his argument is refuted, but also because of what happens to him (and maybe we can even dare to make an improbable parallel between his meeting with Sonya and Midḥat's with Munīra). We can, however, safely affirm that *al-Raj*[c] is less ideologically unambiguous than *Crime and Punishment*. Can we therefore say that it is artistically or technically superior?

69 It is important to notice that this first encounter with the characters' attitudes is portrayed through Ṣafiyya's neutral perspective: 'She didn't understand everything they were saying' (Takarlī 1980: 77/57). In this case Ṣafiyya's limited awareness (ignorance) fulfils the role we have already seen fulfilled by little Sanā[ɔ]. Still, we can already

understand from this one example that Midḥat's father is conservative but fundamentally moderate and tolerant.

70 Cf. Dostoevsky 1866: 258–65. Despite this similarity Midḥat's character is fundamentally different from Raskolnikov's. For instance, we read about the former: 'He wasn't temperamentally inclined to commit crimes for the sake of having it [a full life, getting rich, and so on] all' (Takarlī 1980: 151/*117*).

71 Cf. the bitter irony when Ḥusayn cracks a joke about his death and in fact unwittingly predicts Midḥat's (Takarlī 1980: 153/*118*). The novel contains other 'prophetic' passages.

72 Ironically, the scene closes the chapter where Midḥat's theories of calculated selfishness are more completely formulated during his dialogue with Ḥusayn, see earlier paragraphs.

73 Cf. Raskolnikov's nightmares, especially in section I, Chapter 5, section III, Chapter 6. Dostoevsky 1866: 54–9, 275–8.

74 Cf. Yūsuf Idrīs's short story *Uqtul-hā* (1981; *Kill her!*, 1985) where Suzanne shocks Muṣṭafā by gently accepting that he strangle her.

75 From Midḥat's monologue: 'An unstable society with no future; a society on the edge of the abyss; a society of indigestion, stupidity, fear, hatred, hypocrisy; where you eat when your stomach's full, don't know what's going on in the world, can't avoid sexual complexes, and are obsessed with poverty. It's a society which has no relationship with its true members and offers you nothing in exchange for the stupid conditions it imposes' (Takarlī 1980: 150/*115*).

76 Even if this conclusion too is problematized by the novel, as we will see later when we will rely on Cobham's reading of it (Cobham 2002: 186).

77 These unexpressed truths are reminiscent of Mīkhāʾīl's impotent silences *vis-à-vis* Rāma's rejections. However, when it comes to defining identity and political ideas Mīkhāʾīl and Rāma can turn very outspoken as compared to Munīra, Midḥat, Karīm and Ḥusayn.

78 On Genette's warning against a too rigid use of theoretical categories such as his various 'focalizations' within the context of al-Takarlī's novels, see Caiani 2004: 62.

79 Cf. Grossman 1965: 357–8.

80 Cf. Grossman 1965: 358 where Dostoevsky is quoted pondering about a plan (the one which actually prevailed) for *Crime and Punishment*: 'Another plan. Narration by the author, who is a sort of invisible omniscient being, never leaving Raskolnikov's side for a single minute.'

81 See how Genette discusses similar relaxations in the use of the internal focalization in Proust's *A la recherche du temps perdu* (1919–27) but then absolves them of defining Proust's narrative *polymodality* (i.e. the novelist passes at leisure from the consciousness of the hero to that of his narrator and the other characters, sometimes applying rigorously the internal focalization of the hero, at other times turning into a more classical omniscient external narrator), Genette 1972: 207–11.

82 For Qays al-Sāᶜidī, writing for the magazine of the Iraqi communist party, Munīra is the symbol of the Iraqi communist party, while ᶜAdnān is the Baᶜth party (Sāᶜidī 1997).

83 As Cobham goes on to say: 'However, the description of how ᶜAdnān forces himself on Munīra and what he does to her is unequivocally violent and non-consensual' (Cobham 2002: 186).

84 One could write a whole study on the importance of parenthetical passages in *al-Rajᶜ*. The other important one is the whole thirteenth chapter which divides chapter twelve into two parts.

85 This is why Walther reads this feeling of Munīra's as her reaction to the rape (which is, strictly speaking, incorrect), Walther 1995: 137.

86 The feeling of immediacy can be conveyed by a first person narration in the present tense. Such narration would give the reader the illusion that the narrator is relating what happens as it happens, but would also be extremely difficult to sustain in a rigorous fashion throughout a long work of fiction.

87 For an interesting parallel, see how Gary Rosenshield, in the second chapter ('First- versus. Third-Person Narration') of his monograph on *Crime and Punishment*, shows the same shortcoming in Dostoevsky's provisional first person draft of the novel where Raskolnikov is recalling what had happened, Rosenshield 1978: 14–25.

88 It is striking how Karīm and Munīra are the two characters who, for different reasons, cannot influence the course of events. The former is an extremely weak character who is utterly unable to balance his self-obsession with any kind of positive reaction to life's blows. Munīra's character presents similarities with Karīm's, but unlike him she shows some unusual strength in coping with dramatic situations; however, because of external social circumstances (her loss of virginity before marriage in the Iraqi society of the 1960s obviously increases her dependence on a man), she is still in the position of being unable to change her life effectively. Therefore, it is possible that the shift in the narration occurs only in the case of these two characters, in order to dramatize their subordinate status (either socially or self-imposed). Karīm himself admits to being *ᶜājiz* (impotent): he is unable to cope with the loss of his friend Fuᵓād and with his love for Munīra, he is afflicted by a sense of guilt which is justifiable only through his childish self-obsession (here the 'I' form seems to be very appropriate). As we have hinted earlier, Munīra and her cousin Karīm form one of the two crucial pairings of characters in the novel (the other one being Midḥat/Ḥusayn).

89 Of course, the juxtaposition of different narratives can have more than one application and effect. In Ḥusayn's chapter (the fourth), we have a passage depicting Ḥusayn trying to explain to his cousin Midḥat the reasons behind his decision to leave children and wife and run away to Kuwait (Takarlī 1980: 114–17/*86–9*). The first person of Ḥusayn's direct speech is intertwined with paragraphs narrated by a third person omniscient narrator. The two narratives deal with the same subject (the night Ḥusayn did not return home) but through two completely different perspectives. The effect of this contrast is lightly comic (despite the seriousness of the topic). The first person narrator focuses on his highly abstract, existential and philosophical concerns, while the third person narrator chronicles what actually happened. These more factual details (playing poker in a whorehouse, flirting with a prostitute and eventually getting drunk) are not available to Midḥat who unceremoniously reacts to what Ḥusayn tells him with the question: 'What's this rubbish you're talking?' (Takarlī 1980: 118/*89*).

90 Milan Kundera comments on the 'chronological displacement' in his novel *The Unbearable Lightness of Being* (1984) as follows: 'The events of Part Six occur after the events of the seventh and last part. Because of that dislocation, the last part, despite its idyllic quality, is flooded with a melancholy that comes from our knowledge of what is to happen' (Kundera 1986: 77). Obviously, in al-Takarlī's case, the 'idyllic situation' is replaced by Midḥat's discovery of Munīra's truth.

91 Here it will suffice us to point to a few plausible explanations for this novel's pessimistic ending. External intervention in personal matters and the burden of history on individual lives are among the writer's major preoccupations, as is evident also at the end of *al-Masarrāt* where the young man Ghassān is killed at the beginning of the Iran–Iraq war. Also here the character seems oblivious to the danger posed by wider conflicts, and focuses merely on private matters. The impossibility of Midḥat's survival could simply be a matter of chance. This is what we would like to call 'the Dürrenmatt solution': *The Pledge* (1958) is, until just before the end, a perfect detective novel. But the author subverts an entire novelistic genre and avoids the classic finale – the solution of the murder. The murderer dies in a car crash when he is about to fall into the

cunning trap laid by the policeman. Another reason for *al-Raj^{c}*'s ending must presumably be the author's scepticism regarding the ability of Iraqi society to renew itself, at least in the short term. Cf. also Cobham 2002: 191–2.

92 Similarly, Said argues that Auerbach is probably encouraged in his stern condemnation of Goethe, making him 'represent too much', by the 'horrors of the present'– the early 1940s in which he was writing (Said 2003: xxviii–xxix).

93 Bakhtin quoted in Testa 2002: 291.

4 INTERTEXTUALITY

1 In the last novel of the *Rāma* Trilogy, Mīkhā$^{\circ}$īl acknowledges that the ancient poets, whose verses he often quotes, did not leave anything unsaid (Kharrāṭ 1996a: 276). In Khūrī's *Yālū*, the protagonist's grandfather, Father Afrām, claims that all books derive from one secret, divine book (Khūrī 2002: 110–11).

2 '[L]e texte est un tissu de citations, issues des mille foyers de la culture. [. . .] l'écrivain ne peut qu'imiter un geste toujours antérieur, jamais originel; son seul pouvoir est de mêler les écritures' (Barthes 1968: 65).

3 The Italian critic and novelist writes in his *Reflections* on his first novel *The Name of the Rose*: 'I rediscovered what writers have always known (and have told us again and again): books always speak of other books, and every story tells a story that has already been told' (Eco 1983: 20).

4 'Reading and lived experiences are not two different universes. Each of these experiences, in order to be interpreted, calls for certain readings and merges into them. That books are always born from other books is a truth which only seemingly contradicts another truth: that books are born from factual life and human relationships' (Calvino 1964: 15–16).

5 We are using this term even if alliteration more normally refers to the repetition of the first consonant, whereas in these passages the repeated letter is not necessarily the first.

6 We might read al-Kharrāṭ's claim that his alliterations were naturally inspired with Eco's anecdote about Lamartine in mind: 'Talking about a famous poem of his [. . .], Lamartine said that it had come to him in a single flash, on a stormy night, in a forest. When he died, the manuscripts were found, with revisions and variants; and the poem proved to be the most "worked out" in all of French literature' (Eco 1983: 11). Ḥasan claims that al-Kharrāṭ's first two novels are governed by a meticulous structure, despite the author's insisting on his writing being the fruit of spontaneous outbursts (Ḥasan 1996: 126).

7 In *Rāma*, the passages are the aforementioned *ḥā$^{\circ}$* and *mīm* sections (Kharrāṭ 1979: 100/*88*, 105/*92*). In *al-Zaman*, we find the following sections: *hamza* (Kharrāṭ 1985: 19–20); *hā$^{\circ}$* (74); *^{c}ayn* (110); *sīn* (164); *jīm* (227); *sīn* and *ṣād* (258) and *ghayn* (368). In *Yaqīn*, we have a *sīn* passage (Kharrāṭ 1996a: 70, which is not as consistent as the others); *bā$^{\circ}$* (93–4); *wāw* (160–1); *ḍād* (215); *fā$^{\circ}$* (226) and *ṭā$^{\circ}$* (288).

8 On the other hand, Musawi suggests that the words of these passages are connected by both sound and meaning: he quotes extensively from the *ṭā$^{\circ}$* section (Kharrāṭ 1996a: 288), explaining that it conveys the ideas of nostalgia and rapture (Musawi 1999: 172–3).

9 This article is useful for understanding al-Kharrāṭ's own work too because it deals with questions (such as the inspiration of the *turāth*) which are also important factors in relation to al-Kharrāṭ's own fiction. For a brief analysis of the meaning of Arabic letters cf. Ryding 1997 (curiously dealing with the same authors as those mentioned by al-Kharrāṭ) and Appendix I ('Letter Symbolism in Sufi Literature') of Annemarie Schimmel's monograph on Sufism, Schimmel 1975: 411–25.

10 Sāmī^{c}Alī's original reading relates this distinctive feature of Kharrāṭian writing to mystical, *ṣūfī* beliefs: al-Kharrāṭ reproduces in his writing the mystical (pantheistic) unity amongst the various different elements of the world when he employs alliteration: the words he uses are different from one another but they are all united by a letter (cf. 'Alī 2000: 162–3).

11 Al-Kharrāṭ's personal style with all its linguistic eclecticism has not been immune from criticism. Both Musawi and Darrāj, for example, criticize him (Musawi's judgement on al-Kharrāṭ is ambivalent: for his positive comments, see later). Summarizing and synthesizing their points, we can affirm that in their view al-Kharrāṭ's texts are not novels but the self-indulgent ('self-pleasuring') and artificial exercises of an aristocratic aesthete (Musawi 2003: 371–2). One positive aspect of al-Kharrāṭ's first novel which Darrāj seems willing to concede is that its author succeeds in combining Farīd al-Dīn al-^{c}Aṭṭār's mystical passion 'with Breton's philosophy, to give a unique (or almost unique) text characterized by passion, loss, the intimacy of union and the suffering of being apart'. Then he adds that al-Kharrāṭ's text attempts to deal with this burning passion but in fact only deals with 'the blazing language' expressing it (Darrāj 1999: 266). In other words, the focus of fiction is here on the process, the search for a suitable medium for expressing a certain concept or situation, the way a story is narrated.

12 We find many examples of this in al-Tanūkhī's (939–94) *al-Faraj ba^{c}d al-shidda* 'Relief after Distress'. For example, in one of the many stories in this work, a sick young boy, thinking that he is going to die, asks his father to allow him to be left alone with his wet nurse so he can avoid the company of his servants. The boy's father, who is telling the story, says: 'He said to me: [...] what I ask you is that you keep them away from me [...] since they are my age and if I see them healthy, while I know I am dying, my affliction and my illness will increase my weakness so that my death will come earlier' (Tanūkhī 1978: 224). For other examples of the use of direct speech in classical Arabic literature, see Ibn ^{c}Abd Rabbi-hi's (860–940) version of the *ḥadīth* concerning the Quraysh delegation to the legendary pre-Islamic Yemeni king Ibn Dhī Yazan: the tale is narrated through the main characters' (the king and ^{c}Abd al-Muṭṭalib) perspectives and attitudes. These are expressed in their own words: by means of direct speech the reader comes to know their feelings and psychological status (Ibn ^{c}Abd Rabbi-hi 1965: 23–8). See also Tanūkhī 1973: 179, where a character is obviously made to utter his thoughts.

13 As far as classical prose is concerned, we should also consider the need of the author–compiler to appear as a reporter, an historian and not an author of fiction. Hence the narrator himself, or one of his sources, does not know what such and such has thought, but knows only what he or she has said.

14 There are many examples showing how the author systematically employs the verb *qāla* when a dialogue takes place between the protagonists. This repetition is typical of classical prose, while in modern Arabic fiction dashes tend to be used to introduce speech (for such a systematic use of the verb *qāla*, see for instance Kharrāṭ 1979: 196; Kharrāṭ 1985: 294–5). It appears more clearly, however, that al-Kharrāṭ's use of the verb *qāla* is conscious and must be evocative, if not highly significant, when this occurs in passages in which Mīkhā$^{\supset}$īl addresses himself. Not only does the writer feel the need to say that his character is actually saying what he thinks, but he also introduces every utterance with the verb 'to say':

He said: Despite that, the imprisoned beast is never really set free from its cage.
He said: Does it want to remain inside it, is that what it wants?
He said: It does not raise its claw to break it, nor even merely to scratch it.
Then he said: The cage is neither open nor is it easy to break, that is true, but it is not completely impossible to break. Oh, if only he were strong and crazy enough!

And he said: I want to drown in the nudity of being, even from within the cage.
He said: Without naming it.
He said: The brick of stone.

(Kharrāṭ 1985: 257)

15 Jean Fontaine has the following to say about *al-Zaman*: 'Peut-être sont-ce alors les dialogues qui marqueraient davantage l'évolution. Encore que beaucoup de ces échanges sont transcrits dans l'absolu avec l'inchoatif *qāla* sans réelle connotation de prise de parole' (Fontaine 1986: 46).

16 We have to underline that we are dealing with a mere formal feature here. In fact, there are many differences separating al-Kharrāṭ's prose from classical prose: in the former, for instance, the psychological portrayal is very much in the foreground.

17 Cf. the frenetic rhythm obtained by the use of the verb 'to say' in part 2 of T. S. Eliot's *The Waste Land* ('A Game of Chess'), Eliot 1922: 56–7.

18 Here it is possible to compare this inability of Mīkhā°īl to communicate with that of Midḥat and Munīra in *al-Raj*[c] (analysed in the previous chapter). Khalīl (*vis-à-vis* Yūnis) in *Bāb* and al-[c]Ayshūnī (*vis-à-vis* Fāṭima) in Barrāda's *al-Ḍaw*° are also characters who find it difficult to communicate. In this latter novel, the protagonist (al-[c]Ayshūnī) has an imaginary dialogue with a Ghaylāna (Fāṭima's mother), with whom he had a relationship many years before, in which he asks her general, existential questions and then silently comments on her answers (Barrāda 1993: 95–101). This imaginary dialogue is reminiscent of Mīkhā°īl's with Rāma as it is also based on the '*lam yaqul la-hā*' device. More significantly, Ghaylāna (who after splitting up with al-[c]Ayshūnī goes to Spain where she becomes a prostitute), like Rāma, emerges as a strong and independent woman whose views are more practical and pragmatic, less abstract (and pretentious perhaps) than those of the male protagonist.

19 In other words, a reader can enjoy the way al-Kharrāṭ shapes his philosophical or aesthetic stances without knowing that these are allusions to, say, Coptic folk literature or Islamic mystical poets or Western modernist novelists. Additionally, al-Kharrāṭ's lexical and syntactical complexity is not always bound to his intertextual allusions. It is also necessary to underline that al-Kharrāṭ's language is not always the Arabic of a sophisticated, somehow elitist, intellectual. He is also appreciated as one of the most successful authors to merge modern standard Arabic (*fuṣḥā*) and the vernacular ([c]*āmmiyya*) into one expressive and precise literary language (cf. 'Alī 2000: 160–1). He can be classified as one of the writers who continue the process of development of the literary language inaugurated by Egyptian authors such as Yaḥyā Ḥaqqī and Y. Idrīs, mainly through the influence of [c]*āmmiyya* (in their case Egyptian). It is curious to find in the same novel, *Yaqīn*, an increasing use of both Egyptian [c]*āmmiyya* and lengthy alliterations.

20 For a comprehensive intertextual study of the re-writing of *The Arabian Nights* in Ḥabībī's works, see Sessona 2002. Sessona stresses how his novels rely on intertextual references to the Arabic literary heritage, in order to both voice the author's disaffection with the present, and reinforce his links with the cultural past (Sessona 2002: 45). On the other hand, F. J. Ghazoul stresses how *The Arabian Nights* has provided Mahfouz with a suitable basis for his political allegory in his *Layālī Alf layla* (1982); for an analysis of the novel, see Ghazoul 1996: 134–49.

21 For synopses and analyses of the novel in English, see Allen 1995: 195–208; Mehrez 1994: 96–118; Meyer 2001: 55–60 and Musawi 2003: 265–71.

22 Although Meyer seems to suggest that in Ḥabībī and al-Ghīṭānī the *turāth* is there mainly to provide a vehicle for the irony with which they comment in an indirect way on political matters (cf. Meyer 2001: 71–2). Such is the extent and scope of these

writers' use of *turāth*, however, that it would seem to point to wider artistic reasons (the whole of al-Ghīṭānī's impressive novelistic production relies on Arabic literary models of the past, including the *khiṭaṭ* genre and the mystical work of Ibn ᶜArabī; cf. Allen 1995: 123).

23 Allen 1995: 199.

24 As we have noted in the previous chapter, Musawi observes that at the core of *Yaqīn* there is a reworking of the Shahrazād/Shahriyār trope, in which narrating is denial of death (Musawi 1999: 164).

25 For a more detailed discussion of the character of Rāma, see 'Rāma and the Egyptian Character' (Caiani 2005: 37–42).

26 As early as 1919, Muḥammad Nājī adopts Isis within a modern nationalist discourse as the symbol for Egypt in his monumental oil on canvas entitled 'The Awakening of Egypt, or the Procession of Isis' (Baron 1997: 113).

27 In *Rāma*, Demeter, the ancient Greek version of the goddess Isis, is also mentioned with the same connotations of a deity able to bring about birth, rebirth, life. The natural connotations of the myth are obvious. For a brief explication of the significance of Isis and other myths mentioned in the novels, cf. Hornblower and Spawforth 1996.

28 This is the epithet of *al-Sayyida Zaynab*, the granddaughter of the Prophet. She is the patron saint of women and the infirm (with a mosque containing her shrine in Cairo, she is particularly popular in Egypt).

29 It seems clear that Rāma here embodies the feminine nature *par excellence*. We could also argue in passing that later novels by al-Kharrāṭ, namely *Turābu-hā* and *Yā banāt Iskandariyya* (1990), offer (through al-Kharrāṭ's usual intertwining of present time, memory and vision) a large number of female visions rather than characters, which tend to form an ideal, depersonalized female whole (the Other, the idealized beloved). In fact, Hammond mentions an 'ultimately unidentifiable feminine authority' (Hammond 2000: 40). As far as *Turābu-hā* is concerned, al-Nowaihi underlines how the female characters are depersonalized into an archetypal beloved, hence, as we have seen earlier in *Rāma*, 'each individual woman that Mikhael [Mīkhāᵓīl] encounters is unique, but contains within her all other women' (Nowaihi 1994: 52). Notice that the heroes of *Turābu-hā* and *Yā banāt* are also called Mīkhāᵓīl.

30 See how Tawfīq al-Ḥakīm and other Egyptian intellectuals apply the same notion of eternal rejuvenation to the Egyptian nation (Gershoni and Jankowski 1986: 146–7).

31 Here al-Kharrāṭ quotes a phrase from the declaration of faith at the end of the Coptic divine liturgy (according to Saint Basil) which refers to Christ's nature: 'Truly I believe that his divinity parted not from his humanity for a single moment nor a twinkling of an eye' (*The Coptic Liturgy* (*According to Saint Basil*)).

32 Before the Ghazoul–Verlenden English translation of *Rāma* appeared, Ghazoul had published the English translation of all the passages where the dragon is mentioned in the novel (Ghazoul 1999), these are in our edition: Kharrāṭ 1979: 80–1/*70*, 131/*117–18*, 203/*186–8*, 224/*207*, 244/*227*, 270/*252* and 348/*1*, where the novel ends with al-Ḥallāj's verses quoted later.

33 We go from Ghazoul's assumption that the inner story of the dragon within *Rāma* is ironic, although she does not explain how (Ghazoul 1999: 167), to the claim of al-Kharrāṭ's Italian translator, Leonardo Capezzone, based on the novelist's own words, that the dragon 'paradoxically is void of meaning' (Capezzone 1993: 141). The Egyptian writer Badr al-Dīb relies on a passage in *Rāma* (in which Rāma says to Mīkhāᵓīl: 'You slew the dragon', Kharrāṭ 1979: 223/*206*) to interpret the dragon as love (al-Dīb quoted in Fārūq 1997: 154). On the other hand, Fārūq himself shows how the meaning of the dragon is not so well defined (for instance, if we refer to other passages, Rāma quotes the fable of the knight killing the dragon in order to win his beloved).

He adds that the dragon is more to do with Mīkhāʾīl's solitude and inability to merge with the other: it is 'also the feeling of estrangement and alienation in this habitual, familiar world' (Fārūq 1997: 154).

34 Al-Kharrāṭ proposes this interpretation in the Hafez interview mentioned earlier: 'The dragon is the absolute and he is this [sic] consummately sacred and satanic within man. In this sense evil is absolute, inasmuch as good is absolute, but they are both human, and relative, also contingent and eternal' (Hafez 1982: 236–7).

35 Sometimes the connection is explicit: for example, in one of his short stories, *Aqdām al-ʿaṣāfīr ʿalā al-raml* "Birds" Footmarks on the Sand', the narrator mentions the writer's second collection of short stories *Sāʿāt al-kibriyāʾ* 'Hours of pride' (1972): 'I saw the red covers of "Hours of Pride" turning white amongst tongues of fire' (Kharrāṭ 1983: 49). Similarly, in Khūrī's *Mamlakat*, we have an explicit reference to one of his earlier novels, *al-Wujūh al-bayḍāʾ* 'White Faces' (1981): 'The civil war in Lebanon had transformed into *White Faces*' (Khūrī 1993: 28/*22*). Al-Kharrāṭ's fictional *oeuvre* can be seen as a monumental whole. Mīkhāʾīl, the protagonist of his first novel, reappears throughout his successive fiction, emerging as the author's *alter ego*. Even Rāma and the dragon come back in the author's fictional works, along with recurring themes and similar situations. As for the dragon, it also appears at the end of *Yā banāt*.

36 Revelation 12, in which the dragon appears, is entitled 'The Woman and the Dragon', and in Arabic 'al-Marʾa wa-'l-tinnīn'.

37 One of the examples of Egyptian symbolism in early Christian art is the pairing of St George and the dragon which calls to mind 'the god Horus depicted spearing Set, often portrayed as an evil serpent' (*An Introduction to the Coptic Art of Egypt*).

38 The following passage is our translation of the Arabic version of the passage found in *al-Zaman*. This is based on a French (Morard 1985: 21) and an English (MacRae 1977: 256–7) translation of the same Coptic passage. We will indicate in notes every disagreement between the Arabic (al-Kharrāṭ's?) and the other translations.

39 In Gnostic terms we have to differentiate between God (*al-rabb al-abadī*) and the demiurge, the god creator (*al-rabb*): 'By definition, a righteous and benevolent God could not be the source of evil and disorder in the universe. And since the creator God of the Old Testament can be understood to have acted in capricious and questionable ways (as for example with Job), it would naturally follow that he is not the righteous and benevolent father; rather, he proves to be merely a blind and ignorant fashioner of worlds [the demiurge]' (Hedrick 1986: 4).

40 'I had seen it' (كنتُ شاهدتُه) in *al-Zaman*. Both the English and French translations have Eve as the subject of the verb ('a glory which she had seen', MacRae 1977: 256; 'la gloire qu'elle avait vue', Morard 1985: 21).

41 This is one of al-Kharrāṭ's recurrent topics (indeed we could say that his many works are a continuous elaboration of the same themes). As Hafez and Cobham have underlined in commenting on his short story *Jurḥ maftūḥ* (1969): 'The brother–sister relationship was a prominent part of ancient Egyptian mythology. It was not considered incestuous, but rather as analogous to the relationship between body and soul' (Hafez and Cobham 1988: 220).

42 Cf. the French translation: 'Elle me fit connaître une parole de Gnose, concernant Dieu l'Éternel' (Morard 1985: 21).

43 After Mīkhāʾīl has been talking to Rāma about *al-maʿrifa*, knowledge, we read: 'She looked at him. She is the one who knows [*hiya allatī taʿrif*]' (Kharrāṭ 1985: 79).

44 This last sentence does not immediately follow the beginning of the passage in our other sources. Both French and English translations differ from al-Kharrāṭ's Arabic version: 'après cela, notre coeur devint ténèbres' (Morard 1985: 23); 'after these (events) we became darkened in our heart(s)' (MacRae 1977: 257). It is probable, however, that the Arabic *al-rabb* here means God, and not the demiurge. Hence, God's

becoming darkness in the heart of Adam and Eve points at their losing their Gnosis and glory.

45 Hallaq writes about al-Kharrāṭ: 'chez [al-Kharrāṭ] le thème de la femme et celui de la connaissance, dans les sens sémitique et grec du terme, sont intimement liés.' He then defines *Rāma*: 'une suite de variations sur ce thème de la quête qui permet à l'homme d'entrer en possession de soi, de son environnement intérieur comme de son environement matériel' (Hallaq 2001: 163).

46 According to *midrash* literature, Adam's first wife is Lilith (this would explain Genesis 1:27 which seems to point at a simultaneous creation of male and female). In the text referred to by al-Kharrāṭ Naamah (Na^{c}ama) is the Lilith of the Jewish tradition and Lilith (Līlīt) is her sister.

47 The first, spiritual, Eve is here associated with Naamah (the Lilith of the Jewish tradition) who refuses to 'lie beneath Adam because she is equal to him' (Kharrāṭ 1985: 296; in Kharrāṭ 1996a: 207, Lilith is mentioned as the first Eve).

48 This is only one of al-Kharrāṭ's many allusions to the images of Islamic mystical poets. Another example is the image of the unity between wine and cup (Kharrāṭ 1996a: 193; cf. also *Lu^{c}bat*'s opening quotation from al-Muḥāsibī's – 781–837 – *Kitāb al-tawahhum*, Barrāda 1987: 3/*unnumbered page*). Another use of mystical topoi is evident in the evocative appearance of birds (and mythical creatures, such as the dragon): Schimmel talks about how '[t]he traditional connection of the soul with the bird, and the designation of the mystical language as "language of the birds," gives this imagery another overtone' (Schimmel 1975: 424).

49 Each of these, except Coleridge, is mentioned in *Yaqīn*: Shelley's sonnet *Ozymandias* and Keats's ballad *La Belle Dame Sans Merci* are said to be amongst Mīkhā$^{\supset}$īl's youthful reading (Kharrāṭ 1996a: 271). Moreover, some of the ideas attached to their characters are re-stated in *Yaqīn*. For example, according to Musawi, some passages of the novel are reminiscent of Coleridge's imagery in his *Rhyme of the Ancient Mariner*; Mīkhā$^{\supset}$īl identifies with Keats's abandoned knight (prisoner of his love for the *belle dame*); he is Byron's Don Juan who, along with Don Quixote, emerges in the protagonist's consciousness as a free spirit challenging laws and gods. Crucially, Musawi goes on to write about the pairing Don Juan/Mīkhā$^{\supset}$īl: 'Don Juan is active, whereas al-Kharrāṭ's narrator is prisoner of the amorous rapture which cannot be solved except through recollecting, reviving and also "reconstructing" [allusion to Mīkhā$^{\supset}$īl the archaeologist]. All this does not resort to external experiences as much as it strives to reconstruct the relationship through narrating' (Musawi 1999: 169).

50 Bakhtin gives the novel a broad definition: he talks about the concept of 'novelness' rather, applying it to a number of works of different genres (prose and poetry) and from different epochs (from the 'Greek novels' to Dostoevsky's novels). One of the characteristic features of 'novelness' is the focus on the present (as opposed to the focus on a mythical past typical of the epic; Bakhtin 1975: 3–40, 'Epic and the Novel').

51 The passage quoted by Menand in relation to Eliot's conscious desire to revive tradition is taken from the essay 'The Function of Criticism' (1923): 'And, as our instincts of tidiness imperatively command us not to leave to the haphazard of unconsciousness what we can attempt to do consciously, we are forced to conclude that what happens unconsciously [common inheritance and cause unite true artists of any time] we could bring about, and form into a purpose, if we made a conscious attempt' (Eliot 1932: 24).

52 We might pause here to ponder on how much Eliot's discourse was already dealing with intertextuality as some formulate it today. The following is taken from 'The Function of Criticism', 1923: 'I thought of literature then [in 1919, at the time of "Tradition and the Individual Talent"], as I think of it now, of the literature of the world, of the literature of Europe, of the literature of a single country, not as a collection of the writings of individuals, but as "organic wholes", as systems in relation to which, and only in relation to which, individual works of literary art, and the works of

individual artists, have their significance' (Eliot 1932: 23–4). It has to be said that today the stress is more on how writers, being well aware of intertextual connections, explicitly expose them in their works (cf. the following chapter about metafiction).

53 The President was killed in 1981 by a member of *al-Jamāᶜa al-islāmiyya*, an incident recalled in the novel. This information is relevant since in *al-Zaman* Rāma is involved in a leftist plot to murder Sadat!

54 These have not been fabricated by the author but are *verbatim* quotations of original letters sent to newspapers.

55 The increasing concern about sociopolitical issues in the *Rāma* Trilogy is reiterated in *Yaqīn*. In the latter novel though, the letters are not present and such issues are explicitly, but exclusively, treated in the couple's dialogues, especially in the unusually orderly sub-plot of Rāma's trip to Upper Egypt in which she witnesses the aftermath of acts of violence suffered by Copts at the hands of Islamist radicals.

56 We have seen earlier how sometimes Mīkhāᵓīl's elaborate and lyrical sentences conveying lofty concepts contrast to Rāma's much more prosaic vernacular. In *Yaqīn*, a lengthy passage in which Mīkhāᵓīl explains how her body is pure, beyond its bodiness, and so on, is followed by Rāma telling him: 'Do me a favour, enough of that. My body ain't pure!' (Kharrāṭ 1996a: 83–4).

57 Some examples: the miracle of the resurrection of Lazarus is mentioned at p. 54/*44*; p. 56/*45–46* contains a quotation from Ezekiel (see later). It is interesting to see that Khūrī alludes to the Bible's exegetical literature as al-Kharrāṭ does: the narrator in *Mamlakat* is explaining to his lover Mary the meaning of her Hebrew name ('the rebellious') and refers to two Marys as the two Eves (in al-Kharrāṭ Naamah and Lilith): 'The first Mary rebelled against Him [Adam], according to the story. The second Mary accepted Him. But where is the true rebellion – in refusal, or acceptance?' (Khūrī 1993: 58/*47*).

58 The uprootedness of the young generation of Palestinian refugees is amplified by another intertextual reference, this time to a non-literary text. Fayṣal, a young Palestinian from the refugee camp of Shatila, narrates a dream he had in which the people of the refugee camp return to Palestine. Once there, he realizes that he is lonely, as his friends from the camp have returned to the places their families came from. He tries to persuade his friends to build a camp like Shatila in Palestine so that they will not be separated. Fayṣal's dream, as reported in *ᶜāmmiyya* in Muḥammad Malaṣ's book about his documentary on the dreams of Palestinians (probably *al-Manām. Mufakkirat film*, Beirut: Dār al-ādāb, 1991), is quoted in *Mamlakat* (Khūrī 1993: 32–3/*26*). This shows that, even if in Khūrī's novels literary references are predominant, we also find a limited use of documents (like the letters and pieces of news used by al-Kharrāṭ).

59 Since the Arabic version of the biblical passage does not differ significantly from the 'New International Version' English translation of the Holy Bible, we have chosen to quote *verbatim* that version of the passage (1989 edition, p. 1,096).

60 Cf. the ambivalent image of the salt (*milḥ*) in Khūrī with that of the wound (*jurḥ*) in al-Kharrāṭ, discussed in Caiani 2005: 43.

61 'You are the salt of the earth' (Khūrī 1989: 14/*9*). Ironically, for Samᶜān Fayyāḍ, a secondary character in *Riḥlat*, the salt of the earth is Russia! (Khūrī 1989: 125/*118*).

62 The Bible is parodied when Little Ghāndī starts his restaurant business using the leftovers from the restaurant of the American University in Beirut. This is depicted in similar terms to the creation of the Earth as described in Genesis (Khūrī 1989: 187/*173–4*).

63 The same concern is expressed, as we have seen earlier, through the use of the journalistic texts in Barrāda's *Luᶜbat*.

64 The same comic effect is rendered in the passage quoted by Ghandour (Ghandour 2000: 192) depicting the Reverend Amīn's reference to the Sermon on the Mount ('Blessed are the meek, for they shall inherit the earth', Matthew 5: 5) to Little Ghāndī.

Reverend Amīn adds that Ghāndī should consider himself lucky because, just like John the Baptist, he saw the green horses. Ghāndī replies: 'Send my best to John the Baptist, Your Highness' (Khūrī 1989: 37/*33*).

65 Khūrī and al-Kharrāṭ's affiliation to the political Left could also help explain their progressive, anti-sectarian attitude. Al-Kharrāṭ was a Trotskyite in his youth (cf. his novel *Ṭarīq al-nisr* 'The Way of the Eagle', 2002, in which he draws from his youthful political experiences) and Khūrī's affiliation to militant Communist groups is also echoed in his works: for example, Khalīl in *Bāb* says: 'we wanted to liberate the individual, not just the land [Palestine]' (Khūrī 1998: 53/*46*). The title of al-Kharrāṭ's most recent novel is taken from Proverbs 30:19.

66 'Men have walked with certainty on water/But he who died of thirst/Is closer to certainty than those men' (Kharrāṭ 1996a: 7).

67 The crucial historical event which condemns Adele to exile is the 1963 *coup-d'état* in Iraq which ends *al-Raj*^{c}.

68 This is a novel which, as we will see in the next chapter, is also about reading and writing and their relationship to consciousness (cf. Cobham 2004).

69 Like the Kharrāṭian man whose nature is to strive to achieve knowledge at all costs.

70 Tawfīq confesses: 'It occurred to me that boring books [. . .] for example an experimental novel, especially an Arabic one, might help me to sleep' (Takarlī 1998: 459).

71 We can draw a comparison between these two kinds of insertions and the use of music in films. There is a basic difference between a song in a film played or sung by an actor and one which is part of the film soundtrack.

72 The legend has it that the poet reached a place in Anatolia and, when he was about to die, saw the tomb of a princess who had died there. After having asked for information about her, he recited the two lines, obviously referring to the princess and himself as the two strangers.

73 Yālū at first joins the fighting enthusiastically, naively thinking he is a hero who has to defend his homeland. His choice can, however, be explained: first, joining the fighting is a way to rebel against his family (his mother hopes that he will follow in the footsteps of her father and become a priest). Second, the war seems at first to provide him with some sort of direction in his life: even if on the crudest of levels, war gives young Yālū a means of self-expression ('spitting out words'), and it gives him protection (Khūrī 2002: 294).

74 Some of them are, however, likely to be lost on the average reader – for example the one to Propp. Some of these references will be analysed in the following chapter, as they have a significant metafictional value – for example the one to Rushdie.

75 Darwīsh's verses are also read by, and referred to, Shams in *Bāb*; Khūrī 1998: 467–8/*444*.

76 In our case, Fāṭima, like her French muse, tries to fight boredom by having sex with men whom she meets by chance and with whom she refuses to establish any sort of relationship. Her reasons for doing this, and, more generally, for her life as a whole are significantly different from those of Mademoiselle Beaunon (Barrāda 1993: 146 *passim*).

77 Yet another example of such a superficial intertextual intertwining is provided at the end of Khūrī's *Mamlakat* where Khūrī's narrator draws a parallel between a story he is narrating and the one which appears at the beginning of Rushdie's *Midnight's Children* (Khūrī 1993: 98).

78 Al-Kharrāṭ's writing has features in common with that 'subjective realism' which Hutcheon defines as a characteristic of the writing of Joyce, Proust, Virginia Woolf, Pirandello, Svevo and Gide. The focus with such writers is on the character's inner processes: they, like al-Kharrāṭ, 'doubt the claim of external reality to being real, and chose instead to substitute an inner world of subjectivity and imagination' (Hutcheon 1980: 25). As we have seen earlier in more detail, the importance of language and the

experimental, radical use of it in al-Kharrāṭ is reminiscent of Joyce, and, as we will see in the following chapter, Khūrī's fiction is in some respects very close to Rushdie's.

5 METAFICTION

1 Cf. Barthes 1968. Obviously, the fact that the author is aware of using or referring to other texts does not necessarily limit his or her creativity (as we have shown by discussing al-Kharrāṭ and Khūrī's texts).

2 These issues are discussed earlier with reference to Bakhtin's concept of polyphony (cf. Bakhtin 1963: 56–7 quoted earlier).

3 On the concept of the author as a function, see Michel Foucault's observations (Foucault 1969).

4 It is therefore striking that Musawi almost completely ignores the Lebanese author in his monograph on the postcolonial Arabic novel (where he dedicates chapter IX – 'Cultural Contestation and Self-Definition in Arabic Metafiction' – to metafictional writing; Musawi 2003: 337–73).

5 As underlined in Meyer 2001: 129 *passim*.

6 As noted in Chapter 2, these self-referred comments can be ironic: 'I won't say I don't know, for I have said that so many times in this novel' (Khūrī 1993: 102/*83*).

7 In the short story *al-Tannūr* (1972; *The Oven*, 1981), al-Takarlī gives us a masterful example of a quintessential unreliable narrator. Through a first person narrative, a man is mentally rehearsing his defence strategy before standing trial. As he changes his idea on the version of events he is going to give a number of times, the reader gradually discovers how and why he is hiding the truth.

8 The metafictional features of al-Takarlī's *al-Masarrāt* have been analysed in Cobham's article 'Reading and Writing in *al-Masarrāt wa-'l-awjā*ᶜ by Fuᵓād al-Takarlī' (Cobham 2004) from which the translation of this passage is taken.

9 As Cobham hints in her article, in this passage about moral responsibility the omniscient narrator uses the first person plural in order to involve us, the readers (Cobham 2004: 31), whereas a more superficial interpretation would have the passage referring to the mistakes Tawfīq has made *vis-à-vis* his life's women: he is suffering for having married Kamīla whom he does not love, but he is paying even more for not having been able to marry Adele whom he really loved.

10 Through representing what is familiar in a skilfully unfamiliar way art makes us see familiar objects and actions anew, as if for the first time: the automatism of perception is thus removed (Shklovsky 1917).

11 The same passage is quoted in Allen 1995: 124, n. 133.

12 At the very end of the novel (Takarlī 1998: 460–4), Tawfīq incidentally realizes that the green holdall which Ghassān (his young friend who, in the meantime, has died in the Iraq–Iran war) left him is full of money. Ghassān has not left anything which could have helped Tawfīq understand what he meant by this gift. The protagonist is conscious that his position is like that of a reader who has to make sense of the meaning of a complex symbol: what did the author (Ghassān, an amateur writer) mean by it? What did he want him to do with it? Is he meant to use the money to help Fatḥiyya, who is pregnant with Ghassān's child?

13 Tawfīq's numerous readings include Artsybashev (one of his favourites), Camus, Dostoevsky, Hemingway, Ṭāhā Ḥusayn, Mahfouz, Tolstoy and Turgenev.

14 Peter Currie, describing how many contemporary American novels are metafictional, expresses a neutral attitude (for example he writes: 'the tendency of recent fiction to reflect critically on the nature of its own fictionality is as much worthy of commendation for rejecting once and for all the myth of 'organic form' as it is open to the reproach of idealism, of retreating from an empirical reality', Currie 1987: 56). As for

Linda Hutcheon, she writes in the introduction to the book quoted by Aghacy: '*Narcissistic Narrative: The Metafictional Paradox* was originally conceived as a defence of a kind of fiction which began to run rampant in the 1960s [Metafiction]' (Hutcheon 1980: 1).

15 An edited version of what follows will be published in a forthcoming article by the present author under the title '"My Name is Yālū." The Development of Metafiction in Ilyās Khūrī's Work'.

16 The focus is still on marginalized characters, as Yālū epitomizes the anti-hero who is unaware of the consequences of his actions. From a stylistic point of view, *Yālū* continues to use the same economical language as the preceding texts and like them imitates oral story-telling techniques, such as the use of embedded stories and multiple narrators.

17 First of all, Yālū, like many of the protagonists of the novels analysed here, responds with silence to the challenges presented to him. This is an obvious disadvantage when it prevents him from defending himself against police accusations. As a child he was afflicted with a speech defect: the Civil War taught him 'to spit out his words' (Khūrī 2002: 61), providing him with some form of self-expression, albeit a thoroughly inadequate one (giving him, for instance, the illusion of being a hero, teaching him to use words devoid of meaning). Later in life, he would persuade himself that he had spoken his mind to people, when he had actually been talking to himself (e.g. with his friend Ṭūnī in Paris; Khūrī 2002: 67–8). More importantly, as he will become aware later, his inability to articulate his thoughts and feelings hampers him in all aspects of his life.

18 The third person narrative in *Yālū* is similar to the one adopted by al-Takarlī in *al-Raj*^{c}, which has been analysed in Chapter 3.

19 The chapters are untitled and unnumbered. They are, however, clearly divided from one another. The chapters containing Yālū's own written accounts are Chs III (179–87); V (205–19); VII (261–9); IX–XV (287–362) and the final one, XVIII (375–9). The remaining ones are narrated in the third person.

20 These involve harassing couples parked at night in the wood adjacent to the villa and occasionally taking their money or raping the female companions of the drivers. There is nothing in the text to suggest that Yālū is not sincere when he appears unaware of the effects of his actions, although this self-absorbed, unthinking attitude obviously does not make him innocent, as he himself acknowledges later when writing makes him more aware of the nature of his actions.

21 Yālū and Khalīl are similar in the ways they criticize the older generation, as represented by their respective father figures (Father Afrām and Yūnis). In both *Yālū* and *Bāb* the discourse of the older generation is latent rather than fully expressed. In *Yālū*, the protagonist holds his grandfather responsible for depriving Ghābī of her chance to be loved (by her lover Ilyās who, Yālū discovers, might well be his true father). This is only one of the old man's many blameworthy actions and is seen as the cause of Ghābī's lack of concern for Yālū (Khūrī 2002: 262–3).

22 The third person narrator even reminds us how writing is used as the most common form of torture in the Arab world for political dissidents if they survive, as Yālū does, the brutal 'torture of the bottle' (Khūrī 2002: 228–9). The references to the torture of writing (whether corresponding to actual practices or thoroughly fictional), to the nightmare of the blank page, to writing as an activity which requires complete isolation and is met with scorn (see the judge's complete dismissal of and utter contempt for Yālū's papers), are all self-referential, as they can be understood as ironic comments on the writing of fiction in a country like Lebanon.

23 Sciascia's character complaining about the machinery of justice is probably unjustly convicted, while Khūrī chooses as his fictional anti-hero a petty thief and serial rapist who is obviously guilty.

24 In Krzysztof Kieslowski's *A Short Film about Killing* (1988), we are first exposed to a cruel and totally gratuitous murder carried out by a young man at the expense of an innocent taxi driver. In the second part of the film, the young murderer is convicted and executed: we are clearly invited to compare the two violent acts and conclude that they are equally cruel and gratuitous. Even if the young Polish man is in some way comparable to Yālū in that he seems oblivious to the consequences of his actions, Khūrī's narrative is more tolerant towards its protagonist than Kieslowski's camera is: there is no mistaking in the latter that the young Polish murderer acts cruelly and criminally, and his act is quite unacceptable. Khūrī, on the other hand, by exclusively presenting his protagonist's consciousness, makes us understand the wider context – social, political and moral – in which Yālū carries out his acts of violence (Khūrī 2002: 335–6). The contrast between Yālū's own acts of violence and those he is subjected to at the hands of the law is striking.

25 For instance, when Yālū first decides to write of his own free will, outside the constraints of the investigations, he sets out three ideas: a person has to decide between living his life and writing about it; people cannot help betraying one another; people spend their time stealing ideas from one another (Khūrī 2002: 258–9). The thought of stealing ideas is a concept dear to Khūrī (it is echoed in Father Afrām's literary theory of the one divine, universal book from which all the writers of the world copy; see earlier), but here Yālū quite plausibly reaches the same conclusion after he realizes that he has stolen the idea of desire/betrayal from Randa (it has to be said that the overall transformation of Yālū's consciousness is not as plausible as the acquisition of this idea).

26 In *al-Masarrāt* Tawfīq, the amateur literary critic, praises and criticizes famous novels according to their authors' ability to show how the personality of a certain character has come into being, what circumstances have shaped his mind, what has motivated his actions (Takarlī 1998: 120, 158–9; Cobham 2004: 33).

27 There is even a graphic difference between Yālū's first written confessions and those appearing after chapter IX: these latter are made up of indented paragraphs identical to those of the third person chapters (e.g. the first two, for example).

28 As with al-Kharrāṭ's Mīkhāʾīl, the union of man with the divine/absolute is striven for but never achieved. However, if in al-Kharrāṭ's works this failure points at a philosophical and mystical reading of human life, in Khūrī's, man is prevented from attaining spiritual and material fulfilment by social injustice and abuses of power.

29 The verses are taken from Darwīsh's *Jidāriyya*, Darwīsh 2000: 532.

30 One of the novel's last sentences, in which Yālū writes that he does not want a sad finale to his mother's story, in which 'she walks on her own in the city streets, stumbling in her shadow' (Khūrī 2002: 379) reconnects us with the opening scene of the novel, in which Yālū stands in front of the interrogator's desk, with the sun's rays coming from the window behind the man. Yālū is blinded by the light and cannot see anything but the halos of light and an unidentified woman walking 'on her own in the city streets, stumbling in her shadow' (Khūrī 2002: 9). It is as if Yālū is prevented from having a life different from the one narrated in the novel not only by obvious disadvantageous circumstances (like lack of material means and social and political structures) but also by his lack of imagination and self-awareness.

31 Yālū is almost by definition the unreliable narrator as he is forced to write in order to fabricate lies. Even when he (increasingly consciously) turns writing into a tool with which to explore his own experiences, like Khūrī's other narrators, he is forgetful and unsure.

32 Here we will first deal with method 2 (the narrator in novels such as Khūrī's *Mamlakat* and *Riḥlat* and Rushdie's *Midnight's Children* being the authorial persona), then with method 1 (the narrator in *Bāb* is not the authorial persona).

33 Relying on Octavio Paz's considerations on novelistic humour, Kundera stresses how through humour a novelist such as Rushdie gives an ambivalent value to his writing

(which, in his *Satanic Verses*, was famously mistaken for an outright attack on Islam by the Iranian theocracy; cf. Kundera 1993: 4 ff.). We will go back to this topic in the conclusion.

34 Myths can also be fabricated to serve more prosaic purposes. In *Riḥlat*, Abū ᶜAbbās al-Yatīm makes a living out of narrating to tourists and curious people the legend of the Italian nun who survived a shipwreck by walking on water (Khūrī 1989: 144–6/*136–7*). When Alice tells him that he is a swindler and a liar, he replies that this is what people want from him: 'If I lie, they believe me, if I don't lie, they don't believe me. But I don't lie; I say what I've heard, and what I've heard is true, because I've heard it, right?' (Khūrī 1989: 146/*138*). On the other hand, Yālū is forced to find a way to write about facts which never took place to make his confessions conform to the authorities' wishes. He models his imaginary meeting with Haykal (of the al-Naddāf clan) in al-Ashrafiyya (a quarter of Beirut) on a meeting which actually took place (Khūrī 2002: 327–8).

35 Al-Kharrāṭ is aware of the fact that some of the lengthy passages in *Yaqīn* are straightforward examples of social criticism. Rāma, who is in the middle of describing the situation of extreme poverty and promiscuity in which the victims and the perpetrators of those violent acts live, asks: 'Does this sound like a social report?' (Kharrāṭ 1996a: 208). When Rāma finishes narrating the story of her meeting with a girl whose lies caused the outbreak of a violent episode, we have a lengthy, extremely detailed summary of the event, which is a sort of reportage quoting from eye witnesses' accounts and newspaper articles (Kharrāṭ 1996a: 153–8). The reportage is introduced with the sentence: 'They told one another a detailed account of the story' (Kharrāṭ 1996a: 153). Turkish novelist Orhan Pamuk opens his novel *Snow* (2002) with a series of quotations, including the following from Stendhal's *The Charterhouse of Parma*: 'Politics in a literary work are a pistol-shot in the middle of a concert, a crude affair though one impossible to ignore. We are about to speak of very ugly matters' (Pamuk 2002: unnumbered page). Pamuk duly obliges as he skilfully deals with politics (the battle between secularists and Islamists in contemporary Turkey) in a novel which also includes metafictional elements.

36 In other words, Khūrī is neither saying that because of the imperfections and the bias of writers and historians, the 'very ugly matters' of politics and history do not exist, nor that one should refrain from imitating Stendhal and try to 'speak of' such matters.

37 Cf. what is stated by Benjamin about the remembering author and the importance in writing of 'the weaving of his memory, the Penelope work of recollection', quoted at the end of Chapter 2.

38 For other observations about this passage, see Ghandour 2000: 200–1.

39 Even the ability to forget can be as vital as that of remembering. As we have seen earlier, this concept is at times didactically stated in *Bāb*. In *Riḥlat*, Alice says that the most beautiful thing about human beings is that they forget. She is made to quote the definition in *Lisān al-ᶜArab* (Khūrī 1989: 65/*62*, 83/*79*): 'He is called a human being because he forgets' (cf. Khūrī quoted in Mejcher 2001: 11). Cf. other comments on the same pun (*insān*, *yansā*) in *Mamlakat*: Khūrī 1993: 95/*77*.

40 In his analysis of *Mamlakat*, Meyer underlines how Khūrī addresses the question of individual memory by means of his reworking of a folk tale, that of Jurjī the monk (Meyer 2001: 113–15). Meyer concludes that Khūrī, in his use of folk tales and oral narrative, tries to resurrect individual memory: the 'war in Beirut tore its memory apart, yet this process of forgetting engenders renewed memory' (Meyer 2001: 115).

41 A similar sense of guilt for having survived is evident in the Italian novelist Primo Levi's autobiographical works on his experiences as a captive at the Auschwitz concentration camp (cf. *If This Is a Man*, 1947).

42 The author and his narrators' fears of being alienated from the real world, of being misunderstood or separated from the common people, are the same as those felt by al-Kharrāt's Mīkhāʾīl (cf. Caiani 2005: 42 ff.).

43 Cf. Nowaihi 2000: 384.
44 The final chapter of the novel 'Which of you remembers my mother?' (the whole chapter is a *Ta^{c}tīm* section; Barrāda 1987: 127–49) is an interior monologue from al-Hādī which well describes these bitter feelings and the sense of defeat of the writer's generation: to the political themes is added a yearning for lost childhood (embodied in the figure of the dead mother), expressed in highly lyrical language, reminiscent of al-Kharrāṭ's writing.
45 For a completely positive critical evaluation of *Lu^{c}bat*, see Nowaihi 2000.
46 For instance, the diary entry about receiving Fāṭima's letter (Barrāda 1993: 186–7) opens the fourth chapter which contains the letter itself (Barrāda 1993: 107). In the second chapter, al-^{c}Ayshūnī, who is addressing Fāṭima in the second person, quotes a diary entry in which he relates his meeting with Ghaylāna again after many years (Barrāda 1993: 77); the same entry appears in the last section of the last chapter which includes all his diary entries (Barrāda 1993: 187).
47 Fāṭima is working as a maid for a wealthy Gulf Arab couple and witnesses the scene of smashing plates at a party in Southern France, held on the occasion of the wedding of a son of the couple.
48 It is significant to refer what Barrāda writes in this introduction to Khūrī's associating writing with memory and forgetting. Ultimately, Barrāda's hero is concerned about writing as an act which can produce two contradictory effects: it can help forget traumatic experiences (political in *Lu^{c}bat*, personal in *al-Ḍaw$^{\supset}$*); or it can be 'an indelible tattoo in our depths which awakens our passions when everything around us is hopelessness and futility' (Barrāda 1993: 7).
49 There is a similar confession in Fāṭima's letter to the painter: she tells him that, maybe, writing will help her understand her past experiences (Barrāda 1993: 110).
50 See earlier, for Khūrī's observations about writing as the connection between the present time of the writer and the past time of the lived experience.
51 For a discussion on the crisis and alienation of the Egyptian intellectual as depicted in al-Kharrāṭ's first novels, see Caiani 2005: 46–7.
52 The difficulties of such a task are explained by *Riḥlat*'s narrator who, considering Alice, Little Ghāndī and their like sadly observes: 'How can I tell the story of a life never lived by its characters, a life that passed by them?' (Khūrī 1989: 141/*133*).
53 'Individualization and characterization are residues of the realistic novel. They are no longer necessary' (al-Kharrāṭ quoted in Halim 1994: 18).
54 Cf. Musawi 2003: 360–1.

6 CONCLUSION: ON LITERARY INNVOVATION (PART 2)

1 Whereas the term 'critical realism' mentioned earlier relates to the content of novels, this neo-realism implies a change in novelistic form.
2 Al-Kharrāṭ mentions as some of the works most representative of this trend the novels of Ibrāhīm Aṣlān (b. 1935) and the early fiction of Bahā$^{\supset}$ Ṭāhir, in Egypt; the works of the Syrian writer Zakariyyā Tāmir (b. 1931) and those of Khūrī (Kharrāṭ 1993: 15–17). Jacquemond mentions Ṣun^{c}allāh Ibrāhīm's *Tilka al-rā$^{\supset}$iḥa* (1966; *The Smell of It*, 1971) as probably the first and most influential novel of this kind. He also quotes from a more recent novel, *al-Ṣaqqār* 'The Falconer' (1996) by the Egyptian Samīr Gharīb ^{c}Alī (b. 1966), to illustrate this style (Jacquemond 2003: 120–1).
3 Al-Kharrāṭ obviously includes himself in this group of writers, along with Moroccan Aḥmad al-Madīnī (b. 1936) and Syrian Ḥaydar Ḥaydar (b. 1936) amongst others (Kharrāṭ 1993: 17–18).
4 While al-Kharrāṭ does not seem to differentiate significantly between this style and that of the 'interior current' (Kharrāṭ 1993: 19), Jacquemond connects this trend to

South American literature and to the reworking of indigenous folk literature of the previous current (Jacquemond 2003: 122).

5 Jacquemond notes how this modernist current in Egypt has been mainly promoted by Christian writers. However, whereas al-Kharrāṭ has achieved literary respectability and even critical prestige, Jacquemond writes of other non-realistic writers like Badr al-Dīb and Nabīl Na[c]ūm (b. 1944) as sorts of 'poètes maudits', at times snubbed by critics (Jacquemond 2003: 123–4).

6 Meyer states that this feature is what gives Khūrī's work 'a postmodern feel' (Meyer 2001: 271).

7 Meyer fails to provide evidence for this and for other claims such as the one that 'most Arab readers who comment on Khoury express the impression that he is the best Arab novelist writing today' (Meyer 2001: 272).

8 He is overlooked in monographs which study the development of the post-Mahfouz novel (such as *Infirāṭ al-[c]iqd al-muqaddas. Mun[c]aṭafāt al-riwāya al-[c]arabiyya ba[c]d Maḥfūẓ* 'The Breaking of the Sacred Pact. Turning Points of the Arabic Novel after *Mahfouz*' (1999) by Musawi and al-Kharrāṭ's own critical works, not to mention Darrāj's *Naẓariyyat al-riwāya wa-'l-riwāya al-[c]arabiyya* 'The Theory of the Novel and the Arabic Novel' (1999).

9 We suspect that his being overlooked as a true innovator is due to the fact that he is regarded as a rather straightforward realistic writer.

10 As we have pointed out earlier, the few critical articles published in English focus almost exclusively on the themes of his novels.

11 As we have seen earlier, his strategy is to let Mīkhā[ɔ]īl's inner self talk: what we see of the world is elaborated from within our inner selves. Therefore, there is no point in having a third person omniscient narrator providing us with an outline of each character.

12 Even if this is not the author's priority, in *Yaqīn* al-Kharrāṭ is moving towards a more fully characterized Rāma who strives to disentangle herself from Mīkhā[ɔ]īl's depiction of her. According to Paul Valéry, the goal of criticism is 'to discover which problem the author posed himself (knowingly or not) and to find whether he solved it or not' (Valéry quoted in Brenkman 2006: 833). Let us ask ourselves: what is Khūrī trying to say in *Bāb* with his depiction of the couple Yūnis–Nahīla? One of the aspects of this relationship which he wants to show is how the hero's real life is often different from the idealized picture we have in our mind: what the hero does is not always good, and innocent people might suffer because of his actions, people whom we do not often see or consider, the Nahīlas confined to their background. How does Khūrī decide to highlight this phenomenon? Through Khalīl, he makes Nahīla speak up against Yūnis and at the same time offers an extremely positive, idealized portrayal of her. Maybe this choice is successful in making a straightforward point. Nonetheless, Khūrī would have been even more successful, had Nahīla been presented as a normal human being with weaknesses and shortcomings too (as we have seen earlier, this is what al-Takarlī does with his initially idealized Munīra). Khalīl reproaches Yūnis for talking about an over-idealized love story between him and his wife, Nahīla, as depicted by Yūnis: this love story does not exist, it is as unreal (and dangerous, as the text makes clear) as the over-idealized depiction of Palestinian people as innocent victims who are unable to make mistakes. How does Khalīl fight this dangerous idea? By showing how Nahīla is perfect. Is it successful to fight an over-idealization (Yūnis's marriage) with another over-idealization (Nahīla's)?

13 Waugh goes on to write that '[r]edundancy is provided for in literary texts through the presence of familiar conventions. Experimental fiction of the aleatory variety eschews such redundancy by simply ignoring the conventions of literary tradition. Such texts set out to resist the normal processes of reading, memory and understanding, but without redundancy, texts are read and forgotten' (Waugh 1984: 48). Even if we have made analogous observations in relation to some novels by Khūrī and Barrāda, it is fair to

say that in these texts there is always a mixture of fictional elements, some of which are rather traditional.

14 A critic who, like Hutcheon, is dedicated to the study of metafictional writing would probably question the negative connotation of Darrāj's definition of al-Kharrāṭ as a *ṣāniᶜ lughawī* (cf. Hutcheon 1980: xiv).

15 Again, Auerbach writes of the Homeric style that its basic impulse was 'to represent phenomena in a fully externalized form', then he adds: 'Nor do psychological processes receive any other treatment: here too nothing must remain hidden and unexpressed. [. . .] Homer's personages vent their inmost hearts in speech; what they do not say to others, they speak in their own minds, so that the reader is informed of it' (Auerbach 1946: 6).

16 Other critics have found the stress on the couple's refined tastes and way of living refreshing: M. M. Badawi writes about al-Kharrāṭ's early novels: 'Al-Kharrat's work constitutes an interesting and welcome change from the claustrophobic political atmosphere of that of many of his contemporaries' (Badawi 1993: 174).

17 See for instance in *Yaqīn* the Upper Egyptian characters of the maid to the archaeological mission Umm Barhūm and the carriage driver Aḥmad.

18 The nature of Gnosticism (which, as we have seen, partly informs al-Kharrāṭ's Trilogy) is extremely elitist: only the elected are saved; but Mīkhāʾīl does not seem to belong to the elected.

19 Cf. Bakhtin's similar point on Dostoevsky quoted at the beginning of Chapter 3.

20 As we have observed elsewhere: 'It is noteworthy that Mīkhāʾīl's vision of his homeland basically coincides with that of those Egyptian nationalist intellectuals with secular tendencies who, after the 1919 revolution, were particularly active in shaping a new image of Egypt. The character Mīkhāʾīl sometimes seems to [. . .] mirror [. . .] those thinkers' ideas (such as Pharaonism). [Muḥammad Ḥusayn] Haykal is a case in point: he was a prominent figure in the nationalist debate and many of his theories find an echo in the Kharrāṭian hero. For instance, "Haykal attached particular importance to the fact that Pharaonic customs could be found continuing in both the Coptic and the Muslim communities in Egypt" (Gershoni and Jankowski 1986: 157). It is to be noted that these theories (stressing the unity between Muslims and Copts and their equal status, downplaying religion as a unifying factor) were obviously particularly appealing to the Copts, despite the fact that they were mainly promoted by Muslim secularist thinkers (such as Tawfīq al-Ḥakīm, Ṭāhā Ḥusayn and Haykal himself). The most important Coptic presence in the nationalist debate of the time was that of Salāma Mūsā (Carter 1986: 96), who, al-Kharrāṭ tells us, is amongst the handful of Arab modern writers with whom he "interacts" (Hafez 1994: 245).' Caiani 2005: 39.

21 In some passages of the Trilogy, Rāma can be seen as an idealized symbol of the homeland, like the character of Zahra in Mahfouz's *Mīrāmār*. As we have stated at the end of our article on al-Kharrāṭ's representations of Egypt, however: '[Rāma] is also questioned and criticized while Mahfouz's heroine remains an ideal symbol safely distanced from any significant criticism (Zahra's only negative aspect is her excessive innocence). Mahfouz uses Zahra to underline how different characters (all embodying a well-defined political affiliation and a social class) relate to her. [. . .] al-Kharrāṭ focuses more on Mīkhāʾīl than on Rāma, but the latter still emerges as a character who is more complex and less passive than Zahra. More than that, al-Kharrāṭ focuses on an idea, a concept, an image of his nation which is mainly Mīkhāʾīl's, but, more importantly, is volatile, a sort of "image-in-progress," an image which is first idealized only to be questioned later. Hence, the eternal and idealized Rāma as Isis is paired with the unfaithful Rāma woman-nation whose fickle behaviour makes her lover suffer (cf. how harshly Rāma is regarded by a secondary character in Kharrāṭ, 1979: 215–16). Rāma is sometimes the victim, sometimes the aggressor. Rāma, and al-Kharrāṭ's other heroines, are by no means static images; they evoke in the beholder

(Mīkhā°īl/al-Kharrāṭ and the reader) contrasting, ambivalent feelings and perceptions' (Caiani 2005: 48).

22 Even in other works by al-Kharrāṭ (like the short stories *Jurḥ maftūḥ* – 1969 – and *al-Tuhma*, 1991; *The Accusation*, 1996), it is clear that the hero can be held responsible for the heroine/Egypt's suffering (cf. Caiani 2005: 46).

23 Even if the argument for tolerance and unity is made throughout *Yaqīn* almost obsessively, we should stress that a genuine attempt is made to understand the causes for these acts of violence. Again, despite sharing the belief that Egypt is one despite its religious differences, Rāma and Mīkhā°īl offer different reasons for the emergence of intolerant and violent Islamist groups: the first stressing material and spiritual poverty, the second a deeper social malaise.

24 Similarly, the same dilemma can arise when we consider Khūrī's depiction of the Holocaust in *Bāb* (which we have criticized earlier): can it be justified by the author's need not to demonize Jews?

25 If Barrāda's overt and somewhat superficial experimentation in *Lu*ᶜ*bat* represents a unique case amongst the novels studied, *al-Ḍaw*° is more reminiscent of al-Kharrāṭ (in its introspective and at times lyrical passages) and al-Takarlī (in its skilful manipulation of the narrative structure).

26 Kundera complains that today in the West most novels are written outside the history of the novel, they are novelized pieces of writing (ranging from novelized score-settling to novelized childbirths), which 'are each one like the next, are completely consumable in the morning and discardable in the afternoon' (Kundera 1993: 17–18). Similarly, 'literary criticism has become a mere (often intelligent, always hasty) *literary news bulletin*.' Because of this degeneration, Kundera argues, a work like Rushdie's *Satanic Verses* has been surrendered to 'completely arbitrary judgements' (Kundera 1993: 24).

27 Hallaq's argument is therefore contradictory: first it states that literature is not supposed to change reality, then it claims that literature is the first, founding step of social reform (a reform which will probably bring about some future changes).

28 If we rely on the observations made by Terri DeYoung on the differences between the modernist concern about the past (e.g. Eliot's anxiety over his relationship with his predecessors) and the postmodernist concern about spatiality (a writer's relations with other writers from different places and cultures), we could say that both types of concerns (and inspirations) are present in the work of the contemporary Arab novelist (cf. DeYoung 1998: 3).

29 This is the case of al-ᶜAyshūnī, who idealizes pre-independence Tangiers with its cosmopolitan population, amongst whom is his adoptive father, a Spanish man who allows him to lead a privileged life and introduces him to art (in this case, the character of the European is extremely positive). In some of al-Kharrāṭ's novels, other than the Trilogy, we have a similarly positive depiction of pre-independence Alexandria with its international population. For a good example of how Arab writers reflect critically on the new, post-independence leadership of their countries, see the short story *Anṣāf al-thā°irīn* (1981; *The Half Revolutionaries*, 1991) by Y. Idrīs.

30 In his *Rā°iḥat al-burtuqāl* 'The Smell of the Orange' (1992), the narration is filtered through the eyes and mind of the unnamed protagonist. Here, as in al-Kharrāṭ's novels discussed earlier, there is no well defined dividing line separating what really happens to the hero from what he imagines, thinks or remembers. The characters whom the hero comes across in his mysterious night trip are all surrounded by mystery and uncertainty. As is the case with al-Kharrāṭ's and Khūrī's heroes, he is likely to question the reliability of his own memories (who was the girl with whom he passed some months in a small flat while hiding from the police? Is there only one female character in the novel? Or are the teacher, the wife ᶜIzza and Mājida Fikrī different women?).

BIBLIOGRAPHY

Abdel-Malek, K. and Hallaq, W. (eds) (2000) *Tradition, Modernity, and Postmodernity in Arabic Literature: Essays in Honour of Professor Issa J. Boullata*, Leiden: Brill.

Abu-Deeb, K. (2000) 'The Collapse of Totalizing Discourse and the Rise of Marginalized/Minority Discourses', in Abdel-Malek and Hallaq (2000) *Tradition, Modernity, and Postmodernity in Arabic Literature: Essays in Honour of Professor Issa J. Boullata*, Leiden: Brill. 335–66.

Abū Sayf, Y. (1987) *al-Aqbāṭ wa-'l-qawmiyya al-*ᶜ*arabiyya*, Beirut: Markaz dirāsāt al-waḥda al-ᶜarabiyya.

Accad, E. (1990) *Sexuality and War: Literary Masks of the Middle East*, New York and London: New York University Press.

Adonis (1972) 'al-Lugha, al-thaqāfa, al-wāqiᶜ', in *Zaman al-shi*ᶜ*r*, Beirut: Dār al-ᶜawda. 128–40; trans. Nancy Berg (ed.) and Nur Elmessiri (1987) 'Language, Culture, and Reality', *Alif*, Vol. 7: 112–20; reprinted in Ghazoul and Harlow (1994) *The View from Within*, Cairo: The American University in Cairo Press. 27–33.

Aghacy, S. (1996) 'Elias Khoury's The Journey of Little Gandhi: Fiction and Ideology', *International Journal of Middle East Studies*, Vol. 28, No. 2: 163–76.

ᶜAlī, S. (2000) 'Lugha tatawassaṭ al-jasad', in *Idwār al-Kharrāṭ. Mughāmir ḥattā al-nihāya*, Cairo: Markaz al-ḥaḍāra al-ᶜarabiyya. 160–3.

Allen, R. (1982) *The Arabic Novel: An Historical and Critical Introduction*, Syracuse: Syracuse University Press.

—— (1995) *The Arabic Novel: An Historical and Critical Introduction*, 2nd edn, Syracuse: Syracuse University Press.

Allen, R. Kilpatrick, H. and de Moor, E. (eds) (1995) *Love and Sexuality in Modern Arabic Literature*, London: Saqi Books.

Antoon, S. (2003) '[Review of Sakkut (2000)]', *Journal of Arabic Literature*, Vol. XXXIV, No. 3: 298–300.

Auerbach, E. (1946) *Mimesis. Dargestellte Wirklichkeit in der abendländischen Literatur*; trans. Willard R. Trask (2003) *Mimesis. The Representation of Reality in Western Literature*, Princeton and Oxford: Princeton University Press.

Badawi, M. M. (ed.) (1992) *Modern Arabic Literature*, Cambridge: Cambridge University Press.

—— (1993) *A Short History of Modern Arabic Literature*, Oxford: Clarendon Press.

Badawī, M. (1993) 'Al-Naṣṣ al-Ishkālī wa-tadmīr al-ᶜalāqa al-marjaᶜ fī thunāᵓiyyat Idwār al-Kharrāṭ', in *al-Riwāya al-ḥadītha fī Miṣr*, Cairo: al-Hayᵓa al-miṣriyya al-ᶜāmma li-'l-kitāb. 93–123.

Bakhtin, M. M. (1963) *Problemy poetiki Dostoevskogo*, trans. Caryl Emerson (ed.) (1984) *Problems of Dostoevsky's Poetics*, Minneapolis and London: University of Minnesota Press.

—— (1975) *Voprosy literatury i estetiki*, trans. Caryl Emerson and Michael Holquist (eds) (1981) *The Dialogic Imagination. Four Essays*, Austin: University of Texas Press.

Barakāt, Ḥ. (1975) 'Arabic Novels and Social Transformation', in R. Ostle (ed.) *Studies in Modern Arabic Literature*, Warminster: Aris and Phillips. 126–39.

Baron, B. (1997) 'Nationalist Iconography. Egypt as a Nation', in Gershoni and Jankowski (1986) *Egypt, Islam and the Arabs: The Search for Egyptian Nationhood, 1900–1930*, New York and Oxford: Oxford University Press. 105–24.

Barrāda, M. (1987; 2nd edn 1992) *Lu^c^bat al-nisyān*, Rabat: Dār al-Amān; trans. Issa J. Boullata (1996) *The Game of Forgetting*, Austin: University of Texas at Austin Press.

—— (1993; 2nd edn 1995) *al-Ḍaw^ʾ^ al-hārib*, Casablanca: Nashr al-fanak.

Barth, J. (1967) 'The Literature of Exhaustion', *The Atlantic*; reprinted in Barth (1997) *The Friday Book. Essays and Other Nonfiction*, Baltimore and London: The Johns Hopkins University Press. 62–76.

—— (1980) 'The Literature of Replenishment', *The Atlantic*; reprinted in Barth (1997) *The Friday Book. Essays and Other Nonfiction*, Baltimore and London: The Johns Hopkins University Press. 193–206.

—— (1997) *The Friday Book. Essays and Other Nonfiction*, Baltimore and London: The Johns Hopkins University Press.

Barthes, R. (1968) 'La mort de l'auteur', reprinted in Barthes (1984) *Le bruissement de la langue*, Paris: Éditions du Seuil. 61–7.

—— (1984) *Le bruissement de la langue*, Paris: Éditions du Seuil.

Batatu, H. (1978) *The Old Social Classes and the Revolutionary Movements of Iraq. A Study of Iraq's Old Landed and Commercial Classes and of its Communists, Ba^c^thists, and Free Officers*, Princeton: Princeton University Press.

Benjamin, W. (1929) 'Zum Bilde Prousts', in *Die Literarische Welt*; trans. H. Zohn (1999) 'The Image of Proust', in *Illuminations*, London: Pimlico. 197–210.

Blavatsky, H. P. (1888) *The Secret Doctrine*, Los Angeles: The Theosophy Company, 1925.

Bloom, H. (1997) *The Anxiety of Influence. A Theory of Poetry*, 2nd edn, New York and Oxford: Oxford University Press.

Booth, W. C. (1983) *The Rhetoric of Fiction*, 2nd edn, Chicago: The University of Chicago Press.

—— (1984) 'Introduction', in Bakhtin (1963) *Problemy poetiki Dostoevskogo*; trans. Caryl Emerson (ed.) (1984) *Problems of Dostoevsky's Poetics*, Minneapolis and London: University of Minnesota Press. xiii–xxvii.

Boullata, I. J. (1996) 'Translator's Introduction', in M. Barrāda *Lu^c^bat al-nisyān*; trans. Issa J. Boullata (1996) *The Game of Forgetting*, Austin: University of Texas at Austin Press. 1–12.

Brenkman, J. (2006) 'Innovation: Notes on Nihilism and the Aesthetics of the Novel', in F. Moretti (ed.) *The Novel. Volume 2. Forms and Themes*, Princeton and Oxford: Princeton University Press. 808–38.

Breton, A. (1924) *Manifeste du surréalisme*, reprinted in *Manifestes du surréalisme* (1962), Paris: J. J. Pauvert; trans. R. Seaver and H. R. Lane (1972) 'Manifesto of Surrealism', in *Manifestoes of Surrealism*, Ann Arbor: University of Michigan Press. 1–47.

Cachia, P. (1990) *An Overview of Modern Arabic Literature*, Edinburgh: Edinburgh University Press.

Caiani, F. (2004) 'Polyphony and Narrative Voice,' in Fuʾād al-Takarlī's *al-Raj^c al-ba^cīd*', *Journal of Arabic Literature*, Vol. XXXV, No. 1: 45–70.

—— (2005) 'Representations of Egypt in some Works by Idwār al-Kharrāṭ', *Middle Eastern Literatures*, Vol. 8, No. 1: 35–52.

Calvino, I. (1964) 'Prefazione', in I. Calvino *Il sentiero dei nidi di ragno*, edn used 1972, Torino: Einaudi. 7–24.

—— (1979) *Se una notte d'inverno un viaggiatore*, trans. William Weaver (1981) *If On a Winter's Night a Traveller*, New York: Harcourt Brace Jovanovich.

Capezzone, L. (1993) 'Postfazione', in E. al-Kharrat *Le ragazze di Alessandria*, trans. L. Capezzone, Roma: Jouvence. 141–49.

Carter, B. L. (1986) *The Copts in Egyptian Politics*, London, Sydney and Dover/New Hampshire: Croom Helm.

Chatman, S. (1978) *Story and Discourse. Narrative Structure in Fiction and Film*, Ithaca and London: Cornell University Press.

Cirlot, J. E. (1958) *Diccionario de simbolos tradicionales*, trans. J. Sage (1962) *A Dictionary of Symbols*, London: Routledge K. Paul.

Cobham, C. (2002) 'The Long Way Back: Possibilities for Survival and Renewal in *al-Raj^c al-ba^cīd* by Fuʾād al-Takarlī', *Arabic and Middle Eastern Literatures*, Vol. 5, No. 2: 181–94.

—— (2004) 'Reading and Writing in *al-Masarrāt wa'l-awjā^c* by Fuʾād al-Takarlī', *Journal of Arabic Literature*, Vol. XXXV, No. 1: 25–44.

Conrad, J. (1924) 'Henry James', in *Notes on Life and Letters*, London and Toronto: J. M. Dent and Sons Ltd. 11–19.

The Coptic Liturgy (of Saint Basil). Available: http://www.coptic.net/prayers/StBasilLiturgy.html (accessed 1 February 2007).

Currie, P. (1987) 'The Eccentric Self: Anti-Characterization and the Problem of the Subject in American Postmodernist Fiction', in M. Bradbury and S. Ro (eds) *Contemporary American Fiction*, London: Edward Arnold. 53–70.

Darrāj, F. (1999) 'Idwār al-Kharrāṭ: al-mutanāhī wa-'l-lā mutanāhī fī riwāyat al-muḥlaq', in *Naẓariyyat al-riwāya wa-'l-riwāya al-^carabiyya*, Beirut and Casablanca: al-Markiz al-thaqāfī al-^carabī. 255–83.

Darwīsh, M. (1987; 6th edn 1994) *Dhākira li-'l-nisyān*, Beirut: Dār al-^cawda.

—— (2000) *Jidāriyya*, reprinted in *al-A^cmāl al-jadīda* (2004), Beirut: Riyāḍ al-rayyis li-'l-kutub wa-'l-nathr. 437–537.

DeYoung, T. (1998) *Placing the Poet. Badr Shakir al-Sayyab and Postcolonial Iraq*, New York: State University of New York Press.

Dostoevsky, F. M. (1866) *Prestuplenie i nakazanie*, trans. Richard Pevear and Larissa Volokhonsky (1993) *Crime and Punishment*, London: Everyman's Library.

—— (1881) *Bratia Karamazovy*, trans. D. Magarshack (1958) *The Brothers Karamazov*, London: Penguin Books.

Eco, U. (1983) *Postille a 'Il nome della rosa'*, trans. W. Weaver (1984) *Reflections on The Name of the Rose*, London: Minerva.

Eliot, T. S. (1922) *The Waste Land*, reprinted in *Selected Poems* (1954), London: Faber and Faber. 49–74.

—— (1932) *Selected Essays*, edn used 1951, London: Faber and Faber.

Fārūq, S. (1997) *Jamāliyyāt al-tashaẓẓī: dirāsāt naqdiyya fī adab Idwār al-Kharrāṭ wa-Badr al-Dīb*, Cairo: Dār sharqiyyāt li-'l-nashr wa-'l-tawzī^c.

Faulkner, W. (1929) *The Sound and the Fury*, edn used 1995, London: Vintage.

Fontaine, J. (1986) 'Le Nouveau Roman Égyptien. 1975–1985', in J. Fontaine *Romans arabes modernes*, edn used 1992, Tunis: Institut des belles letters arabes. 7–54.

Foucault, M. (1969) 'What Is an Author?', trans. Josue V. Harari, in Lodge (1988) *Modern Criticism and Theory. A Reader*, London and New York: Longman. 196–210.

Friedman, N. (1955) 'Point of View in Fiction', in Stevick (1967) *The Theory of the Novel*, New York: The Free Press. 108–37.

Gaskell, G. A. (1960) *Dictionary of all Scriptures and Myths*, New York: The Julian Press.

Genette, G. (1972) *Discours du récit* (in Figures III); trans. Jane E. Lewin (1980) *Narrative Discourse*, Oxford: Basil Blackwell.

—— (1982) *Palimpsestes: la littérature au second degré*; trans. Channa Newman and Claude Doubinsky (1997) *Palimpsestes. Literature in the Second Degree*, Lincoln and London: University of Nebraska Press.

Gershoni, I. and Jankowski, J. P. (eds) (1986) *Egypt, Islam and the Arabs: The Search for Egyptian Nationhood, 1900–1930*, New York and Oxford: Oxford University Press.

Ghandour, S. (2000) 'History, Religion, and the Construction of Subjectivity in Elias Khoury's *Riḥlat Ghāndī al-Ṣaghīr*', in Abdel-Malek and Hallaq (2000) *Tradition, Modernity, and Postmodernity in Arabic Literature: Essays in Honour of Professor Issa J. Boullata*, Leiden: Brill. 186–202.

Ghazoul, F. J. (1996) *Nocturnal Poetics, The Arabian Nights in Comparative Context*, Cairo: The American University in Cairo Press.

—— (1999) 'Rama and the Dragon, by Edwār al-Kharrāṭ', *Journal of Arabic and Middle Eastern Literatures*, Vol. 2, No. 2: 167–72.

Ghazoul, F. J. and Harlow, B. (eds) (1994) *The View from Within*, Cairo: The American University in Cairo Press.

Ghīṭānī, J. (1971) *al-Zaynī Barakāt*, Cairo: Dār al-shurūq, 1989.

—— (1984) 'Jadaliyyat al-tanāṣṣ', *Alif*, 4: 71–82; trans. Samia Mehrez (1994) 'Intertextual Dialectics', in Ghazoul and Harlow (1994) *The View from Within*, Cairo: The American University in Cairo Press. 17–26.

—— (1988) *Zayni Barakat*, trans. F. Abdel Wahab, London: Penguin.

Grossman, L. (1962; 2nd edn 1965) *Dostoevskii*, Moscow: Molodaya Gvardia Publishing House; trans. M. Mackler (1974) *Dostoevsky. A Biography*, London: Allen Lane.

Hafez, S. (1982) 'Ḥiwār ma^{c}a Idwār al-Kharrāṭ', *Alif*, 2: 90–113; trans. Maggie Awadalla (1994) 'The Relative and the Absolute in Avant-Garde Narration', in Ghazoul and Harlow (1994) *The View from Within*, Cairo: The American University in Cairo Press. 228–45.

—— (1994) 'The Transformation of Reality and the Arabic Novel's Aesthetic Response', *Bulletin of the School of Oriental and African Studies*, Vol. 57, No. 1: 93–112.

—— (2000) 'The Novel, Politics and Islam. Haydar Haydar's Banquet for Seaweed', *New Left Review* 5, September/October: 117–41.

Hafez, S. and Cobham, C. (eds) (1988) *A Reader of Modern Arabic Short Stories*, London: Saqi Books.

Ḥakīm, T. (1933) *^{c}Awdat al-rūḥ*, Cairo: Maktabat al-ādāb wa-maṭba^{c}atu-hā.

Ḥalāwī, J. J. (1995) 'Ḥiwār ma^{c}a al-riwā$^{\circ}$ī Fu$^{\circ}$ād al-Takarlī', *al-Ādāb* September/October/November: 24–29.

Halim, H. (1994) 'The Face of Memory', *Al-Ahram Weekly* 14 July–20 July: 18–19.

—— (1996) 'Mikhail and the Dragon', *Al-Ahram Weekly* 27 June–3 July: 18, 22.

Hallaq, B. (1998) 'Autobiography and Polyphony', in R. Ostle, E. de Moor and S. Wild (eds) (1998) *Writing the Self*, London: Saqi Books. 192–206.

—— (2001) 'Transgénérique et modernité dans la littérature arabe', *Arabic and Middle Eastern Literatures*, Vol. 4, No. 2: 157–66.

Hammond, M. (2000) 'Subsuming the Feminine Other: Gender and Narration in Idwār al-Kharrāṭ's *Yā Banāt Iskandriyya*', *Journal of Arabic Literature*, Vol. 31: 38–58.

Ḥasan, Ḥ. (1996) *Yaqīn al-kitāba. Idwār al-Kharrāṭ wa-marāyā-hu al-mutakassara*, Cairo: al-Majlis al-a^c^lā li-'l-thaqāfa.

Hassan, W. (2002) 'Postcolonial Theory and Modern Arabic Literature: Horizons of Application', *Journal of Arabic Literature*, Vol. XXXIII, No. 1: 45–64.

Haydar, P. (1996) 'Preface', in I. Khūrī (1996) *The Kingdom of Strangers*, trans. Paula Haydar, Fayetteville: The University of Arkansas Press. v–viii.

Hedrick, C. W. (1986) 'Introduction', in C. W. Hedrick and R. Hodgson (eds) *Nag Hammadi, Gnosticism, and Early Christianity*, Peabody/Massachusetts: Hendrickson Publishers. 1–11.

The Holy Bible (1989) New International Version, Classic edn, London, Sydney, Auckland and Toronto.

Hornblower, S. and Spawforth, A. (eds) (1996) *The Oxford Classical Dictionary*, 3rd edn, Oxford: Oxford University Press.

Hutcheon, L. (1980) *Narcissistic Narrative. The Metafictional Paradox*, New York and London: Methuen, 1984.

—— (1988) *A Poetics of Postmodernism*, London and New York: Routledge.

—— (1989) *The Politics of Postmodernism*, London and New York: Routledge.

Ibn ^c^Abd Rabbi-hi (1965) *al-^c^Iqd al-farīd*, A. Amīn, A. al-Zayn and I. al-Abyārī (eds). Cairo: Maṭba^c^at lajnat al-ta^ɔ^līf wa-'l-tarjama wa-'l-nashr, 1949–1965.

Ibrāhīm, Ṣ. (1974) *Najmat Aghusṭus*, Damascus: Ittiḥād al-kuttāb al-^c^arab.

—— (1992) *Dhāt*, Cairo: Dār al-mustaqbal al-^c^arabī; trans. Anthony Calderbank (2001) *Zaat*, Cairo: the American University in Cairo Press.

Idrīs, S. (1997) 'Al-Tajrīb wa-'l-tajdīd fī al-riwāya al-^c^arabiyya', *al-Ādāb*, May/June: 19.

Idrīs, Y. (1981a) 'Uqtul-hā', in Idrīs (1982) *Uqtul-hā*, Cairo: Maktabat Miṣr. 81–100.

—— (1981b) 'Anṣāf al-Thā^ɔ^irīn', in Idrīs (1982) *Uqtul-hā*, Cairo: Maktabat Miṣr. 63–79.

—— (1982) *Uqtul-hā*, Cairo: Maktabat Miṣr.

An Introduction to the Coptic Art of Egypt. Available: http://www.coptic.net/articles/CopticArtOfEgypt.txt (accessed 1 February 2007).

Iser, W. (1976) *Der Akt des Lesens*, Munich: Fink; trans. W. Iser (1978) *The Act of Reading. A Theory of Aesthetic Response*, London and Henley: Routledge and Kegan Paul.

Jabrā, J. I. (1969) *al-Safīna*, Beirut: Dār al-nahār; trans. Adnan Haydar and Roger Allen (1985) *The Ship*, Washington, DC: Three Continents Press.

—— (1978) *al-Baḥth ^c^an Walīd Mas^c^ūd*, Beirut: Dār al-ādāb; trans. Adnan Haydar and Roger Allen (2000) *In Search of Walid Masoud*, Syracuse: Syracuse University Press.

Jacquemond, R. (2003) *Entre scribes et écrivains. Le champ littéraire dans l'Égypte contemporaine*, Paris: Sinbad/Actes Sud.

James, H. (1884) 'The Art of Fiction', reprinted in Roger Gard (ed.) *The Critical Muse: Selected Literary Criticism* (1987), London: Penguin. 186–206.

Joyce, J. (1922) *Ulysses*, edn used 2000, London: Penguin.

Kanafānī, G. (1963) 'Rijāl fī-'l-shams', in Kanafānī (1972) *al-Āthār al-Kāmila. Al-Riwāyāt*. Beirut: Mu^ɔ^assasat al-abḥāth al-^c^arabiyya. 33–153; trans. Hilary Kilpatrick (1978) *Men in the Sun*, London: Heinemann.

—— (1966) *Mā tabaqqā la-kum*, in Kanafānī (1972) *al-Āthār al-Kāmila. Al-Riwāyāt*. Beirut: Muʾassasat al-abḥāth al-ʿarabiyya. 154–233; trans. May Jayyusi and Jeremy Reed (1990) *All That's Left to You*, Austin: The University of Texas Press.

—— (1972) *al-Āthār al-Kāmila. Al-Riwāyāt*. Beirut: Muʾassasat al-abḥāth al-ʿarabiyya.

Kermode, F. (1992) 'Wannabee', *London Review of Books*, Vol. 14, No. 19 (8 October): 14.

Kharrāṭ, I. (1959; 3rd edn 1995) *Ḥīṭān ʿāliya*, Alexandria and Cairo: Dār wa-maṭābiʿ al-mustaqbal.

—— (1969) 'Jurḥ Maftūḥ', trans. Catherine Cobham (1984) 'An Open Wound', *Journal of Arabic Literature* 15: 122–34; reprinted in Hafez and Cobham (1988) *A Reader of Modern Arabic Short Stories*, London: Saqi Books. 201–22.

—— (1972) *Sāʿāt al-kibriyāʾ*, Beirut: Dār al-ādāb.

—— (1979) *Rāma wa-'l-tinnīn*, edn used 1990, Beirut: Dār al-ādāb, trans. Ferial Ghazoul and John Verlenden (2002) *Rama and the Dragon*, Cairo and New York: The American University in Cairo Press.

—— (1983) *Ikhtināqāt al-ʿishq wa-'l-ṣabāḥ*, Cairo: Dār al-mustaqbal al-ʿarabī.

—— (1985) *al-Zaman al-ākhar*, Cairo: Dār shahdī.

—— (1986) *Turābu-hā zaʿfarān*, edn used 1999, Cairo: Dār al-Aḥmadī li-'l-nashr.

—— (1989) *City of Saffron*, trans. Frances Liardet. London: Quartet Books.

—— (1990) *Yā banāt Iskandariyya*, Beirut: Dār al-ādāb; trans. Frances Liardet (1993) *Girls of Alexandria*, London: Quartet Books.

—— (1991a) *Amwāj al-layālī*, Cairo: Dār sharqiyyāt li-'l-nashr wa-'l-tawzīʿ.

—— (1991b) 'The Mashriq', in R. Ostle (ed.) *Modern Literature in the Near/Middle East. 1856–1970*, London: Routledge. 180–92.

—— (1993) *al-Ḥasāsiya al-jadīda*, Beirut: Dār al-ādāb.

—— (1994a) *Ḥarīq al-akhyila*, Cairo: Dār wa maṭābiʿ al-mustaqbal.

—— (1994b) *al-Kitāba ʿabra al-nawʿiyya*, Cairo: Dār sharqiyyāt li-'l-nashr wa-'l-tawzīʿ.

—— (1995) 'al-Kitāba fī zaman mutaghayyir', *al-Ādāb* July/August: 26–30.

—— (1996a) *Yaqīn al-ʿaṭash*, Cairo: Dār sharqiyyāt li-'l-nashr wa-'l-tawzīʿ.

—— (1996b) *Muhājamat al-mustaḥīl*, Damascus: Dār al-madā li-'l-thaqāfa wa-'l-nashr.

—— (1998) 'Random Variations on an Autobiographical Theme', in R. Ostle, E. de Moor and S. Wild (eds) (1998) *Writing the Self*, London: Saqi Books. 9–17.

—— (1999) *Aṣwāt al-ḥadātha*, Beirut: Dār al-ādāb.

—— (2001) 'Kullu-nā multazim', *Nizwa*, Vol. 25 (July): 37–45.

Khūrī, I. (1989) *Riḥlat Ghāndī al-ṣaghīr*, Beirut: Dār al-ādāb; trans. Paula Haydar (1994) *The Journey of Little Gandhi*, Minneapolis and London: University of Minnesota Press.

—— (1990) 'The Unfolding of Modern Fiction and Arab Memory', *Journal of the Midwest Modern Language Association*, Vol. 23, No. 1 (Spring): 1–8.

—— (1993) *Mamlakat al-ghurabāʾ*, Beirut: Dār al-ādāb.

—— (1996) *The Kingdom of Strangers*, trans. Paula Haydar. Fayetteville: The University of Arkansas Press.

—— (1998) *Bāb al-shams*, 2nd edn, Beirut: Dār al-ādāb; trans. Humphrey Davies (2005) *Gate of the Sun*, London: Harvill Secker.

—— (1999) 'al-Riwāya wa-'l-baḥth ʿan lugha jadīda', *Akhbār al-adab*, 4 July 1999: 14.

—— (2002) *Yālū*, Beirut: Dār al-ādāb.

Kiberd, D. (1992) 'Introduction', in Joyce (1922) *Ulysses*, edn used 2000, London: Penguin. ix–lxxxix.

Kieslowski, K. (1988) 'A Short Film about Killing', in *Dekalog: The Ten Comandments*, Poland 1988 (Poland: Zespol Filmowy 'Tov').

Kilpatrick, H. (1992) 'The Egyptian novel from *Zaynab* to 1980', in M. M. Badawi (ed.) (1992) *Modern Arabic Literature*, Cambridge: Cambridge University Press. 223–69.

Kundera, M. (1986) *L'art du roman*, Paris: Gallimard; trans. Linda Asher, (1988) *The Art of the Novel*, London: Faber and Faber.

—— (1993) *Testaments trahis*, Paris: Gallimard; trans. Linda Asher (1995) *Testaments Betrayed*, London and Boston: Faber and Faber.

Liardet, F. (1989) 'Introduction', in I. Kharrāṭ (1989) *City of Saffron*, trans. Frances Liardet. London: Quartet Books. vii–x.

Litz, A. W. and Rainey, L. (eds) (2000) 'Ezra Pound', in A. Walton Litz, Louis Menand and Lawrence Rainey (eds) *The Cambridge History of Literary Criticism. Volume 7. Modernism and the New Criticism*, Cambridge: Cambridge University Press. 57–92.

Lodge, D. (ed.) (1988) *Modern Criticism and Theory. A Reader*, London and New York: Longman.

McHale, B. (1987) *Postmodernist Fiction*, London and New York: Routledge.

MacRae, G. W. (1977) 'The Apocalypse of Adam', in Marvin W. Meyer (ed.) *The Nag Hammadi Library in English*, Leiden: E. J. Brill. 256–64.

Mahfouz, N. (1967) *Mīrāmār*, Cairo: Maktabat Miṣr; trans. Fatma Moussa-Mahmoud (1978) *Miramar*, Cairo: The American University Press.

Mehrez, S. (1994) *Egyptian Writers between History and Fiction*, Cairo: The American University in Cairo Press.

Mejcher, S. (2001) 'Elias Khoury: the necessity to forget – and remember', *Banipal*, Vol. 12 (Autumn): 8–14.

Menand, L. (2000) 'T. S. Eliot', in A. Walton Litz, Louis Menand and Lawrence Rainey (eds) *The Cambridge History of Literary Criticism. Volume 7. Modernism and the New Criticism*, Cambridge: Cambridge University Press. 17–56.

Meyer, S. G. (2001) *The Experimental Arabic Novel*, New York: State University of New York Press.

Morard, F. (1985) *L'Apocalypse d'Adam*, Québec: Les Presses de l'Université Laval.

Munīf, ^{c}A. (1975) *Sharq al-Mutawassiṭ*; edn used 1987, Beyrut: al-Mu^{ɔ}assasa al-^{c}arabiyya li-'l-dirāsāt wa-'l-nashr.

—— (1977) *al-Nihāyāt*, edn used 1994, Beyrut: al-Mu^{ɔ}assasa al-^{c}arabiyya li-'l-dirāsāt wa-'l-nashr; trans. Roger Allen (1988) *Endings*. London: Quartet.

Musallam, S. (1983) 'Abṭāl 'al-Raj^{c} al-ba^{c}īd' bayna al-iḥbāṭ wa-'l-ightirāb', *al-Aqlām*, Vol. 18, No. 2 (February): 38–43.

Musawi, M. J. (1999) *Infirāṭ al-^{c}iqd al-muqaddas. Mun^{c}aṭafāt al-riwāya al-^{c}arabiyya ba^{c}d Maḥfūẓ*, Cairo: al-Hay^{ɔ}a al-miṣriyya al-^{c}āmma li-'l-kitāb.

—— (2003) *The Postcolonial Arabic Novel. Debating Ambivalence*, Leiden and Boston: Brill.

Nowaihi, M. (1994) 'Memory and Imagination in Edwar al-Kharrat's *Turābuhā Za^{c}farān*', *Journal of Arabic Literature*, Vol. 25: 34–57.

—— (2000) 'Committed Postmodernity: Muḥammad Barrāda's *The Game of Forgetting*', in Abdel-Malek and Hallaq (2000) *Tradition, Modernity, and Postmodernity in Arabic Literature: Essays in Honour of Professor Issa J. Boullata*, Leiden: Brill. 367–88.

Ostle, R., de Moor, E. and Wild, S. (eds) (1998) *Writing the Self*, London: Saqi Books.

Pamuk, O. (2002) *Kar*, Istanbul: –letişim; trans. M. Freely (2004) *Snow*, London: Faber and Faber.

Peled, M. (1995) 'Sexuality in Jabrā's Novel, *The Search for Walīd Mas^{c}ūd*', in R. Allen, H. Kilpatrick and E. de Moor (eds) *Love and Sexuality in Modern Arabic Literature*, London: Saqi Books. 140–53.

Pellat, C. (1966) 'Ḥikāya', in B. Lewis, V. L. Ménage, Ch. Pellat and J. Schacht (eds) *The Encyclopaedia of Islam. Volume III*, Leiden: E. J. Brill/London: Luzac & Co., 1971. 367–72.

Rabaté, J. (2001) 'Una lingua straniata. Gli stili del modernismo', in F. Moretti (ed.) *Il romanzo. Volume I*, Torino: Einaudi. 747–73.

Rayān, A. (ed.) (1998) *Ṣawt ṣārikh fī al-shawāri^{c}. Qirā^{ɔ}a fī a^{c}māl Idwār al-Kharrāt*, Cairo: al-Hay^{ɔ}a al-miṣriyya al-^{c}āmma li-'l-kitāb.

Rosenshield, G. (1978) *Crime and Punishment. The Techniques of the Omniscient Author*, Lisse: The Peter De Ridder Press.

Ruocco, M. (1999) *L'intellettuale arabo tra impegno e dissenso*, Roma: Jouvence.

Rushdie, S. (1981) *Midnight's Children*, edn used 1995, London: Vintage.

—— (1988) *The Satanic Verses*, edn used 1998, London: Vintage.

Ryding, K. C. (1997) 'The Alchemy of Sound: Medieval Arabic Phonosymbolism', in Asma Afsaruddin and A. H. Mathias Zahniser (eds) *Humanism, Culture, & Language in the Near East*, Winona Lake/Indiana: Eisenbrauns. 155–63.

Said, E. W. (1989) 'Afterword', in E. Khoury, *Little Mountain*. London: Collins Harvill. 135–47.

—— (2003) 'Introduction to the Fiftieth-Anniversary Edition', in E. Auerbach (1946) *Mimesis. Dargestellte Wirklichkeit in der abendländischen Literatur*; trans. Willard R. Trask (2003) *Mimesis. The Representation of Reality in Western Literature*, Princeton and Oxford: Princeton University Press. ix–xxxii.

Sa^{c}īd, M. (1999) '"Bāb al-shams" bayna 'l-tasjīl wa-muqtaḍiyyāt al-fann', *al-Ādāb*, March/April: 101–3.

Sā^{c}idī, Q. (1997) 'al-Raj^{c} al-ba^{c}īd. Shakhṣiyyāt wa-afkār', *al-Thaqāfa al-jadīda*, No. 298. Available: http://www.iraqcp.org/298thakafa/art11.htm (accessed 1 February 2007).

Sakkut, H. (2000) *The Arabic Novel: Bibliography and Critical Introduction 1865–1995*, Cairo and New York: The American University in Cairo Press (6 volumes).

Schimmel, A. (1975) *Mystical Dimensions of Islam*, Chapel Hill: The University of North Carolina Press.

Sciascia, L. (1971) *Il contesto. Una parodia*, trans. Adrienne Foulke (2001) *Equal Danger*, London: Granta Books.

Sessona, A. Z. (2002) 'The Re-Writing of The Arabian Nights by Imīl Ḥabībī', *Middle Eastern Literatures*, Vol. 5, No. 1: 29–48.

Shalan, J. (2002) 'Writing the Nation: The Emergence of Egypt in the Modern Arabic Novel', *Journal of Arabic Literature*, Vol. 33, No. 3: 211–47.

Shaykh, Ḥ. (2001) *Inna-hā Lundun yā ^{c}azīzī*, Beirut: Dār al-ādāb.

Shklovsky, V. (1917) 'Art As Technique', reprinted in Lodge (1988) *Modern Criticism and Theory. A Reader*, London and New York: Longman. 16–30.

Shukrī, Gh. (1990) *al-Aqbāṭ fī waṭan mutaghayyir*, Cairo: Kitāb al-ahālī.

Stagh, M. (1993) *The Limits of Freedom of Speech. Prose Literature and Prose Writers in Egypt under Nasser and Sadat*, Stockholm: Almqvist/Wiksell International.

Stevick, P. (ed.) (1967) *The Theory of the Novel*, New York: The Free Press.

Sun, A. X. D. (2004) 'Mao-ti', *London Review of Books*, Vol. 26, No. 13 (8 July 2004). 12–13.

Takarlī, F. (1960) *al-Wajh al-ākhar*, edn used 1989, Beirut: Dār al-ādāb.

—— (1972) 'al-Tannūr', reprinted in Hafez and Cobham (1988) *A Reader of Modern Arabic Short Stories*, London: Saqi Books. 105–15.

—— (1980) *al-Raj^{c} al-ba^{c}īd*, edn used 1993, Beirut: Dār al-ādāb; trans. Catherine Cobham (2000) *The Long Way Back*, Cairo: The American University in Cairo Press.

Takarlī, F. (1985) *Les voix de l'aube*, trans. Martine Faideau and Rachida Turki. Paris: Jean-Claude Lattès.

—— (1998) *al-Masarrāt wa-'l-awjā*[c], Damascus: Dār al-madā li-'l-thaqāfa wa-'l-nashr.

Tanūkhī (1973) *Nishwār al-muḥāḍara*, [c]Abbūd al-Shāljī (ed.) Beirut: self-published, 1971–1973.

—— (1978) *al-Faraj ba*[c]*d al-shidda*, [c]Abbūd al-Shāljī (ed.) Beirut: Dār Ṣādir.

Testa, E. (2002) 'Stile, discorso, intreccio', in F. Moretti (ed.) *Il romanzo. Volume II*, Torino: Einaudi. 271–99.

Thāmir, F. (1992) 'al-Raj[c] al-ba[c]īd: dhurwat al-ṣawgh al-fannī li-'l-riwāya muta[c]addidat al-aṣwāt', in F. Thamir (1992) *al-Ṣawt al-ākhar: al-jawhar al-ḥiwārī li-'l-khiṭāb al-adabī*, Baghdad: Dār al-shu[ɔ]ūn al-thaqāfiyya. 79–93.

Walther, W. (1995) 'Distant Echoes of Love in the Narrative Works of Fu'ād al-Tikirlī', in R. Allen, H. Kilpatrick and E. de Moor (eds) *Love and Sexuality in Modern Arabic Literature*, London: Saqi Books. 131–9.

—— (1997) 'Studies in Human Psyche and Human Behavior under Political and Social Pressure: the Recent Literary Works of Fu'ad al-Takarli', *Arab Studies Quarterly*, Fall: 21–36.

Wardānī, M. (1992) *Rā*[ɔ]*iḥat al-burtuqāl*, Cairo: Dār sharqiyyāt li-'l-nashr wa-'l-tawzī[c].

Waugh, P. (1984) 'What is Metafiction and Why are They Saying Such Awful Things About it?', reprinted in M. Currie (ed.) (1995) *Metafiction*, London and New York: Longman. 39–54.

Wendell, C. (1972) *The Evolution of the Egyptian National Image. From its Origins to Aḥmad Luṭfī al-Sayyid*, Berkeley/Los Angeles/London: University of California Press.

Westphal, B. (2001) 'Postmodernismo e letteratura', in G. M. Anselmi (ed.) *Mappe della letteratura europea e meditteranea. Volume III. Da Gogol' al Postmoderno*, Milano: Bruno Mondadori Editori. 311–38.

INDEX

Notes: Publication names are in italics, as are words transliterated from Arabic (but not the names of persons or characters). References such as '178–9' indicate (not necessarily continuous) discussion of a topic across a range of pages, whilst '142n22' indicates a reference to note 22 on page 142. A reference in the form '142nn' indicates that the topic is referred to in multiple notes on page 142. Wherever possible in the case of topics with many references, these have either been divided into sub-topics or the most significant discussions of the topic are indicated by page numbers in bold. To distinguish clearly between characters in the novels discussed and the novels in which they appear (which often bear the name of the principal character), all references to fictional characters are followed by '(char.)'.

For Product Safety Concerns and Information please contact our EU representative GPSR@taylorandfrancis.com
Taylor & Francis Verlag GmbH, Kaufingerstraße 24, 80331 München, Germany

www.ingramcontent.com/pod-product-compliance
Lightning Source LLC
Chambersburg PA
CBHW071515100726
47908CB00004B/1173